# HARD
# NOSE
## The Story of the 1986 Giants

# HARD NOSE

## The Story of the 1986 Giants

**JIM BURT**
**with Hank Gola**

**HARCOURT**
**BRACE**
**JOVANOVICH**

San Diego   New York   London

Requests for permission to make copies of
any part of the work should be mailed to:
Permissions, Harcourt Brace Jovanovich, Publishers,
Orlando, Florida 32887.

Library of Congress Cataloging-in-Publication Data

Burt, Jim.
  Hard nose.

  1. New York Giants (Football team)   I. Gola, Hank.
II. Title.
GV956.N4B87   1987      796.332'64'097471      87–17678
ISBN 0-15-138575-0

Designed by Michael Farmer
Printed in the United States of America
First edition
A B C D E

To Colleen for all her years of loyalty, love, and understanding; to Jimmy, my pride and joy; to Dad, who taught me everything I know about life; and to Mr. Kempf, who was always there when I needed him.

*Jim Burt*


To the memory of my dad, Hank Sr., whose spirit lived with me from the start; to Lillian who believed in and encouraged me from the start; and to Henry and Julianne for making my life complete.

*Hank Gola*

# Contents

*Photographs follow pages 86 and 214.*

# Acknowledgments

The authors wish to thank Billy Ard, Bill Belichick, John De-lery, Vinny DiTrani, Peter Finney, Jr., David Fishof, Greg Gallo, Greg Garber, Kathy Kaynak, Art Kehoe, Randy Lange, John Madden, Phil Mushnick, Kyle Palmer, Bill Parcells, Johnny Parker, John and Sue Peasley, Paul Rotella, Lou Saban, Steve Serby, Jim Smith, Barry Stanton, and George Young, for their help in the book's production; David Vigliano, for conceiving the idea; and our editor, B.J. Robbins, for putting up with us.

# Acknowledgment

# I

**BUFFALO**


**Kickoff**

How does it feel to step into a dream?

Weird and wonderful, that's how. For years, my fantasy was to be standing on our sidelines as the final minutes ticked down to a Super Bowl championship. Every grunt, every pain, and every ounce of sweat had been dedicated to that special moment when I could say, "We're better than anybody else," and have the whole world agree with me. On January 25, 1987, that moment arrived—as real as the Rose Bowl scoreboard at Super Bowl XXI. New York Giants, 39. Denver Broncos, 20.

I should have gone berserk, bonkers, whacko. Instead, my dream took hold of me and swept me into a time warp of satisfaction—as if this was a gourmet treat to savor, not devour.

*Where's Jimmy?* I thought. *I've got to bring him down here.*

It was just too good a moment not to share. I looked back to where my family and friends were standing and shouting. The ten of them were easy to spot because they were all wearing No. 64 jerseys, with numerals you could read, not like mine. And so I sent for my son, Jim Jr., so that he could enjoy the feeling with me.

I put Jimmy on my shoulders and thus began ten minutes that seemed like an eternity. We floated together on a cloud, sharing the second-best moment in my life—topped only by the day Jimmy was born and the first time I held him and he squeezed my finger with his fist. But that was different, the beginning of a human life. *This* was a climax, the Super Bowl. And my boy, five years old, was experiencing something I had waited for my whole life.

I couldn't bring Jimmy into the locker room with me, but my father got in later, after it had already emptied out. Dad threw his arms around me in a bear hug, saying, "Jimmy, I'm happier than a pig in shit."

"Me too, Dad. Me too."

That's what was really special about winning the Super Bowl. And that was when my dream turned back twenty years to Buffalo, to a voice at the top of the stairs . . .

"Johnny! Jimmy!"

The roar belonged to a rather stocky, very aggravated man whose belly was bouncing over the waistband of his boxer shorts, which were all he was wearing at that particular time.

My father. Don Burt. He had been called in to break up a hockey fight. Table hockey, that is. The game with the levers and rods, which I as an eight-year-old was treating with all the intensity due the Stanley Cup playoffs. The person who had done the calling was me. The person who was doing the pummeling was my brother John, four years older, at least thirty pounds heavier, and the table hockey nemesis for whose defeat I had been preparing so diligently for weeks.

Moments like those provided me with my first training for the NFL. Trying to beat John in everything—that was competition. Standing up to my dad's infamous German temper— that took guts. I've tackled Eric Dickerson with his goggles glaring and I've been double-teamed by the Hogs. But nothing has ever been as terrifying to me as the sight of my father at the top of those stairs.

This was supposed to be the day sweet revenge would be mine. John had been knocking me around the table rink since we first took up the game. Losing always drove me crazy, so when John took off for a night with his friends, I would slip down to the "ice" and practice plays until two or three in the morning, when my blistered fingers begged for mercy.

My persistence was quickly rewarded. It wasn't long before I had perfected an entire playbook of moves that would surely be the end of my brother's domination. The puck we used was not the flat, cheap thing that came with the game but a sleek modification with a roller ball in the middle so that it would whiz around the surface. I swear I had that thing moving as if by remote control. I was able to start the puck by flipping it to one of my metal defensemen and with a *snap*, I could careen that puck around the boards, catch it with my other defenseman and push it up to my wing.

*Poom.* Slip it back. *Poom.* It was unbelievable. If either of my two defensemen had the puck, John was dead. I'd set it in the track so he couldn't possibly poke-check it and with a slight flick, I'd get it to my center iceman. Wayne Gretzky had nothing over this guy. I'd bring him in nice and slow on the breakaway with two options. A quick twist would lift the puck into the top corner of the net. If I just pushed the man forward, the puck would lodge in the opposite side of the net. John had to guess—and on this night of nights, he was guessing wrong.

I was savoring the taste of vengeance. I wasn't yet a gracious winner. In fact, I was merciless.

John did what he had to do to quiet down the crowd. He stalked over and started beating me with both fists—only there wasn't a striped shirt around to send him off for fighting. The only defense I had was to appeal to the referee in the upstairs room by screaming at the top of my lungs, "Daaaaad!"

My father, who was relaxing in bed with the newspaper, oblivious to our big game, reacted coolly at first. "Shaddup," he'd yell down. The implied threat in my father's voice was my way of getting John to settle down for just a little while. Then, *poom, poom, slip,* score. I'd aggravate John so he'd come over and start beating on me again. Next thing we heard was Dad's bark with the irritation factor turned up: "Down!" he'd yell, as if we were dogs. So we heeled, for the time being.

When I completed the hat trick, it was enough to get our father out of bed and the two of us into deep shit. Our hardwood floors would send the warning. Steadily and loudly.

*Boom . . . Boom . . . Boom.*

We took off like scared rabbits down to the basement. *Boom. Boom. Boom.* His step was quicker now. Down there, we took our separate hiding positions, but we could hear him growling. "Johnny! Jimmy! Get up here!"

Uh oh. The moment of truth. We knew that if we made him walk down another flight of stairs, he'd really kill us. We had to make the move. There was only one route—right past him. John, being the older one, had to go first. Dad got hold of him and whacked him six or seven times. I then braced myself for the worst but when my turn came, I took only a couple of shots. He knew John had already gotten me six or seven times so he'd even it out, two for me, seven for him. In the NFL, you'd call it a makeup call. Back then I called it "Thanks, Dad."

That's how it all started for me, Jim Burt, nose tackle for the Super Bowl XXI champion New York Giants. Boy, that sounds good. Pardon me, but we used to be called the Same Old Giants, the "Same Old" being a derisive label for a team that kept finding unique ways to lose. But in 1986, we found out about winning. Our offense caught up to our defense in both ability and confidence and by the time we rolled into Pasadena, we had a team that simply refused to lose.

It was a magic year—a season in which the two biggest goals of my career, Super Bowl and Pro Bowl, were fulfilled for the first time after six back-breaking seasons in the NFL, and twenty-seven crazy years on planet Earth. As you're about to see, nothing came easy to me. I started my pro career from the bottom, a dirt-bag free agent just a few mistakes away from the waiver wire—which in a way made me luckier than a lot of my teammates who weren't as intimately familiar with the opposite side of success.

Fighting just came naturally to me. Good thing, because I had to fight for everything I ever got, which only made the getting that much sweeter. You've probably noticed. I'm the grateful Giant who climbed into the stands to slap hands with our fans after we won the NFC championship. What a moment it was for me, a hard-nosed kid from a proud, blue-collar town.

Buffalo. The name of the city even *sounds* like work—a beast of burden as opposed to more glamorous towns. But it was my playground then and the games were not for the chicken-hearted. Simple survival demanded courage, and like it or not I found myself charging headlong into challenges, proving wrong anyone who dared to say no. Emotion first, brains later. Manifested as defiance, that trait took me deep into trouble, which I faced with a solid right hand and an irrepressible sense of humor, not always in that order. Manifested as tenacity, it helped me reach goals some people said I couldn't—like making it in the NFL, for example.

Growing up wasn't pretty but it left me with a rather simple philosophy: Let nothing interfere with the achievement of a goal or the pursuit of *fun*. To that end, I can be doggedly loyal, reliable, and even a pain in the ass. When people ask Bill Parcells about me, he begins by explaining that football is not a game for well-adjusted people. He's also fond of saying that I'm a few quarts low. Bill, who is close to empty himself, should have seen me in my salad days.

You might say that my house was ruled by a code of antics. I grew up with two older sisters: Kathy—so strong we called her "Hoss" after the character in "Bonanza"—who was seven years older than me, and Sally, the chief policy advisor of the family, eight years my senior. Then there was John; a much younger brother, Dana; and a younger sister, Jeannie. My mother, Jean, had her hands full and sometimes *I* had my hands full of Mom, having antagonized and then sprinted away from the three older ones so that I could wrap myself around her legs and have her swat them away. Scolding didn't help much; it was in one ear and out the other. Sometimes, even pots and pans wouldn't work. All I can say is, after raising us and putting up with my father, I'm sure my mother will go straight to heaven.

Dad gave me plenty of slack as a kid, although when I went too far, my neck would end up in the proverbial noose. Today he is one of my best friends, a hardworking man I've tried to pattern my life after.

There's a story I'll always remember that sums up my relationship with my father. I was only eight years old when Dad took the entire family up to a swimming hole in Canada. There was a high dive there and none of my older brothers or sisters would let my father talk them into going off it. Finally, Dad said he was going to dive from it with me. I was scared, probably more than the other kids, but I trusted my father so much that I took his hand and climbed up to a spot on the cliffs. Down below, the water looked like a sacrificial well.

Off we went, hand in hand, father and son. And after that, I couldn't get enough of that dive, even though the others still didn't dare try it. To me, that's a big part of life. Taking that chance, trusting someone you know and love.

I was a lucky kid in that I got to spend a lot of quality time with my father. He worked hard Monday through Friday, sometimes twelve or fourteen hours a day. But he could put that behind him and play hard on the weekends at golf, bowling, or poker. Since I was always around Dad, I really learned poker. As an eight-year-old, I hustled all my brothers' friends, cleaning them out of all their change.

Even then, I knew the value of a dollar because I was already introduced to hard work and I didn't mind it a bit. My father had, and still has, his own Pepsi-Cola distributorship. From the time I was five years old, I helped him with his truck route, delivering the soda, or "pop" as we call it, to a string of stores in South Buffalo and Lackawanna.

John would come along too, of course. There was no twisting our arms to get us to go. We took pride in helping out on the truck. Dad used to do all that heavy work by himself so he looked forward to the days when we could join him. At first, when I was very young, I would just sort the empties while John helped load and unload. It didn't take long, however, before my competitive instincts had me trying to match John case for case.

Already grown into a big kid, John found the work easier than I did and he'd show off his strength, which made me mad. Soon, I'd be going after the full cases. I'd struggle like anything to stay on my feet but I just *had* to keep up with my brother. Dad wouldn't say a thing, unless one of the store owners did. Then he'd tell me to take it easy. I didn't, of course, but he knew I wasn't going to listen to him anyway.

Besides, it was good for me. All those full cases of soda, especially stacked one on top of the other, provided John and me with early weight training. I didn't lift any weights until my freshman year at the University of Miami, but those soda cases worked just as well. The job was always hard, no matter what season it was. In summer the orders would be heavy and we'd work from eight to seven. In the winter, we'd be fighting the elements.

In Buffalo, that means snow. Every day. And snowbanks. Everywhere.

In order to unload the truck, you'd have to lift the case out, climb into the snowbank and hoist it over the other side. If you had help, you could rest the case on the snowbank and use a two-man relay system. If not, forget about it. You were on your own. That never bothered Dad. The sight of him working was awe-inspiring. He wore short-sleeve shirts even on the coldest days and only a pair of rubbers over his work shoes. It didn't take long before he was soaking wet.

The cases had to be stacked five to a hand truck, or wheeler. Most of the stores on our route had stairs, which meant you had to lift up the loaded hand truck step by step, usually about seven or eight of them. That was the worst part because it was always wet, which made the footing treacherous. You'd have to get your weight under the truck and pull. If you slipped, there went I don't know how many dollars' worth of lost pop.

Counting cases was one way John and I kept score. Comparing the calluses on our hands was another. My father's hands were loaded with calluses from the fingers all the way to the palms. By the time I was seven or eight, my hands had thick ones, too. You could slap my hands all day and they wouldn't hurt. We used to wear those calluses proudly like badges, and at the end of the week, we'd show them off.

In the winter, when we wore gloves, whoever had the biggest holes in the fabric by the end of the week won. I'd cheat a little by using bottle openers to cut my holes bigger. John could never figure it out. I was always scheming.

Once, when I was fifteen, Dad went off on a golfing trip and left us in charge for the weekend. John helped another driver on Friday, and on Saturday the two of us were supposed to do Dad's route. Dad had all the stops lined up for John.

Or so he thought. He never would have believed what was about to happen. When John left for his route on Friday, I went to work, too. Early in the morning, I got into my father's Oldsmobile and took off for the garage where his truck was parked. Remember, I was fifteen. In New York State, driver's licenses are issued at age sixteen. No problem, though. At fourteen I had driven with my dad in the car—me at the controls, Dad scrunched up between the driver's door and me. My dad was a little crazy, too. Bill Parcells would probably say he wasn't exactly well-adjusted either.

There was one occasion when Dad and his regular golfing partners had finished their usual eighteen holes. As always, they started sucking down the Genesee beers until it got dark. They'd usually fill the table with cans, but on this day, they really outdid themselves. Guess who drove home? Yep. My dad was next to me, of course, just in case I screwed up. But on that day I think he was sleeping. In fact, I know it because I had to help him into the house, take out his false teeth, and hide them from Shadow, our dog. Shadow would chew up two or three pairs of dentures every year. Dad would have to eat soft foods for three or four days and, through his gums, he'd keep making threats about getting rid of the dog.

Back to me in the garage. My father's car had automatic transmission so it was simple to master. I just had to keep my head on a swivel for the cops. But the hard part came when I got to the garage. My dad's truck was tucked tightly in between the others. The beams and other obstacles created quite a problem in my mind since this was my first solo run and I had to play it cool with the other drivers and garage attendants.

Dad would have flipped his cork. But did I care? Of course not. I did know, however, that if I screwed up, it was *over*. But in my ongoing competition with John, this was going to be the ultimate challenge. It was the same feeling I had later in the championship game against the Redskins; I was too scared to lose—too scared to do anything else but play my ass off. This was Russian roulette, all or nothing.

We always left the keys in the truck, and I started her up. I'd experimented with the stick shift before so I had some idea about gears. Off I went. Somehow, I maneuvered her out of the garage and there I was on the open road, about twelve miles away from the plant where I had to fill the truck with the day's load of pop. Then I headed for the thruway.

I was careful not to let anyone in on the right and made sure nothing happened on my left. I just stayed in the right-hand lane, real slow, with my head right next to the side-view mirror. I wanted to make sure I didn't cross into the next lane because this truck was pretty wide.

The danger of it all made it exciting even though I was only doing about forty-five miles an hour, cautious as anything. I backed her up to the loading dock, got the pop and did the whole route. It went without a hitch.

When I got home, I told John about my coup and he was pretty ticked off at me because he had wanted to take credit for doing the route himself. On Sunday, Dad got home and I told him. But instead of letting me have it, he shook his head and said, "You're shittin' me." He wasn't sure if I was kidding him or not.

So I pulled the wad of cash from the day's deliveries out of my pocket and showed it to him. I was pretty proud of myself. He just looked at me and started to laugh. He walked away shaking his head and never said another word about it. I had really pulled one off and dodged a bullet.

That's what I mean about his letting me have some slack. And in our neighborhood in Buffalo, I needed it. Up through the eighth grade, we stuck it out in the inner city. We had a corner house across from the public school I attended. Actually, I spent kindergarten through fifth grade at St. Gerard's, but the sisters there slapped me with so many rulers, I got the twitches. I'd be daydreaming at my desk and they'd sneak up behind me and whack me as hard as they could either behind the neck or across the knuckles. Those nuns were meaner than Dick Butkus and Ray Nitschke put together. They had me under *control*. That's why I got out of there and transferred to Public School 82.

P.S. 82 bordered on the projects, at a time when racial tension was high and a number of riots had broken out around Buffalo. Even kids like myself were swept into the war, if you could call us kids. My son, Jimmy, is now six, and I can't imagine him fighting for his life the way I did—the way I had to— at that age.

When I was six, I signed up for my first year of Little League football, an activity that came complete with bonus lessons in hand-to-hand combat. You see, football practice was on the other side of the projects. I could either go around them, a mile-long detour, or go through them and take my lumps.

The way I saw it, I didn't have a choice. The way we were raised, you didn't back down from anything. Without considering the alternatives or the consequences, I would jump on my bike in my football gear and plunge straight through the middle of trouble. If anyone started something, I'd try to finish it. I was getting into fights every day. I didn't care. I was getting the crap beat out of me by John at home, so it didn't matter. Anything they could dish out, I'd already been through.

I got in my shots, but sometimes it wasn't enough. There were just too many other shots coming at me the other way. Still, I kept ticking and I never called my brother for help. I always took my bike back through there alone the next day again. Nothing discouraged me—and, as it turned out, I had one great advantage over all of them. My hard head.

Football practice was the great equalizer. My favorite drill was the one where two guys lined up about twenty-five feet apart. One guy got the ball. The other—this was my favorite part—got to run over him. I'd just put my head down and *whomp!* I'd knock these guys for loops, even though I wasn't that big then. I was six years old when I started that and before long, I really started to earn some respect in the neighborhood.

A number of years later, the neighborhood violence went too far. John was jumped by a gang and left for dead. The last thing he remembered hearing was the suggestion that they run him over with their van; he heard another voice say, "Don't bother, he's already dead." He dragged himself home with both eyes blackened and his back scarred by cigarette burns and buckle marks. Even then we stayed. But the final straw came when I was accused of demolishing another kid's bike. True, I'd been fighting with him, but it was his cousin who actually did the damage and blamed me. My dad gave me a beating for it, even though I was screaming that I didn't do it. If I had, I would have taken the whipping graciously.

Knowing that I would have, too, my sister Sally figured there was something more to the story. So she and I went over to the kid's house. His mother came to the door and politely invited us in. As we were telling our story, the kid's cousin—the real culprit—entered the room and pulled a kitchen knife. He and I started scuffling and I managed to pry the knife from him. But I also found myself trapped with this maniac because the woman had panicked, locked the door, and called her husband. My little brother, Dana, who was waiting outside, heard the commotion and ran back to our place to get Dad.

When Dad arrived, he shoved the door open. The kid's mother began explaining why she locked us in, but Dad didn't want to hear it. He grabbed Sally and me and we all got out of there. When we got home, the kid's father called and Sally got on the phone. He was yelling and screaming at her and she motioned to my father to get on the phone. The guy was making all sorts of threats and Dad told him that if he wanted to, he could bring his ass on over. We all took our battle stations to wait for him but he never showed. That night, with Sally arguing the case in favor of, we decided we were going to move.

I didn't know then how that decision would so radically affect the next five years of my life. I guess we *had* to get out of the inner city—but looking back, I'm not sure if it was the right thing to do. Nevertheless, the Burts and the Bills left Buffalo in the same year and found a home in the same patch of high-income suburbia.

Our family moved into a house not far from where Rich Stadium was being built, in Orchard Park. Even the name sounded wimpy. I'd been street-hardened by the city and now I was being turned loose in a cul-de-sac society. I was in for a major case of culture shock. There was a different set of rules in the suburbs and a whole population of snooty suburbanites ready to pass judgment. I felt stifled by an alien, imposed set of values that wouldn't have cut it back in Buffalo. I had already been conditioned. I didn't need to be accepted. And certainly, after years of watching my back in Buffalo, I wasn't about to trust people easily.

The kids were different . . . soft. Authority seemed insincere, as if the people in charge were on some sort of power trip. I wouldn't say I rebelled, exactly. I just didn't respect anyone enough to listen. I got a taste of that insincerity soon after we moved in and especially during my first freshman football practice at Orchard Park High School.

I thought these guys were all pansies compared to the city kids I'd been knocking heads with in the Buffalo youth leagues. Most of the Orchard Park guys were out for contact football for the first time. I'd already been doing it for seven years and had the fundamentals down cold—along with a trained-killer outlook.

When we lined up for tackling drills I was chomping at the bit. I thrived on that stuff but all these guys were afraid to get in there and stick their nose into something. In Buffalo, we'd be fighting to get in line, instead of hanging back as these kids were.

I was little, too, about 130 pounds, wiry, but certainly no

bigger than anyone else on the field. And I was killing them. I'd take them off their feet and plant them like the pansies they were. Not that I thought it was any big feat. I guess they didn't like me very much but it really didn't matter. I know I didn't like them.

At the same time, the coach of this chicken outfit seemed to be more concerned with organization and discipline than with plain football. The school was clean, the equipment was brand-new and all the coaches wore color-coordinated shorts. I didn't know anything about all that. I just knew how to play, and the adjustment wasn't coming easily. During the stretching exercises I was goofing around and the coach had me run penalty laps. He eventually got so annoyed, he told me to report to him before school the next day, when he was going to teach me a lesson and run me until I dropped.

I didn't show. At practice that afternoon, he said, "You're off the team. You don't get along with any of the players, anyway," he went on, ignoring the fact I'd only been to practice two or three times. "And you didn't show up this morning."

I pleaded my case a bit so he said he would take up the matter with the team. I certainly didn't have any friends there. Big deal. When he took a vote whether to kick me off or keep me, I was ousted by a nearly unanimous margin. I only got one vote and that came from a real derelict. No one liked him. That's why he liked me.

So, no freshman football. *What's wrong with these guys?* I thought.

I didn't realize, nor would I have cared if I *had* realized, that there was a whole town asking the same question about me. I was getting a reputation around this small town of small minds—as a problem kid from the inner city. What I called scrappiness, they called juvenile delinquence.

One man, however, refused to listen to all that crap. He was a hard-nosed guy named Jerry Kempf, an ex-Marine and coach of the Orchard Park hockey team.

He needed one more player to fill his roster, and a couple of kids I knew had recommended that he take a look at me.

I remember our first meeting got off to a bad start. Typically, I showed up fifteen minutes late for the tryout, my subconscious way of testing him, and he let me know immediately that he wasn't going to stand for it. At the same time, I knew there was something different about the unpretentious way he exerted authority. Instinctively, I started calling him Mr. Kempf. I still do to this day.

At first, Mr. Kempf didn't have any idea who I was. I was only thirteen—I would be playing with fifteen- and sixteen-year-olds—and I weighed only 130 pounds. *Who's this scrawny little wimp?* he must have thought. So he asked me, "Who are you?" "Jim Burt, sir," I answered. Then I overheard him asking Peter Schmafeld, one of the kids who recommended me, "I thought you said this kid was tough and aggressive?"

"Wait till you see him play, Coach," Peter replied. That fired me up. It was all I thought about as I put on my equipment. Once I got on the ice, the puck never left my stick. I was just streaking up and down the ice and when I was on defense I was throwing hip checks at people. I was all over the rink and I never once came off the ice. Then I started getting tired and wondered when Mr. Kempf would give me a break. But once I realized he was testing me to see if I'd quit and slow down, I went even harder. That set the tone for a great relationship—and the first great outside influence on my life.

I wanted to do well for this coach, who had given me a shot even though others in the community were bad-mouthing me; with no freshman football to worry about, I threw myself into hockey. When I set my mind on something, I'd just do it and do it and do it. I wasn't very good at hockey when I first started playing in Buffalo—and I wanted to be. So I'd go down to my garage, set up the net, and stickhandle around the poles for three, four, five hours. I'd picture myself on the ice (the same kind of thought pattern I go through now with football, visualizing myself on the field). The poles would be defensemen and I'd slip them and score.

I patterned myself after Gil Perreault, the star center iceman of the Sabres, whose trademarks were his slick moves and the way he could control the puck. I developed into a decent skater and stickhandler. Just decent. I still wasn't that good. But in my freshman and sophomore years, I played on four or five different teams, working at it every chance I could. I guess it's the same old story. Nothing comes easy to me, then or now. But the thing that always intrigues me is the challenge and the competition. There's a certain high that comes from working toward something and achieving it.

I suppose my favorite part of the game was sticking it to the players who thought of themselves as tough guys. They used to call me "Elbows" because of the way I took people into the corners with these big, oversized pads of mine. Let someone start a fight with one of my teammates and I'd bait him into picking something with *me*. Pounding these guys was fun and going into the locker room to laugh about it later was even better. But the funniest part was how the story grew larger every day back in school, until by the end of the week, a scuffle had become a bloodbath.

I remember one wise guy who kept roughing up our guys and mouthing off to Mr. Kempf whenever he skated past our bench. Later in the game, he was ejected for cutting someone with a high stick. As he was leaving the ice, we were trying to get at him but the referees shielded him. He kept mouthing off, though, and once he got on the other side of the boards, he hung himself out over the glass and started swinging his stick at us. That was about all I could take. I snuck off to the side and grabbed his stick. Then I greeted him with a right hand that met him square in the mouth. The next thing I knew, he was spitting teeth at me. I looked up and saw that I had knocked out all of his front choppers.

It turned out that his persistent slashing and high-sticking led to a hearing by the league. He'd injured several players before our incident ever happened and he had already gone through a hearing once. This time, the league threw him out. Justice was served. No teeth. No hockey. No smile.

At one point, I was playing on four different teams, including an amateur all-star squad. We were coached by Mr. Kempf and we'd head across the border into Canada to find suitable competition. This league had a rule that if a player was sent off for fighting, he'd have to serve a three-game suspension. We kept about four extra jerseys on hand for those times. If we were playing at a place far-off enough for them not to notice, I'd suit up as somebody else. Many times, I was Stash, the name on our fourth jersey. I wasn't the only guy who did it, either.

In my junior year in high school, a growth spurt added seven or eight inches and about eighty pounds to my frame, so I started laying off the fighting. Hockey was still a lot of fun, and we won a lot of games with a great bunch of guys. By this time, no one could touch us as a team. The sad part about it was that they were seniors and I was a junior. It was our last year of playing together and it turned out to be my last year of hockey, too.

The better athletes were in the class ahead of me. The athletes in my class seemed to have the same mentality they had on that freshman-year football team. Anyway, Mr. Kempf was no longer the coach and after playing for him, how could I play for anyone else?

You see, Mr. Kempf had been standing by me through some tough times off the ice. My reputation as some sort of thug spilled out of the arena, and older kids in their twenties came looking for me to pick fights. Hockey had only enhanced my hoodlum image; I had a baby face then. They probably thought I was an easy mark. But I handled myself against all of them.

Even families got into the act. There was a time when three brothers came after me, one after the other. And I splattered them, one after the other.

My biggest problem was that I could never walk away from anything. I remember my mother telling me, "Jimmy, now if anybody comes, just walk away, just walk away." I'd say, "Right, Ma," and keep on walking into trouble.

I was a screwup, I really was. I did wacky stunts—but never to harm anybody really. We had fun and we laughed about it. I had a rep, but it didn't bother me. I didn't think much about the consequences. Every weekend, something had to happen, something bizarre, something crazy. School was a joke, too. I'd been a pretty good student in grammar school but at Orchard Park, I finagled my way through. I did as little work as I could and spent as little time as possible in class. Whatever I could get away with, I tried to get away with.

Naturally, everyone knew me as the scourge of Orchard Park, and by my junior and senior years, people were saying, This kid's going to be a bum the rest of his life. It was true that I was wild and at times I was out of control. But you know what? There wasn't one of them who tried to sit down with me and talk sense into me. That was something I'd have to do for myself a few years later.

Dad tried in his own way. He'd tell me I wasn't going to live to see twenty. But at that age, you don't want to hear that stuff from your father. Mr. Kempf cared too, of course, but was too close a friend; I needed someone else in authority to take me in hand and channel my energies into something constructive. I know that's what I do now when I visit schools and see kids like myself. Instead, back then the authority types just harassed me, which only riled me more.

If I could go back, I know I'd still do some of the crazy things to have fun but I know I would have thought more with my head and less with my emotions. I never started any of those fights, but I could have avoided maybe eighty percent of them. Back then, I enjoyed my reputation. I enjoyed being the tough guy. And if someone provoked me, I just went back at him harder—something I've used to my benefit on the football field.

Let me give an example. You walk out of school and there's an older kid waiting for you. The whole school is letting out and watching, sometimes even chanting, "Go, go." You send a friend over to tell the guy you don't want to fight. But he only says that you're chicken. And that's how it went; that's how it started. One time I beat up a kid who tried to run me over with his car in a McDonald's parking lot. He even pressed charges (which were later thrown out of court).

At least I had a few friends I could trust in Orchard Park, especially Kyle Palmer, who was my best buddy. I first hooked up with Kyle as a sophomore and by the end of that football season, we became best friends. Kyle, who was born and raised in the South, said he had never had so much fun in his life before—which had to be right because he was one of the deadheads who helped vote me off the freshman team. One of my first major projects after a year of living in this pansyland was to give Kyle a personality transplant. In doing so, I proudly created my first monster.

The summer before our senior year, we figured we'd get jobs, but how it happened was quite by accident. I'd been invited to a party and went there with Kyle, only to be told Kyle couldn't come in. I guess they remembered what a nerd he had been as a freshman and they were concerned he might crash a good party. I ended up in a scuffle where I was outnumbered and didn't fare too well.

Kyle drove his car back to my house but I was so ticked off, I wanted to cool out by walking home. Unfortunately, the same chumps who got me at the party followed me in their van. When I spotted them, I hurled a rock at their windshield. Well, they jumped me, and let me have it again. When I got home, even my dad was so pissed off that he joined me, Kyle, John, and about three others on a mission of revenge. For the next few hours, we formed a search party for those guys. We were about to give up when, by chance, we checked Rapple's, a bar on my corner. Sure enough, some people there said they had seen the guys and that they were headed for Mickey Rat's, a joint forty-five minutes away on Lake Erie.

It was about 1 A.M. and Dad went home but the rest of the posse headed straight for Mickey Rat's. I had on my battle gear—leather jacket, work boots, and old shitty-ass jeans. When we got to the place, I walked in first and saw the chumps at the Fusbol table. To make a long story short, I was joined by my five friends and we proceeded to redecorate the gang of them, red being the primary color. The bouncers let it go. It was already out of control and we took the place under *our* control. After the smoke cleared, the owner came up to me and asked if I wanted a job. "Sure," I said. He fired half of the bouncers he had and hired me and Kyle. We became the youngest bouncers in town at eighteen, and we worked there the rest of the summer.

The fight a lot of my friends still talk about shouldn't even have involved me. It was one of those I could have avoided. We were at a drive-in and one of the guys in our group started throwing gravel. Some of it hit another car. Now, I wasn't even close to the scene and I really didn't want to participate. The guy in the car, a big guy with his high school football jersey on, charged out and asked who threw the rocks. A kid named Cornelius, a real weasel, said, "He did," pointing to me.

I really didn't want any part of the whole thing until the guy in the football jersey did an unwise thing. He charged at me and smacked me in the chest. Casually, I took a sip of beer and set the bottle down on the car I had been leaning on. Then I drilled him with about four rights, jackhammer style. I did some damage, drew some blood, probably rearranged his face. Later, I went up to him and offered him a beer. He and his buddy came over and drank with us the rest of the night.

Mr. Kempf had a lot of rules, but there was one in particular I had trouble with. No one dates the coach's daughter. But you know me and rules.

I'd seen Colleen around school but never paid any attention to her, except to tell her dad what she did wrong. I loved to stir up trouble. I'd take something that wasn't that big a deal and build it into a major crime. For instance, she'd smoke cigarettes in school and I'd egg Mr. Kempf on as I told him the story: "You mean to tell me you let your daughter smoke? You don't let us do this and that. How could you let your own daughter get away with that stuff? Unbelievable."

He'd reply, his face beet-red, "We'll see. I don't allow that stuff in my house." Then he'd walk away pissed off and determined to make life as miserable as possible for Colleen.

That didn't put me on her list of favorite people. I didn't care. I was too interested in sports and she definitely wasn't. But interests change. One day, I started looking at her differently, as if she were actually alive.

We ended up in the same car at a drive-in theater, packed about eight kids to a car. She thought it was neat when at 235 pounds, I managed to hide on the floor and avoid paying for the ticket. Then I offered to go Dutch with her the rest of the night. A little wit. A little intellect. Soon her opinion of me was completely turned around. She began thinking of me as a nice cuddly teddy bear. What a con artist.

Mr. Kempf began to notice that I was hanging around his house all the time, but he thought it was because of little Steven, Colleen's younger brother and a hockey player himself. One day, Colleen summoned up the nerve to ask her dad what he thought of the idea of her dating Jim Burt.

"You can't. It's my rule. None of my players can date my daughter."

Colleen told him we'd already been seeing each other for two months. Mr. Kempf dropped the rule.

Our first official date was a Sabres–Islanders playoff game at War Memorial Auditorium. Hey, deep down, I was the romantic type. And what could be sweeter than poetry on ice, with a few good hockey fights mixed in? Besides, the tickets were free because Mr. Kempf gave them to us. Parking was free, too, because I refused to pay for the two-dollar lot. So we left the car ten blocks away. Colleen, who'd always been pampered by her dad, didn't like the hike. I thought I was just being practical. My philosophy: two dollars saved is two dollars earned. Her interpretation: I was cheap.

Colleen will tell you that I loved to pick fights as a kid, which is absolutely untrue. I mean, a guy has to defend his girlfriend's honor, right? We used to go to Chestnut Ridge Park, which was inhabited by a gang of long-haired sleazy types. They'd be sitting on the steps of a restaurant where we liked to eat. Like a gentleman, I'd let Colleen walk on ahead of me. Inevitably, one of the creeps would pinch her behind, which is when I would jump into action by discreetly punching the SOB in the nose. After all, I had to protect Mr. Kempf's daughter.

There was one incident in particular that helped convince me that Colleen was the girl for me. We were visiting my grandfather in St. Petersburg during my freshman year in college—I was at the University of Miami and she was at Bauder Fashion College—and I had to be back in Miami, six hours away, for exams at eight the next morning.

We slept until 2 A.M., then hit the road. I was doing about eighty mph in the middle of redneck Florida when I passed a weigh station. A trooper had caught me on radar.

Time for instantaneous action. I glanced in the rearview mirror and saw that I was way ahead of him—he was just starting his car. I could beat him. So I floored the thing to about a hundred and twenty. But I also knew that if I kept going straight, he'd just radio ahead and get me.

At this point Colleen was scrunched into a ball on the floor of the car as if she were in a Clint Eastwood movie. She was begging me to stop so I'd be in less trouble. Was she kidding?

I had New York plates. Strike one. I had a black Cutlass Salon with a T-roof and red interior. Strike two. I didn't have a license because I never bothered to renew it. Strike three. If this guy ever stopped me, I might still be in jail.

"No way," I said to Colleen as I hit the gas pedal. I zipped off the second exit at about a hundred mph, then pulled off the road into the parking lot of a restaurant, which was closed and pitch dark. I turned off the lights and waited. As soon as the trooper went whizzing by one way, I whizzed by in the other direction. My leg, I'll admit, was shaking. It was one of the two or three times I got away with it, but the only time with Colleen in the car.

Anyway, I figured if Colleen could put up with that, she could put up with anything—and believe me, there was a lot more to put up with. It was easy to see that I'd better marry this girl. A year later, I did. That was the nicest thing about Orchard Park.

# 2

## MIAMI

## "Shit or Get Off the Pot"

Talk about ridiculous. At one point, my entire football career hung in the balance over a grilled cheese sandwich.

I'd already signed to play at the University of Miami for coach Lou Saban, a Buffalo legend. He had been the only coach to bring the Buffalo Bills a championship. First I had to graduate from Orchard Park High, where a certain teacher named Miss Matthews was blocking my path as assuredly as a center for the Washington Redskins.

A little background. I was always a model student, as long as you were building a model of *Animal House.* I usually found a way to shake things up in the classroom—sometimes by choice, sometimes by accident. A good example was metal shop, where I once set a school record for a single class period by sending three kids to the nurse's office. One friend was hit in the face with a hammerhead that flew off its handle as I was reforming a piece of sheet metal. Within minutes, I was reforming someone else's hand with the same hammer. The third incident was my fault entirely. I was horsing around with a kid by brandishing a soldering iron I thought had cooled off. Wrong. When I touched the tip of the iron to the poor kid, his pants caught on fire and his rear end was branded with my mark forever. He screamed. Very loud.

29

This last catastrophe brought the principal steaming into the classroom where he asked me, "What the hell are you doing down here?"

Good question. I'd caused havoc in those hallways for four years, not maliciously, but because everything seemed like good fun to me. I served my share of detention and wrote my share of penitential essays, but it never did lead me off the path of mayhem. *Hey*, I thought, *they expect it from me.* They would have been disappointed if I didn't cross that line of good behavior. After all, I had to keep the school disciplinarian working. That's the way I looked at it. Without me, he might not have had a job.

In any case, Orchard Park High School required its graduates to fulfill a certain number of elective credits. Our core subjects were difficult enough, so Kyle and I decided to look for an elective class that would be a piece of cake.

We found it. Cooking.

Miss Matthews, a well-meaning single woman in her middle thirties, was the instructor. Poor Miss Matthews. I feel sorry for her now, because there was no way she could have been prepared to deal with our shenanigans.

The class was a blast, especially since the students in the period before ours took it so seriously. They prepared all sorts of great-tasting desserts and left them behind in the refrigerator for testing the next day. When Chef Kyle and I arrived for our eighth-period class, *we* performed the all-important taste test. We gorged on their creations, stuffing them into our hungry mouths with both hands, usually leaving a telltale pile of crumbs around the refrigerator. Unfortunately, Miss Matthews was not grading our appetites.

One classmate, a sophomore named Brendan Beguine, was even crazier than I was. One day Miss Matthews got between Brendan, myself, and a chocolate cake he was about to hurl at my face. "Don't you do it. Don't you do it," Miss Matthews shrieked. Brendan did it. He just reached over her shoulder and the cake disintegrated into little pieces all over me and the floor. It continued that way for a year. By the time our term project was due, the few normal people in the class were bug-eyed and Miss Matthews couldn't wait until the semester was over. I don't blame her.

My term project was to prepare a grilled cheese sandwich. If I could not or would not perform this vital display of culinary skill, I'd be given an incomplete grade and would come up short on my required elective credits. In order to graduate, in order to play college football, in order to have any shot at the NFL and the Super Bowl, I had to hand in that sandwich.

You know what my reaction was. I refused. "You've got to be kidding me. I've been here four years and in order to get out, I have to make a grilled cheese sandwich?" The answer was a definitive yes. That was strange as I had thought Orchard Park would have done anything to get rid of me.

Well, they wanted my dad to come into school for a meeting with Miss Matthews and the principal. But after four years of this kind of thing, Dad had enough. As far as he was concerned, this was my problem. Luckily, my sister Sally had more common sense than I did. She offered to help. Some help. . . . She ended up making the whole thing while I watched TV. I swallowed my pride, not the sandwich, and delivered the project on the last day of school. Thus began my college football career.

Miami had been an easy choice because of Lou Saban and because, quite frankly, my reputation had scared off a bunch of other schools. Let me tell you, I was a hell of a high school player and under other circumstances I would have been more heavily recruited. But only Lou had the smarts—or was it nerve?—to go after me.

I played fullback and defensive end in high school and both were much more fun than nose tackle. Defensive end is really a fun position, especially if you have a destructive nature on the field. I really did some damage there, especially in my junior year, when I was only one of two non-senior starters, along with Mike Morsian, a very good outside linebacker. Our defensive line consisted of me, Craig Wolfley, who is now with the Steelers, and Larry Full, who played in the Canadian Football League for a few seasons and now wrestles professionally under the name Lex Luger. Three future pros playing side-by-side must have been some sort of record. I remember teams trying the quarterback option play on us once to each side, and then forgetting about it for the rest of the game.

The quarterback, with the option of pitching out or keeping the ball, had only to take one step forward and I would be in his face, making the big play, something I hardly get a chance to do as a Giant. I felt like Carl Banks or Lawrence Taylor, at least at that level. It's too bad that particular team didn't get to play a full season together. A teachers' strike stopped us after five games. We won them all but never got to play another one. I hope Miss Matthews appreciated that sacrifice.

All in all, it seemed as though nothing was working out for me in Orchard Park; I needed to get away to school. I had to escape some of the guys I was hanging around with. I had to get out on my own, even away from my family. You can only do high school stuff—that's what I called it—for so long, then you've got to buckle down or you're going to end up being a loser. For a long time I wasn't ready to do that, but I finally realized when it was the right time to quit; when it was party time and when it wasn't. When I got to college it was time to get serious. It took me a semester to adjust, but I did, thanks to Lou Saban.

Lou was the person who finally made me take control of my life. When he came to my house to recruit me for his first team at Miami, I knew I wanted to play for him. There was no bullshit about him. Even my father liked him. I also knew that he was sticking out his neck for me. I was the only player he recruited personally. None of his assistants ever saw me. He said that as long as I was willing to make a commitment, he was willing to give me a shot. We made a deal. He took me south as his prodigy, while most of Orchard Park, with the exception of Dad and Mr. Kempf, was betting that I wouldn't last a semester.

At first, I didn't exactly take advantage of my fresh start. Miami was an exciting campus and I was still screwing around and not worrying about the consequences. There's a story at Miami that I hung a kid out of a balcony by his ankles. I used to deny it, but I'm admitting here that it's true. You see, there I was, walking in front of a dorm when a shopping cart came crashing down on the sidewalk, missing my head by a couple of feet. If it had hit me, I would been part of the cement. The gouge left by the impact was huge.

Naturally, I wasn't going to let the madman who dropped the cart get away with it. I was sure what window it had come from so I charged up to the twelfth-story room and grabbed the suspect—your average drugged-out Miami undergrad. Despite his screams, I dangled him out the window so he could see the twisted remains of the shopping cart that had nearly killed me. I told my friends that I was going to let go of his ankles. I was kidding, of course, but he didn't know that.

Word of that incident never reached Lou, thank God, but on Thanksgiving night of that freshman year, I unknowingly pulled what was to be my last turkey of a stunt. Colleen and I and another couple were celebrating the holiday at a place called Big Daddy's. Of course, at Miami that year we were always finding reasons to celebrate. We would just make them up. Anyway, we drank well into the night and when we got back to campus, my friend didn't want to walk back to his dorm. So I took a shortcut—across the intramural football field. I couldn't just drive straight across the lawn, of course. I had to execute a few doughnuts—figure eights and things—along the way. The field looked like a bomb had hit it.

Before we made it across, we were surrounded by campus police cars with their sirens blasting and lights flashing. They took my name and number and let me off.

Well, the next day, Lou got wind of my landscaping project. I was in the weight room when I heard he was looking for me. I didn't want to face his wrath in there, so I headed straight into his office to wait for him. When he got there, he let me have it with all the power his lungs could muster. I'm telling you, he was the loudest, most terrifying man you'd ever want to see in your life—except for my father.

First, Lou, who has the look of a Marine drill sergeant, took the office door and slammed it shut. Then he let loose with a tirade that scared people in the other end of the building. "God, you disappointed me," he said, his face a ripe tomato. "I'm gonna kill you. Just f—— up one more time and you're out. I won't care. The worst thing will be that I could have spent the money on someone else."

What could I do? I just sat there. I didn't move, I didn't speak. I knew he was serious. Suddenly, he just smacked me in the back of my head with his hand. *Whap!* I didn't react. If I'd been hit by another person, I would have struck back. I'd been doing that all my life anyway. But Lou's words were hitting home. I was his handpicked player. He got me out of Orchard Park and now I was about go back there to shovel snow. "Shit or get off the pot," he told me. I got off the pot.

Suddenly, it began to sink in. I would have gone home a failure and proved Orchard Park right. *Failure* scared me more than any other word. For the first time, I could see myself as a bum, just like those twenty-year-old losers in Orchard Park who had nothing better to do than pick fights with me. Something clicked after that incident. I became totally dedicated. I still did crazy things, but nothing to get me in trouble with Lou and not at the expense of my new goal, to make All-American and to play in the NFL.

I always had that dream, but I never really acted upon it until after Saban's "talk." In high school, I excelled because I had natural talent. Here, nothing less than a total effort was going to be satisfactory.

Lou had meant what he said and from that day on, he watched my every move. He watched where I parked my car, how I spent my free time, and made sure I went to every class. He arranged for Dr. Harry "Scooter" Mallios, a fullback on Miami's national championship team in the fifties, to be my academic advisor. Dr. Mallios took care of me so well that the team used to call me his son. All Dr. Mallios had to say was that he was going to tell Lou if I missed a class. I had no desire to run afoul of Lou again.

In other words, I grew up. I never found myself in Lou's office again and the same was true when Howard Schnellenberger took over as head coach during my last two years. My senior year, I was named captain and made All-American. Take that, Orchard Park!

Of course, staying out of trouble didn't mean I had to become a choirboy. By the time I left college, I had established new standards of clean fun that still have them talking in Coral Gables. My nickname was "Bam-Bam" and my specialty was motivation. You've heard of "Moon over Miami"? I helped put it there before the big Florida State game by leading the team around campus clad only in our skivvies. Earlier that day I got the entire team up and out of the dorm, grabbed my curl bar and had us chanting, "We want FSU" as we pumped iron on the campus lawn, much to the astonishment of passersby.

Before big games, I would force the freshmen to wrestle each other, preferably to death. If I wasn't satisfied with the enthusiasm being generated, I jumped in there myself. None of the frosh wanted *that* to happen. They gladly mauled each other instead.

At times, I'd just get the itch to wrestle myself, so I'd coerce my roommates, Art Kehoe and Tony Fitzpatrick, into impromptu tag team matches that could last for hours. At other times I was *forced* into wrestling. There was a naïve freshman by the name of Danny Brown (now the defensive line coach at Louisville), who unwisely woke me up from my sleep. No one disturbed my sack time. He had been out partying that night; now, by my senior year, I didn't like to go out that much. If I did, I drank seltzer water. I still do. Well, Danny Brown came back in a good mood and wouldn't stop poking me, even after I told him to cut it out. Finally, I just locked the door and started throwing the guy around. He came in there about eleven o'clock. He didn't get out till one-thirty. I'd pin him, let him up, and throw him down again. He must have sweated out every ounce of liquor he had in him.

Tony Fitzpatrick—"Fitzy" for short—was my personal project. When he got to Miami as a freshman, Artie and I recruited him as our personal gofer. Lucky guy. He was kind of cocky then, always running his mouth, so I had to take him down a few pegs. One day, he stole my keys and just drove off with my car. When he came back to my room, I pinned him to the ground and shaved off all his chest hairs. The next day at practice, his chest was covered with Band-Aids and he could hardly wear his shoulder pads.

Like me, Fitzy came in as a linebacker, 202 pounds in his case. Before I was done with him, he was a 245-pound nose tackle. I used to drag Fitzy out of bed each morning, force him to do four hundred push-ups, then take him down to the weight room for a couple of torturous hours. There was nothing I made him do that I didn't do myself, however, and it was to pay off for us both. After I left, Fitzy would star on Miami's national championship team and later make it to the pros with the Houston Gamblers of the USFL.

By the end of my freshman year, I was obsessed with being the best player I could be. The coaches already decided that they were going to move me to nose and when I got back to Buffalo for the summer, I threw myself into weight training for the first time in my life. Craig Wolfley hooked me up with Don Reinholdt, who as a power lifter had won the title of the World's Strongest Man. We worked long and hard in his basement gym that summer and when I got back to Miami for my sophomore year, I was ready. I was 238 as a freshman and 242 as a sophomore, but it was distributed differently—less flab and more muscle.

I got to be a starter in my sophomore year after the junior-college transfer ahead of me was injured. I never let go of the job. I really wanted to excel and I knew I had to do more than just lift weights. I knew that I had the heart to make it in the pros, but I felt I had to help my game in every way I could.

For instance, people freak out when they see that I can do a split. Believe me, I'm not a natural gymnast. I used to go through a grueling two hours of stretching every night for two and a half years as part of my kick-boxing program with Harold Roth.

I first saw the guy at the Cuban disco where I worked as a bouncer. He blew my mind by dancing on one leg, with the other held up to his head. Later I asked him how he did it and he showed me a few other tricks.

"See that?" he said, pointing to a plant hanging a foot below the ceiling. In an instant, he kicked it down. I was amazed. I asked him if he could teach me. That kind of flexibility and quickness could give me an edge on the defensive line. "Sure," he said. And that's how I first entered his torture chamber.

Every night, I would sit against a wall and push my legs outward until my muscles were on the brink of tearing. As soon as I hit the point of pain, I held that position for five minutes. It hurt so much that tears would run down my face and my clothes would become totally drenched. I would lay with my legs up against a wall, and Harold would take hold of them and push down until they could go no farther. Then he would put one leg on the floor and force the other to its limit. When I was done, the only way I could get up was to inch my legs back into place.

It took about a year of this routine before I was able to do a full split. For added quickness, I overdosed on racquetball. By the time I started football practice as a junior, the effects were already incredible. My position coach, Harold Allen—talk about great coaches—couldn't believe the added quickness I had. Today I consider it one of my best assets in the NFL.

My routine once the football season was over consisted of the training table, classes, four hours of weight lifting, racquetball, dinner, and three hours of stretching. In between I found time to beat anybody in anything they wanted to try me in. My roommate Artie, for example, was a pretty good backgammon player. I didn't know the game but I forced him into teaching me. Then I wouldn't let him leave until I could beat him consistently. When I got through with Artie, I would drag anyone in from the halls to play me. By the time I got through, nobody could beat me. Losing in anything, you see, infuriated me.

My fitness routine took care of conditioning. Coach Allen took care of my technique. His record speaks for itself. He's sent sixteen defensive linemen into the pros including myself, Don Latimer, and Ruben Carter. He's such a stickler for fundamentals that when I got to the pros I was ahead of a lot of guys. Bill Belichick has said that as a rookie, my technique was more advanced than the veterans'.

The other big thing with Coach Allen was *hustling.* He's a good old boy from the South, and when he told you to move, you moved. There was no back talk with him.

I remember one occasion at Miami when Fitzy and I were late to a meeting. This followed an incident in which we sent a bunch of unwanted pizzas over to Assistant Coach Grace, who ran the athletic dorm.

Fitzy was only a freshman then and before we got to the meeting I told him if he played it cool, Coach Allen might let it slide. Instead, Fitzy came in giggling and laughing. "Burt . . . Fitzy," Coach Allen said, "I want to see you after the meeting."

"Fitz, you dummy," I whispered. I knew we were in for it.

When the meeting was over, Coach Allen took us in the corner. "Boys, boys, boys," he started. He spoke very deliberately. "I will see you at six o'clock in the morning. Make sure you're right on time because if you're not, you'll be back every day for two weeks."

The next morning came and he put us through the wringer. He had us rolling on our stomachs, a hundred yards back and forth, doing crabwalks, forward rolls, push-ups, sit-ups; all sorts of crazy stuff to get us tired as well as dizzy. We were lucky it was morning and the sun wasn't hot yet. But in any case, we had a plan.

Fitzy, you see, had a special talent—acting. He could retch anywhere, on cue. So after taking some punishment, I said, "Fitzy, *now*," and we started rolling all crazy ways and acting as if we were punch-drunk. Then Fitzy wobbled his way over to the other side of the field and started retching. Coach Allen figured we'd had enough.

"All right, boys," he said. "We're gonna have no more of that shit with Coach Grace, will we?"

"No, Coach. No, Coach." Pretending to hold each other up, we started our final lap. To this day, Coach Allen thinks he destroyed us. But he didn't hurt us at all. That time, anyway.

The coach had his days, too. Nothing I ever faced in the pros compared to some of the things Coach Allen used to put us through. I had never been as tired on a practice field as I was then. But I was younger. I didn't know any better than to plow right through it.

At one workout my freshman spring, we were on the field for I don't know how many straight plays while the temperature got up to one hundred dog-day degrees. I was on the second-team defense and the coaches were trying to test us to see how much we had. The same eleven guys stayed out there on defense while they ran the first, second, and third-team offenses on and off. We had guys dropping all over the field. Whenever I could, I'd go off to the sideline and drink as much as possible. But everything I drank, I threw back up. I didn't need Fitzy to fake it.

There was another practice in my senior year when I was out there for ninety-seven straight plays. I know because I counted. I had said something to Coach Allen to piss him off and he ran me so hard I lost sixteen pounds of water. After practice, I sat there for hours just drinking. I was so dehydrated, I couldn't walk.

But I tell you, I loved Coach Allen, the same way I loved Saban. Lou, in fact, should have gotten more of the credit for Schnellenberger's national championship team. Lou recruited most of the players on the club; because those classes were so successful, it helped bring more recruits into the program even after Lou left because of a standoff with administration. I think Lou gets short shrift. He's really the one who got Miami's program going again.

Between Lou, Coach Allen and Dr. Mallios, I turned my energies toward more constructive endeavors. I've always had a knack for dealing with kids—maybe because I've got so much kid in me. Even while I was screwing up back in Orchard Park, I found the time to take my little nieces and nephews on trips to the playground and zoo. Now that I'm a father, there's nothing more pleasurable to me than playing with my son. Without a doubt, he is one of my life's greatest joys.

At Miami, I had my first opportunity to do good for the local kids. My friend John Peasley's girlfriend and future wife, Sue, worked with mentally retarded youngsters as part of her special education training. There was one student, the "problem child" of the class, who would sometimes resort to violence without reason. Sue asked me if I wouldn't mind taking the kid in hand for a day to see if I could have some sort of influence on him.

Well, a few minutes after I picked him up, I could see why he was the problem kid. He started spitting on me. Frankly, it was a pain in the neck and I didn't know how to react. Still, I was very patient with him even though the spitting went on for three or four hours. Finally, when he did it again we were close to a swimming pool and I decided to test his powers of reason—so I grabbed him by the arm, dunked him in the pool and pulled him out again, just as quickly. That seemed to calm him down a little so I knew that there were certain ways of getting through to him, even though my methods might have been slightly unorthodox.

I got him into some dry clothes and the day went on smoothly for a while without any spitting. I'd already forgotten about it when he let another one go right on my shirt. *Damn it*, I figured, *this is it*. I just spat back at him. *Ptooo!* And he spat back at me. *Ptooo!* It went on and on until we both got cotton-mouth.

You know what? We ended up being best buddies. Every now and then he'd get out of hand but I'd just grab him by the arm or wave my finger at him and he'd be fine. Every time I visited him after that day, I could see his face light up as soon as he saw me. And his teacher told me that he was better behaved at school, and that his fighting had stopped.

I'll never forget the time my little friend and I went to a dance at his school. He didn't like to dance so he was just standing around watching. Well, I started acting goofy—I guess that's my calling—by making all sorts of funny faces and going through some strange contortions on the dance floor. He loved it. He kept laughing and soon the *two* of us were out there dancing. We must have kept it up for two hours and even for me it was a workout. When we finally walked out of that place, we sprinted straight for the pool and jumped in, clothes and all.

Working with kids has always been rewarding for me. It's always been my way of putting a little something back. I know how I grew up and that if I had had somebody to guide me along, a lot of things wouldn't have happened. I always try to spend a lot of time with kids at banquets in the hopes that I can leave a good—and lasting—impression. I think that's very important. I don't think kids ought to see athletes acting like spoiled jerks. When you're a kid, you can pick up impressions that can really stick with you.

When little Jimmy was born in 1981—what can I say?—he was everything to me. If it was up to me I'd have five or six kids by now but Colleen wants to wait. Jimmy's so big and she's small. She sometimes has a tough time with him.

Some people say that Jimmy's a chip off the old block. Although he's got some of the tendencies I have now, he doesn't have the wildness I had as a kid. He's growing up in a completely different environment. I'm glad I have the time to spend with him. I want him to have the same values my father handed down to me, but I'm able to control things and guide him more.

I give Jimmy slack, but on certain things—such as school—he gets none. He's got to do the right thing in school and he knows it. It's important that he pay attention and do his best. Every day when he comes home from school I say, "Jimmy, how'd you do?" And then if he made any mistakes, we discuss them.

On the other hand, there have been things broken around the house and I let him slide. He can flip on his head and I don't say a word—because it's also important for him to rough it up. He needs some street smarts because he's going to be out there on his own, too. I'm glad he plays with a lot of older kids.

The other thing is, I'm never too busy for Jimmy (except for game-day morning, when I'm a madman), even during the height of the football season. If it's only for an hour, I make sure I give him my attention every day, regardless of what's on my mind. You can't be a father just fifty-one weeks out of the year. I have never been one to do things halfway. With me, it's all or nothing.

That's why I was so disappointed when I wasn't drafted after three good years at Miami. Harold Allen had been telling me I'd be drafted and I had my heart set on it. It wasn't as if I played in obscurity. I had my best performance ever in our big game at home against Florida State my senior year. It was before that game that I led the skivvy parade, remember, and made the freshmen wrestle. Florida State is always a huge game for the Hurricanes, and to add to the importance, we were both 4–0 at the time. We were pretty good—we had Jim Kelly as our quarterback—but Florida State was favored. They were on a streak of twenty-six regular season wins.

I was up against a replacement center, and I made eleven tackles, forced five fumbles, and batted down three passes, including a two-point conversion try that would have won the game for them. The receiver was wide open and I managed to get my hand up there. We won, 10–9, and I was named national lineman of the week by *Sports Illustrated*. At the end of the year, I even made an All-American team, fulfilling my goal. But I guess no one in the NFL was paying attention.

My problem? I was only six-foot-one. Funny, now that I've had some success, my build seems to be the prototype for nose tackles. With the punishment we take inside, we have to be built lower to the ground, with big, strong legs. Back then, nose tackle was a new position in the NFL. The trend on the defensive line had always been toward big players—rangy "Storks" like Ted Hendricks or massive "Purple People Eaters" like Alan Page.

I couldn't hope to be that imposing. Heart never shows up

on those charts the scouts turn in. So they tagged me with a G-rating, which means undersized, too much of a risk to warrant a draft pick. From what I've heard, certain people in the Giants' organization didn't even think I should have been signed as a free agent. But Bill Parcells and George Young pushed for me.

The weirdest thing about it was that Chris Mara, son of the Giants' owner and a scout for the team, tested five other guys at Miami but never looked at me. In fact, I wasn't tested by a single scouting combine or team. They still had my freshman statistics, including a bogus 5.1 in the forty-yard dash.

I went home to watch the draft on TV. In those days, it was a two-day event. I honestly thought that I was going to be picked in the fourth or fifth round. When it didn't happen, I sat around a little longer, then left to work out my frustrations in the weight room. It was a feeling I've carried with me for a long time.

After I wasn't picked, at least I had my choice of teams and could go to a club where I felt I could get my best shot.'The Giants were collecting nose guards because they would be going to a three-man line for the first time. George Young, who along with Ray Perkins had already called Lou Saban to check me out, phoned to invite me to East Rutherford to look around and meet the coaching staff. I wasn't going to go. My attitude was if they were so interested in me, why didn't they draft me? But Lou talked me into it. I think the Giants asked him to intervene. He advised me to take a shot. What did I have to lose?

Lou was my man, so I went. The only thing was, the Giants never mentioned anything about testing. And when I got to Giants Stadium, I found a field full of rookies, with Ray Perkins putting them through a special mini-camp. I stood there watching them work out when somebody asked me if I cared to do some weight-lifting tests. What was I going to say? I ended up being ranked the strongest guy among the rookies. Later, they asked me to run. What was I going to say? So I got into some gear and ran a 4.85 time in the forty-yard dash, faster than any of their rookie linemen. Likewise, I did pretty well in the agility drills they put me through—so well, in fact, that my line coach Lamar Leachman often tells me, "Boy, that's why you made the team."

Still, I was determined not to sign anything. But the Giants were just as determined not to let me out of there. They'd been filming me and I'd been doing everything well. Bill Parcells, then the defensive coordinator, sat me down on some of the weight-lifting equipment for twenty minutes, assuring me I'd have a chance to make the team. Finally, they sent someone to bring me upstairs to the front office and I told them I still hadn't finished up.

"Boy," Lamar advised me, "when they call you upstairs, you go."

Upstairs, they offered me a contract. I figured What the hell, and signed it. I suppose that if I had gone to somebody else's stadium first, I might have signed with them instead. But the Giants had made sure that the Eagles, Falcons, Bucs, Dolphins, and Steelers didn't get the chance.

I didn't mind going to a losing team. I wanted to compete and I just wanted to be sure I was going to get my shot.

But let me tell you, I walked on eggshells that entire first training camp, despite Perkins' and Parcells' assurances. I was so paranoid about my height that I wore clunky work boots from the first day on so that I'd look taller to the coaches. The only times I took them off were on the field and in the shower. Even then, I'd run in and out quickly so that no one would notice me in my bare feet. People asked me why I wore those boots all the time. I told them it was because they were comfortable. Comfort, hell. My feet were killing me.

The worst night was the one when they cut my roommate,

an offensive lineman whose name I don't even remember. Vinnie Swerc, who's been with the Giants since leather helmets, has the job of knocking on the doors of the poor guys who are going to be cut. It's called a visit from the Turk. Secretly, I think he enjoys it. He just yells through the door in a gruff voice, "Coach wants to see you. Bring your playbook." No explanation required.

The night Swerc the Turk came to get my roommate, I hid under the sheets. I stayed there cowering all night. I was terrified of Vinnie Swerc—though the tables have since turned. Now *he's* got to be on the lookout for some of my hare-brained schemes.

At that camp, I knew I had to work harder than the other guys. The big draft choices get a year or two to prove themselves. I could have been gone after one or two bad plays. I've seen draft choices come into training camp and get away with murder sometimes, when they have that magic ingredient of size. Look at Leonard Marshall during his rookie season. Leonard has really worked hard and today he's a great All Pro. Back then, however, he wasn't showing anything. But he was six-foot-three, he weighed 290, and he was drafted in the second round. If he had been six-two, 265, and done what he did, it would have been adios.

Teams have it figured that out of a hundred players who are undersized, five percent make it. Out of a hundred players at the cutoff size or above, twenty-five percent make it. So they play the percentages. That was my situation. There was no way in hell I shouldn't have been drafted. Had I been drafted, I'm sure I would have been playing a lot earlier, probably starting in my rookie year. But I'm not bitter about it; actually I'm sort of glad things have worked out the way they have. It makes me appreciate things more. And that's probably why I'll never know how good I am—because I always feel I've got to do better. I'll always have the stigma of being a free agent.

I'm lucky I got a chance, too, because I've also seen good free-agent football players come into training camp and not get noticed. I *made* myself a chance. Even though I had a bad ankle, I never let up. I wanted in on special teams, I tried to hustle on every play. I started fights. I wanted to make waves. I wanted to make things happen in games—and get myself noticed.

When that first summer of '81 was through, I'd fought my way onto the team. But it was only the beginning. There was a back injury out there waiting to happen and a whole lot of garbage to plow through before I could get anywhere near my new dream. The Super Bowl.

# 3

## CHICAGO

## Frozen Dreams

In Chicago, they call the wind "the Hawk." Some bird. It eats footballs and, sometimes, whole football teams. The Bears like to think it wears one of those big orange C's on its wings. To them it's an ally.

We were there for our second game of the 1985 NFC playoffs, a macho battle between two similar teams. Many, the Giants included, thought we were the two best in the entire league.

We were two wins away from Super Bowl XX, the ultimate goal. This was the same place where we got off the bus the year before, and ended up losing to the 49ers, who'd go on to win it all. And just like that San Francisco team, the Bears had lost only once all season.

This was going to be old-time football—real physical, the kind I love and the kind we play best. Both franchises had gone from glory years to gory years and both were now on the upswing again. Bear fans were outrageously enthusiastic about their team and even the Chicago weather was in a playoff mood.

The back door of our hotel off Michigan Avenue was almost ripped off its hinges every time it was opened. Lawrence Taylor took a short walk to the store and came back shaking his

51

head. He swore this was the coldest place he'd ever been to on God's earth.

I knew better, of course. I grew up in Buffalo.

Game day checked in at fourteen degrees with a minus-thirteen-degree wind chill at Soldier Field. I wore short sleeves and elbow pads, as oblivious to the cold as I was to those guys in the dark blue shirts breathing ice on the opposite side of the field. The Bears might have been eight-point favorites and at home. But we had just taken apart a 49er team, 17–3, in our wild-card game the previous week. We didn't think there was any way this offense, even with Walter Payton and a leader like Jim McMahon, could be as dangerous as the 49ers'. There wasn't a guy on our defense who wasn't convinced we were going to do the same fun-filled things to the Bears that we'd done to Joe Montana, Roger Craig, and the rest of the 49ers.

The kickers noticed the wind more than anyone in warm-ups. Eric Schubert, wrapped up in a fat parka, was having trouble getting kickoffs thirty yards into the wind—and this was a guy who routinely kicked balls out of the end zone. Our punter, Sean Landeta, who had replaced Dave Jennings that year and had an excellent season, was getting the needle from Jeff Rutledge, backup quarterback to Phil Simms and an erstwhile high school punter.

Rutledge actually told Landeta that he was going to miss one as he himself had done once on a windy night back in Birmingham. Landeta, as cocky as he is paunchy, informed Rutt he'd never missed a punt in his life.

My assignment was Jay Hilgenberg and as I always do, I watched him some in the pre-game and tried to imagine moves I'd make against him. It would be my first time up against Hilgey, a Pro-Bowl center whose uncle starred for the Vikings and whose brother is with the Saints. He's the best center in the NFC. Hilgenberg never quits on a game. A lot of guys soften up by the fourth quarter. He just goes at you harder.

We'd be a key matchup because with this wind, neither team was likely to throw the ball too successfully and our two defenses were 1 – 2 in the league in stopping the run. In the pits, it would be like most NFL games only more so because both teams wanted it so badly. In situations like this, you can feel the tension in the trenches. You can see guys on the offensive line getting into their stance and looking at you out of the side of their eyes. You know they're coming at you and it's like two fighters getting ready in the ring, psyching each other out. That's how it is on the line for every play.

Before the snap, you don't hear a thing. There's a terrific anticipatory silence that's almost eerie. You're immersed in total concentration, looking for the details you saw on the game film. When guys come off the ball they're screaming and groaning. You hear the plastic popping from the helmets and shoulder pads and you concentrate all your energies into beating the guy in front of you. Everything comes at you so quickly, there's often no time to think, just to react. You're lined up against a center and two guards and you're trying to get them to double-team you because it takes them out of action when they're concentrating so hard on you. It's a personal battle and I love it in there.

The Bears got the first break of the game—a Rob Carpenter fumble after we looked like we were going to move the ball on our first possession. It didn't upset me much. Although we knew we couldn't give the Bears many points, games aren't won that early. It's usually the third quarter that decides. All we had to do was stop the Bears and we'd have the momentum again.

That was no problem. We forced them to kick. But our offense was having its troubles, too, and late in the first quarter, Landeta had to punt from his own end zone.

I wasn't paying too much attention. I was buckling my chin strap and getting ready to go back out on the field, figuring the Bears would get the ball close to midfield. Out of the corner of my eye, I saw what I thought was a blocked kick and now know was Landeta whiffing the windblown ball. That SOB Rutledge was right. Shaun Gayle picked it off the ground and ran it in eleven yards for the first score of the game, a gimme touchdown.

Everybody must think we were ready to strangle Sean when he came back to the sidelines, and that Landeta wanted to strangle Rutt. But to tell the truth, we didn't think it would make much difference. We knew we'd have to score more than seven points to win the thing, and a 7−0 first-quarter deficit means little.

Yet that one play became the symbol of our loss that day. People never forgot it, not our fans and certainly not us. One day during the off-season, Parcells was playing golf with his old high school basketball coach and mentor Mickey Corcoran, tight end coach Mike Pope, and offensive coordinator Ron Erhardt. It was a great day for golf, and football had hardly been discussed.

Erhardt had a good round going and was standing over his ball on the sixteenth tee, thinking to himself how he couldn't possibly miss, when the Landeta punt flashed into his mind. He stopped his backswing and said to the others, "How the *hell* did he miss that ball?"

Like I said, though, we weren't panicking at the time and the game settled back down into a defensive battle; and as a defense, we hadn't given them anything. We were kind of lucky because Kevin Butler missed two field goals in that wind, and with 2:00 or so left in the half, it looked as though the Bears were going to be happy with a 7−0 lead. Or at least they weren't going to throw the ball the rest of the half. They were going to run out the clock on the ground. Fine with us. If we stop them, we're thinking, we've still got time for one last drive and a chance to turn things around.

Instead, things turned around on me. Calvin Thomas, their backup running back, came into the game and took a pitch from McMahon to my right. I stepped inside Hilgenberg and was chasing down the play with Hilgenberg behind me. Thomas cut back toward me and I was getting ready to slam him in my hitting position—hands out, face into him at full speed.

Hilgenberg changed that with a little push from behind. I tackled Thomas, all right, but with the ear-hole of my helmet crashing into his shoulder pads. The high-speed collision jerked my neck back and I hit the turf off-balance. I actually bounced back into Harry Carson but I didn't realize it then. I had slipped into the Twilight Zone, where sparkles and dots rode a merry-go-round in my head. If this was Chicago, I must have been at the '32 World's Fair. And wasn't that Babe Ruth calling his home run at Wrigley Field? Actually, it was Dr. Russell Warren, our orthopedic expert, sticking his finger in front of my face. I had managed to get my ass out of there and over to the sidelines and they were putting me through the standard neurological tests.

Then the doctor waved this container of smelling salts in front of my nose. Usually, one whiff snaps you to attention pretty fast, but I was responding to the stuff like a cigar-store Indian. "Oh shit," said Doc Warren.

Through this smoky haze, I could see us blow a chance to tie the score before halftime. We'd managed to move inside their five on a short pass that was turned into big yardage by George Adams; then Simms looked for Bobby Johnson on a fade pattern to the corner of the end zone. The timing pattern had been one of our most successful scoring plays all year. Phil laid the ball up there and Bobby seemed to have a shot at it until he lost it in the glare of the sun. Our luck. Why couldn't it be zero degrees and cloudy?

To make matters worse, Schubert, without his parka, missed the short field goal and we were still behind, 7–0. Joe Morris was hurting, too. He'd been squashed from the blind side by the 308-pound Refrigerator, William Perry, and was even worse off than me.

We would have to find some answers in the locker room. I had to find the smelling salts first.

For the next twenty minutes, I hit on that vial, struggling to regain my senses. By the time we were ready to go out again, Phil Simms was looking less like Harry Carson to me so I knew I was coming back. All Parcells saw, of course, were the eyes bugged out of my head.

I knew I was in trouble when our trainer, Ronnie Barnes, tried to tug my helmet away. It's an old trick. They'll get a teammate to quiz you on your assignments and if you're not responsive, they'll hide your helmet so that there's no way the coach can put you back into the game.

*Bullshit*, I said to myself. It was still 7 – 0 and there was no way I was going to stay out of the game. Luckily, when I got dinged, I had sense enough to wrap my helmet around my arm and I was still clinging to it. So much for Ronnie Barnes. Now all I had to do was convince Parcells.

He started the second half with Jerome Sally at nose and that worried me. The Bears began running the ball against us pretty successfully and it was time for drastic action. I started screaming at Parcells, "I'm okay! I'm okay!" Two, three plays went by and they were still driving, so Parcells said to me, "All right, get in there."

I took an enormous snort of smelling salts and ran onto the field, knowing this next play was going to be big. I tried to be as nonchalant as possible. I knew our coaches' eyes were going to be glued on me and that if I wavered just a little bit, my rear end was going to be nailed to the bench for the rest of the game. I had to try like an SOB not to act hurt.

I also knew that the Bears were thinking that I was still a little buzzed, and that they were going to find out how much

I could take. They were going to come after me and try to knock me out for good. That's just the way it is. I looked over to their huddle and tried not to notice them looking straight at me.

There it was, the same kind of feeling I had when I climbed into the cab of my father's truck, ready for the challenge. This time, though, an All-Pro center was climbing over the ball.

Sure enough, the play was to Payton, straight at me, and I got double-teamed. They really knocked the shit out of me or at least it felt like it. But I had to act like I was fine and after a few plays, I was—at least fine enough to get by.

Every time I came off the field, the smelling salts were my medicine, my private stash. I kept the vial at the end of the bench and tucked it underneath so that the wind couldn't blow it away. I'd just stick the thing up under my nose and breathe in. "This shit's great," I was telling the guys, who were looking at me as if I had just climbed off Mars. I didn't care. I walked over to Byron Hunt and offered him some. "Great shit, Byron."

"What, are you crazy?" he said.

When I think back, I have to wonder how bad I really was, because I can hardly get close to the stuff now. But just then, it smelled pretty good to me.

What Jim McMahon was on, I don't know. If any offensive player was the difference in that game, it was Jim. I've always had respect for him as a leader and feel that he and Phil are very similar in that regard. He's a big-play quarterback and that's the only way you can beat our defense.

McMahon was actually making the wind work for him. He'd underthrow the ball and his receivers were coming back for it while our defensive backs still had their backs turned. Those receptions, combined with a couple of bad coverage break-downs, meant two second-half TDs for the Bears, on twenty-three- and twenty-yard passes to Dennis McKinnon.

I remember two pass plays pretty clearly. We broke coverage on the first one, which set up their first touchdown, and left their tight end Tim Wrightman without anyone within twenty yards of him. I had to hustle my rear end downfield to help on the tackle. Then there was the second touchdown pass—a ball I thought Elvis Patterson, our left cornerback, was going to intercept. McKinnon just took it away from him in the end zone.

With 14:00 left it was 21−0 and we were up shit's creek. After 14−0, it was already a different game. Their defense started to play more aggressively and now it didn't look as if our offense was going to do anything more. They were just coming too hard. Phil, who'd be sacked six times, was getting battered.

I said to Lawrence Taylor, "Hey, we're not going to let them score again. Let's keep this respectable and fight them till the last second. Let's not be a team that quits."

A lot of teams do. The Patriots would do it in the Super Bowl. I know when it's happening. You can feel it in the offensive line and see it in the quarterback's eyes. I didn't want that to be us. I didn't want to go into next season knowing we'd quit here. We had to lay some kind of foundation. I knew it had to come from the defense and I knew L.T. was the man I should talk to.

"I don't think that's going to happen to us," he said.

He was right. The game might have been over but the rough stuff was just starting. The Bears were going to keep it on the ground to waste time but they had plans to punish us. Taylor was going to be their primary target. For five straight plays, fullback Matt Suhey came straight at L.T.'s knees to chop him down.

Later, Suhey said it was the only way he can block someone like L.T., that he'd be a fool to go at him straight up. But Taylor wasn't taking this as a compliment. Remembering Kurt

Peterson's block that cut Harry Carson down with a knee injury in '83, Taylor warned Suhey to get away from his knees and to "block like a man."

Suhey said something back and for some reason, Mike Ditka was yelling at Taylor from the sidelines, too, rubbing it in. I happened to be right behind L.T., who was by now ready to cut Ditka in half.

"Jimmy, you with me? You got my back?" he asked.

"Lawrence," I told him, "we're fighting to the end. Whatever you do, I'm right there with you. You want to go over to their bench, let's go."

We played in that foul mood for the rest of the game. Ditka wouldn't stop and I don't know why. To me, he always seemed a hard guy but a classy coach. I kept my mouth shut because I thought I owed him some respect. A head coach is supposed to control his team, not start a riot, and that's what would have happened. Had L.T. gone over there, I would have been there, too. Somebody would have gotten hurt, and it probably would have been us.

Meanwhile, the Bears kept coming and I had my own rear end to watch. As they had done in the first quarter, they tried posting me up. It'd be a sweep to my right and Hilgenberg would jump back. Jimbo Covert, their six-four, 271-pound All-Pro tackle, wouldn't even try to block his man, Leonard Marshall. He would just fly across the line of scrimmage at me.

It was obvious what they were trying to do—wipe me out and get me out of the game. I'd seen them do it on film and they'd almost killed a few nose guards during the regular season. I knew it was coming. A nose tackle can never look straight ahead facing so many double-teams. I need peripheral vision to take in the whole picture. The first thing I noticed was Covert's long shadow and my immediate reaction was to get down and twist my shoulders on the double-team.

Hilgenberg was pushing me to set me up, but I was lucky. I

moved fast and Covert went flying by without giving me a clean shot. If he had, he would have sent me into next week.

It was one of two small victories in the war. The other was that we did hold them scoreless for the rest of the game. It ended 21 – 0 and we had our pride. But it was over and there was no more fighting to do. The Bears were going all the way. That was obvious to us. We were headed for a cramped, cold locker room somewhere below Soldier Field, where above us their fans were dancing to that annoying Super Bowl Shuffle.

I didn't notice much in my loser's fog. I followed white jerseys into our locker room, walked to my stall, and buried my face in my hands.

That's what makes football so tough for me, the losing. It's the one thing I don't take very well. It affects me. It affects my family. It affects everything around me. We put so much effort into every game, and not just during the previous week's work.

Now I was left with this very empty feeling. You're sore but you didn't get anything accomplished. You slogged through all the hard work, you gave it everything you had. And then you didn't get anything back.

I was lost in that sense of helplessness when Bill Parcells' voice broke the silence.

"Fellas, we lost and I know a lot of you are disappointed," he told us. "But let me tell you something. I want you to remember this feeling because the New York Giants are going to be back next year. We're going to take it all the way."

Bill spoke of Harry Carson and George Martin, the senior members of the team who'd been Giants for over ten years. He was making them a promise and we were making ourselves a pledge. Our championship season was starting here, just as this season was being buried.

I wasn't able to see that clearly then. I had no life in me. I was just dead and the locker room was a blur. I didn't pay any attention to the crowd of reporters around Landeta and around Taylor, who, still angry, scared them away by snarling at them. I do remember L.T. coming up to me in the shower and saying thanks for backing him up. But that's the only thing I remember from the locker room besides Bill's talk.

Colleen was waiting for me outside with her dad, his brother, and some other people. When I came out, I had the hollowest expression on my face. My mouth was open, my jaw was dropped. I mumbled something and walked through them as if they weren't even there.

I got on the bus that took us to our plane at O'Hare. I've been told it was dead quiet on board. I wouldn't know. I walked straight to the back, collapsed across a row of seats, stuck a pillow in front of my face and went to sleep. I woke up at Newark Airport, walked off the plane, and went home, where I slept again. I was dizzy for days, from both the loss and the concussion.

I wondered how long it would take before I would get over it. I never did. Even now, as a Super Bowl winner, the game still lingers in my mind. I'll never forget it.

# 4

## PLEASANTVILLE

## My Boy Bill

**S**ame old Giants.

That's what our "long-suffering" fans were calling us. That's what we were calling ourselves. For two seasons in a row, we had chances to win the NFC East by winning one more game—and we blew them both.

The '84 season came down to a game in St. Louis in Week 15. We led until Mark Haynes, then our All-Pro cornerback, was injured, and Neil Lomax brought the Cardinals back to beat us. The Redskins won the division by beating the Cardinals the next week and we went on as a wild-card team to lose to the Super Bowl champion 49ers in the playoffs, another game I thought we should have won.

In the next-to-last week of the '85 season, we went to Dallas for our most important regular-season game ever. It was a winner-take-all situation and we were the better team, no doubt about it. We got on top early and were going in for another score when Too Tall Jones turned things around by batting up a pass that Jim Jeffcoat returned for a fluke touchdown. Brad Benson had even shoved Jeffcoat out of position to exactly where Jeffcoat and fate found the ball. It was a case of bad luck more than anything else but still, the Cowboys would beat us that day and win the division, leaving us to the Bears.

Single plays like that were deciding our fate. All those negative things were lodged in our minds. We came close but we didn't get it *done*. When we pulled into training camp the second week of July 1986, we didn't feel as if just making the playoffs was going to be good enough anymore. We'd done that three out of the previous five years and we had to take it farther.

It wasn't going to be good enough anymore not to win the division. It wasn't going to be good enough not to get home-field advantage. It wasn't going to be good enough not to go to the Super Bowl. Anything short of Pasadena was going to be just another one of those years.

We told ourselves we had nothing to do with the sorry Giants of the past but, as Joe Morris would say the week of Super Bowl XXI, we were carrying those old ghosts on our backs. We were stigmatized as a snake-bitten franchise, and winning the division in '86 was going to be the first step to our shaking off the demons.

Believing we could reach the Super Bowl, though, was different than reading about it. It seemed every magazine was picking us for the big one and none of us liked it. The thought was nice but it made us uneasy. I mean, we hadn't done anything yet and already we were under pressure to live up to these predictions. It was all the reporters talked about the first few days of training camp—and we were doing our best to duck the issue.

Our defense, as good as it was in '85, was going to be in for a minor overhaul. Bill Parcells believes that a team wins with defense and I couldn't agree more. Just take a look at the old Chargers or even this year's Dolphins to see what a great offense and no D adds up to. But when Parcells spent his first six draft picks on defense—all in the first three rounds—even I wondered if he wasn't getting carried away.

Offensive coaches seemed to be walking around with a "don't ask me" look. But as it turned out, Bill, as usual, was right. All six defensive rookies would make the team: first-round pick Eric Dorsey, a defensive end from Notre Dame who's built like a Greek god; linebacker Pepper Johnson from Ohio State, who fit Parcells' bill for size at six-three, 248 pounds; a pair of second-round defensive backs, corner Mark Collins and safety Greg Lasker; another defensive end, John Washington, a huge guy who looks built for two-gapping; and nose tackle Erik Howard from Washington State, who came into camp and bench-pressed 580 pounds. He was so pumped up, he looked like he was going to explode.

More change would come out of necessity as we got into the pre-season schedule. Our big run-clogging defensive end, Curtis McGriff, pulled a hamstring, and as is sometimes the case with big guys, it was slow to heal and he missed the entire season. That put the oldest guy on our team, George Martin— we call him "Pops"—back into a full-time role; for six seasons, he'd been used primarily in pass-rush situations. It also put the heat on Carl "Killer" Banks to pick up whatever slack was left over from his left outside linebacker position. Banks, a first-round draft pick in 1984, was also going to be used on a full-time basis for the first time in his career.

As it is, training camp is a six-week crash course in ass-busting and tedium. It's always the most grueling part of the season, physically and mentally. You're away from home and cooped up in stuffy dorms with smelly guys and you're practicing twice a day to shock football back into your system. Off-season conditioning is a must, because training camp is no longer used to get players back into shape. It's to refamiliarize bodies with real soreness and pain, brought on by those damned double sessions. They're easy for the defensive linemen— compared to the mental torture *we* go through with Lamar Leachman, our personal Marquis de Sade.

The typical day begins at 7 A.M. and ends with the last meeting at 10 P.M. By that time, your body is worn down and your brain is fried from the nonstop meetings and study. Most guys think it shouldn't be as long as it is—from the second week of July through the third exhibition game. The only guys who benefit from the length are the rookies, especially since they seem to report later and later every year. Coaches love it. They would.

Since I've been a Giant, our pre-season sweatshop has been located upstate in Pleasantville, New York, on the out-of-the-way campus of Pace University. Pace must be the goose-shit capital of the Northeast. The stuff is all over the campus. First rule for rookies: always look where you're walking.

I've also got a personal reason for dreading training camp besides sore muscles and green feet. My back. Every summer since I originally injured it lifting weights in 1982, it either tires out or goes into spasms from the two-a-days. I take pride in my pain threshold and I've fought through a lot of injuries, but when you're hit with severe spasms, you're grounded. You can't walk so you certainly can't play. You're bent over to one side in such a straitjacket of pain that even sleeping is no relief.

This year my back held up until our first pre-season game of the year—a rare Wednesday-night game in Atlanta. There was some stadium conflict with the Braves so the Falcons had to move the game up. Bill Parcells and Falcon coach Dan Henning, bosom buddies from the old days, decided that since the next game was ten days off, this would be a good opportunity to train against each other for three days at the Falcons' complex in Suwanee, Georgia.

We lost the game in Atlanta but our first team played well and held the lead in the first half. We felt pretty good about our performance.

I didn't feel good about by back, however. It tightened up just before our first practice with Atlanta, though I still felt that I could work my way through it.

I should have taken those days off and rested my back, but my competitive drive often gets in the way of common sense. I was excited about practicing against the Falcons. You get tired of going up against the same old guys and this was neat—a chance to really compete. My back was tight and I knew something was wrong but I still wanted to be in there. Plus, I take pride in being able to gut things out and I wanted to make it through all the practices down there. I had made it through the first practice, but two hours later I felt a golf-ball-sized knot in my lower back.

Coming into the second day of practice, my back felt extremely tight, with the same knot in it, but I figured I got through the day before so I could do it again. Besides, only two more days remained. Finally, we got into a live scrimmage and I got what they call a wham block—the tight end came in motion and I went to engage him. My back just went out on me, right where the knot was tight.

I spent the rest of the time down there in my room. When we got back to Pace, I was flat on my back for another week. I missed our second game in Milwaukee against the Packers, when Phil passed us to our first win. Back in Pleasantville, I couldn't move. I couldn't do anything. I took my meals in my dorm room. And I was really depressed. It was brutal.

Then, on top of the excruciating pain in my back, I had this equally big pain in my ass—Parcells. Bill was pissed off at me because I couldn't be on the field. In his mind, it was my fault I was hurt. I would have been better off going home to rest, but he didn't want to make it too comfortable for me.

Every day he'd pester me about when I'd be back.

"As soon as I can," I'd tell him.

"What day?" he'd say.

"Two or three days," I'd reply, just to say something.

"Which is it, two or three?" he'd ask, and I'd say, "Two." I should have said four to give myself some leeway but that's easy to say *now*.

Two days went by—this was after the Packers game—when he asked me if I would be ready to work the next day.

"I don't know," I told him honestly.

"When will you know?" he asked me, predictably enough.

Finally, I said to myself, *I don't give a shit, I'm going, no matter what, tomorrow.* So the next day I was out there in full gear, ready to go. It actually felt pretty good at first. I did a couple of drills and was even able to roll on my hips and hit the sled. Then we had to run.

We were doing a drill where you sprint laterally to the ball and I just couldn't move. I mean, my legs were planted. So I yanked off my helmet and said to Bill, "I can't do it. I can't run." Then I walked over to our assistant trainer, Jimmy Madaleno, told him what happened, and started heading down the stairs to our locker room so I could change and go back to bed.

"Burt, where you going?" It was Parcells, pissed off at me. "Come here. I don't want you going down there. Go stand on the sidelines and watch," he ordered me.

He probably knew what I was going to do because he'd seen me respond to this kind of treatment before. He got me so ticked off, I mumbled a few choice words as I walked back to the field. I watched for a few minutes then said the hell with it. I went through all the drills, even the 9-on-7, where we execute our inside running plays, with Parcells standing behind me every moment. I said to myself, *I'm going to win this battle and get through practice.* I wasn't going to let him win this mental tug-of-war.

When the wind sprints came, I headed over there, too. Then Parcells said, "You don't have to do that, you're hurt." Suddenly, he was concerned. I had it fixed in my mind I was going to run anyway. He yelled over, "Burt, you don't have to run. Come over here and ride the exercise bike." I ignored him. Then he pulled a power play on me and threatened me with a few things, like a thousand-dollar fine. Those were a thousand good reasons why I suddenly decided to use my hearing and jump on the bike.

Dr. Warren came around and asked me how I was doing. He talked to Parcells and I was able to take the next day off. Doc Warren to the rescue again. Seems like he's the only one who can talk sense into Bill. I was back on the practice field Friday. On Saturday night, I played against the Jets in our pre-season home opener.

You might be thinking that Parcells is my worst enemy. He's not. The guy can piss the brass balls off a monkey but he's also a great friend. I feel in my gut that he's one hundred percent for me and I'm one hundred percent for him. I'd go through a wall for the guy. I think he's the reason why a lot of the Giants, including myself, are successful here, while we might not be doing so well somewhere else. He has developed different relationships with many different players with all their varied personalities. But the common denominator comes down to two things: trust and loyalty.

Bill Belichick summed up Parcells as well as anyone can in a profile by Greg Garber of the *Hartford Courant*: "Nothing you can say about him is completely true, or completely false. He's different things to different people, depending on the situation. It's like a roller coaster. You go up two miles an hour, down a hundred, then curve to the left, and curve to the right."

I get dizzy from that roller coaster sometimes but I've learned not to take any of his bullshit personally—because I know his motives and can appreciate them. When he gets nervous about how things are going on the team, he uses you-know-who as a motivational tool by kicking me around. He knows exactly what he's doing and he knows I know exactly what he's doing. The other guys, particularly the younger ones, see him pushing me out on the field with a bad back. He's not doing it just to get to me—because he does it so loudly that everyone can hear it.

Two years ago, I had spasms high up on my back. I could hardly breathe and had a 102-degree temperature. Maybe I even had a case of the flu. He told me he didn't want me to practice but I went out there anyway. And he said: "I really appreciate what you're doing for the other guys."

That's how I know.

Bill is very loyal. He keeps things quiet. Some guys may be absolute horse manure for four or five weeks, but Bill protects them. He never japs them (our term for back-stabbing) in the press, and they appreciate it. On other teams, it leaks out.

Like I said, he deals with the different personalities on our team in different ways. I'm not Lawrence Taylor, I'm not Harry Carson or George Martin, and I'm certainly not Brad Benson, but we've all got special relationships with Bill. I remember, for instance, how Bill used an old player, Danny Lloyd, to get through to Harry when he was depressed and thinking of retirement. Those talks with Danny were one reason why Harry had a resurgence in his career.

Of all the player-coach relationships on the Giants, our two-sided one might be the strongest and the strangest. A lot of guys kid me about it. I just say to them, "Would *you* like to go through what he puts me through?" The reply is always the same: "Hell, no."

In my rookie year, 1981, Parcells had just been hired as defensive coordinator under Ray Perkins to install the 3–4 defense that's now our trademark. Lawrence Taylor came gift-wrapped in the draft as the killer outside linebacker he would need. But to make things work, the nose tackle is the key ingredient to stopping the run. Without a good nose tackle, the 3–4 defense wouldn't have worked, especially in our two-gap scheme.

At that time, no one really knew what to look for in a nose tackle—or at least they tended to draft tall, big guys instead of stocky guys like myself. That's part of the reason, I think, why I wasn't drafted. So there I was, one of twelve guys on the line—nine of them veterans—competing for six spots. Bill Neill was the only other rookie. He was drafted in the fifth round out of Pitt and would win the starting job. Then there were guys like George Small—a monster who'd be better named George Blob.

One by one all the other noses were cut, until they were down to the absolute minimum of six linemen. This was after the Jets' exhibition game, a real good one for me against a center, Joe Fields, whom Bill regarded as one of the three best in the league. I did okay in the game.

This was it. I'd done it. Me, Jim Burt, free agent. A Giant. I was so excited at lunchtime I called my dad to tell him I made the team. Bill Neill and I were joking around on the practice field at Giants Stadium later that day. We were stretching when Parcells walked up to me. He didn't even say congratulations. Instead, he gave me this warning: "Let me tell you something, you little bastard. I can go get ten guys off the street right now to do what you can do. You better work your ass off every day. You make one mistake and you're gone."

So what did I do? I got right back on the phone and said, "Dad, do me a favor. Don't tell any of your friends. Don't tell any of the family. Just keep it to yourself that I made the team because I'm not sure right now."

I wrote in a diary I still keep that Parcells would be a major hurdle for me. Then I started really concentrating on things he'd say. I'd turn them into direct challenges. I'd take them personally. He became the focus, my way of making the team. In college, I motivated myself by shooting for All-American. In the pros, I did it by trying to impress Parcells, my big fish, appropriately called "Tuna" by the players. He got the nickname in New England, some say, because of his questionable skill at the card table. Of course, in those days, I wasn't calling Parcells anything. I was too afraid to talk to him.

That whole 1981 season Parcells had me scared out of my pants. I remember the Washington game, the second week of the year. I had played the last quarter-and-a-half of the season opener against the Eagles because we were getting beat, but I played real well—about five tackles in four series.

It was at least ninety degrees the next week in Washington and I thought I was going to get in there because I had done a good job the week before, and I figured we'd be rotating people because of the heat. I was pacing the sidelines and started harassing Lamar Leachman during the first few series. "C'mon, Lamar," I begged, "put me in, put me in."

He replied in his foghorn Georgia drawl, "Jimmy, if it was up to me I'd put you in, but it's not. It's up to him. Talk to him." He pointed at Parcells.

I hesitated, because after the things he'd said to me I was steering clear of him. But I was also getting more and more ticked off that I wasn't playing. After the third or fourth series of the game, I said to myself, *Look, I don't care what happens. If he cuts me, he cuts me. I'm getting in the game.*

Parcells was standing in front of me on the sidelines calling defensive signals, oblivious to me. Why I did this, I don't know, but I got a running start and put a forearm to his back. I knocked off his headphones, and he ended up about three or four yards on the field.

He just looked at me like I was crazy. I thought, *Oh my God, this is it.* Then he looked at Lamar and yelled, "Get him the hell out of here."

I got in the game two series later.

Parcells remained ticked off at me for the rest of the year. If he said one word to me after that, it was something negative. He was on me hard, and I avoided him because I was paranoid anyway—being a free agent and all.

The season went by and it was pretty successful. We didn't have that great a team but we made the playoffs before losing in San Francisco to the 49ers, who naturally went on to win the Super Bowl.

Parcells was going up and down congratulating his defensive players after that last game. I always had one eye out for him so I was watching carefully as he got to me, even though I was turned facing my locker. He tapped me on the shoulder and said quietly: "Jim, congratulations. Good season. We didn't expect you to make the team." And so on.

Then his voice got real loud.

"But let me tell you something right now. I'm gonna bring in five nose guards next year to take your job. Every day and every minute that you're in this league, you're going to have to work your ass off. You're gonna see. Every minute in the off-season you better work your ass off."

My body was halfway cocked, and I looked at him over my shoulder. I turned around and gritted my teeth at him. "You know what? I wouldn't have it any other way."

He just turned around and walked away.

That's the last thing he said to me that year. I mean he hadn't talked to me all year and then he said something like that to me. I was sure of one thing: *This guy hates me*. When I got home in the off-season, I even had nightmares about it. I couldn't think about anything else. I was training for training camp to show him what I could do. Mini-camp that year was like a Super Bowl for me. We didn't work out in pads, just helmets. But I went full speed at everything. I came out of it with bruises over my whole body, as if I had just been through a regular training camp. And true to Parcells' word, we were seven deep at nose tackle at that mini-camp.

At least they gave me enough respect to put me in the second team ahead of Myron Lapka, who had been a second-round draft pick before he fell out of a pickup truck in some freak off-season accident. Talk about picking guys up off the street. Then they had these other four guys who were built like tree trunks, me, and Bill Neill, who I knew had the spot.

Maybe it was the best thing for me, because all I did was

concentrate on football. When Neill got hurt during the first pre-season game, the first of several knee injuries that would end his career prematurely, I got the job and had a real good pre-season.

That's when Parcells finally started complimenting me. I can remember it vividly because it was the first positive thing he ever said to me. It was our third pre-season game of that 1982 season. We were playing the Jets, who would go to the AFC championship game that year behind an excellent power running game with Freeman McNeil.

At halftime, Parcells shocked me. "I just want to say one thing," he told me. "Son, you did a hell of a job. That's the number-one inside running team in the league, and you shut them down. That's a hell of a job, son."

My eyes got big. *You gotta be kidding me. This guy's complimenting me?* But that was the real start of our crazy relationship. In our first game of the season against Atlanta, I went up against Jeff Van Note, who just happened to be one of the players I had admired most during high school and college, and I played pretty well. Although we lost, Parcells said to me, again in front of the whole team, "That was the best job of two-gapping I've ever seen."

I'd been watching Parcells closely through all this and I was noticing how the team was responding to him. That first year everyone was unsure of him but after two or three weeks, everyone started trusting him like they'd known him for a long time. He created a special bond with us, which is why we played so well in '81. We didn't have a good team at all, but for the defense at least, this positive attitude kept building.

We'd lose a game and expect to be chewed out. But he'd say, "Let me tell you something, you're my guys. You gave one hundred percent and I'm behind you guys, win or lose."

If he had a negative thing to say, he'd pull the guy aside, not blast him in front of the whole team. That started a feeling of pride that grew and grew. By the end of the season, most guys were playing beyond their potential.

Even veterans like Brian Kelley and Brad Van Pelt. Those guys always had the attitude that the Giants were a piece of crap. Now even *they* were saying, Hey, we're pretty good. We finished 9–7, made the playoffs for the first time since 1963, and even won our wild-card game against the Eagles, a team the Giants never seemed able to beat.

I'll tell you, over these last six years Parcells has done some amazing things.

All of this is probably why I was out on the field, with my back still hurting, for that meaningless exhibition game against the Jets. It was the only time in my career that I played tentatively, afraid of being hurt. On the very first play of the game, I was up-ended and smashed my hand hard on the Astroturf. The force dislocated the ring finger of my right hand so that it was at a ninety-degree angle back across my thumb. I just pushed it back into place and headed to the sidelines.

I told Doc Warren I'd dislocated my finger but he didn't believe me. "Where? I don't see anything."

So I made a fist and the thing popped out again as if I were flipping him the bird. He was amazed. He said he'd never seen anything like it. He called the other medical people over to show off his discovery, and started talking mumbo-jumbo about some "A joint." In the meantime, an ants-in-his-pants Parcells was yelling, "When's he gonna be ready?" In a damn exhibition game!

I just told them to tape it up and I played the rest of the game that way. It was the same hand I've broken eight times anyway.

Well, you get the idea what kind of pre-season it was for me—probably the worst since my rookie season. And it was topped off by a tragedy that hit every member of the team. Just as the pre-season ended, we received news that John Tuggle had lost his courageous battle with cancer and had died in a clinic in Tijuana, where he'd been seeking a treatment that wasn't available in the U.S.

Tuggs was one of the toughest, most remarkable individuals I've ever met. Talk about heroes. In '83, he made the team as a fullback after being the very last player taken in the NFL draft. I always admired the way he played the game with his *heart*, something that really showed on special teams. Then, the next pre-season, an examination turned up tumors in his lungs.

He was a fighter. That same summer, he underwent knee surgery and his marriage ended in divorce. Instead of feeling sorry for himself, Tuggs bought a bottle of champagne and toasted the killer disease as a challenge. He was bound and determined to beat it and be back in a football uniform. The weight room became his battlefield. Because of regular chemotherapy treatments, he had to start from scratch. But he built himself into such amazing shape that he was lifting more weight than he ever had before. And he *did* triumph. Though he never played in another game, he made it back for mini-camp in 1984. Believe me, getting that far in his situation was a major accomplishment—a real victory.

He never said anything about the cancer. He just kept working and telling us he was coming through it. I really didn't know whether that was the truth or just his optimism. Sometimes I had to leave the room and break down in tears, after seeing how hard he worked a day or two after another chemotherapy treatment set him back.

Then, during the last off-season training program, we heard he was in the hospital because of a collapsed lung. Brad had talked to Tuggs' girlfriend, who said things weren't so good— but when we called Tuggs on the phone, he was as optimistic as ever. He said he was feeling great and he'd even started giving me encouragement. "Just keep working hard," he said.

The last time I saw him was in the summertime when we went riding our three-wheel all-terrain vehicles together in the woods in Tuxedo Park. He was as crazy as ever. He went up this one hill, so steep even I wouldn't have attempted it. He got caught in the wrong gear and made it up three-quarters of the way before the bike stopped. The damn thing flipped him over backwards and he just picked it up and threw it over his head down the hill. He stood up with marks all over his back, and he just smiled. He was one tough, very special guy.

Tuggs returned to California after that. A few days before he died, he was actually water-skiing—living life as fully as he possibly could. When the season started, we put his number— 38—on the back of our helmets, just as we wore a patch in memory of Spider Lockhart, a Giant great who died from cancer in the off-season. I know what that 38 meant to me all year. I thought about him often, especially during the times of my back problems. I thought of Tuggs and how he battled. *I'm crying with this when Tuggs never did?* And I'm telling you, that was the last time I ever felt sorry for myself.

My contract situation was no more than a mere distraction in camp, simply because I didn't want it to get in the way— though I certainly had my reasons. I was entering my option year and from what the Giants had said after the '85 season, I had expected to sign a new contract before training camp even started. But the Giants never got around to it, and by the time camp started, my attitude was the hell with it, just play. They were probably counting on that, anyway.

You know the Giants have long had the reputation for being cheap—more concerned with a full house than with a winning team. That's bullshit. I've seen Wellington and Tim Mara do some special things for people. John Tuggle for instance. When John was stricken with cancer, the Maras paid him for a couple of extra years and made sure his insurance was covered.

Other owners would have just dumped him. Same thing with Danny Lloyd a few years ago when he got sick.

Yet the Giants will quibble about contracts because that's business and they're not in the business of giving money away. Every time a contract comes up, it's a battle. With all the talent on our team, we rank fourteenth in average player salary. And you can imagine the position *I* was in when my contract last came up—conveniently for them—just when I came off back surgery.

Am I underpaid?

I look at working stiffs making $20,000 or $30,000 a year—and at $170,000 a year, I say definitely not. I'm playing a game that *kids* play—and I'm twenty-seven years old and going into my seventh year. I'm not starving by any means. I've got a nice family, nice things, and a nice home. Too many people are worse off, so I can't complain.

But then again, the only standard I have is what other guys in my position are earning. Out of the three Giants nose guards in 1986, I was the lowest-paid. Even though I've been a starter for three straight seasons, there's a guy playing behind me who made $100,000 a year more than I did over those three years. And when I look at salaries around the league, I was at the five percent level out of the twenty-eight guys who start at nose. A Pro-Bowl nose like Cleveland's Bob Golic makes close to $400,000 while other defensive linemen have $50,000 incentive clauses just for making the Pro Bowl. Mine was $5,000. Underpaid? You bet.

But I'm not the kind of guy to hold out or bitch. I signed a contract in 1983, and regardless of what has happened since, that was it. You sign a three-year contract, you've got to obligate it. That was exactly the crux of the Joe Morris holdout.

Joe actually saw it the same way I did. Legally, he was under contract at last year's training camp because he, like me, had an option year remaining. But the Giants had fed him the same

spiel about option years and had promised to redo his contract. He was under the impression—which management had
given him—that he was not under any contractual obligation.

Some fans wondered how Joe could do what he did. But
look at it this way. Your boss promises to redo your contract
in January and from June on, you're looking forward to it.
January comes and goes and he hasn't done it. That's got to
piss you off.

Joe chose to deal with it his own way. He thought it was the
only way to get anything done and not come out empty-handed,
like I did. He went through all the off-season training programs and worked his ass off in Johnny Parker's weight room.
He cooperated in every way until training camp arrived. When
nothing was accomplished, he took a stand and held out over
what was then a $900,000 difference over four years—the
Giants at $1.8 million, Joe and his agent at $2.7. It looked to
be a major problem, especially at the usual snail's pace at which
the Giants approach these things.

Bill Parcells knew he couldn't win consistently without Joe,
so he intervened. Everyone agreed that Joe would participate
in everything but the contact drills. Joe thought it was a sign
of good faith, but the Giants probably saw it as a sign of weak-
ness.

Joe took some ribbing on the practice field. Harry Carson
was yelling, "What is this, a work stoppage?" But Harry, like
most of the guys, was on Joe's side. I know I was. It was business and Joe just had to do what he had to do.

Then before we left for Atlanta and our first pre-season game,
Parcells told Joe he'd have to make a choice between staying
out entirely or going full in everything. No more deal. In Bill's
opinion, Joe was under contract and he had bent the rules
enough. He thought the Giants' offer was fair. Joe didn't, so
Joe stayed home.

I talked to him all the way through it and I knew he wasn't

giving up because he'd seen other things happen to other players—like Mark Haynes and Earnest Gray, who each went through bitter contract battles and were no longer with the team. Sooner or later they had to sign him. It was obvious we needed him in training camp, especially when George Adams suffered a freak hip injury in one of our first intra-squad scrimmages. It couldn't be properly diagnosed at camp, and turned out to be a chipped pelvic bone that would also put pressure on blood vessels in the area. It would cause George to miss the season—an example of just how tenuous and fragile a player's career can be.

Joe had the advantage. We were on the verge of something great and we needed him. Not too many guys are going to do what Joe can do in our scheme. There's a difference between cutting back and exploding through a hole, which Joe does so well. Some offenses will just stand on their blocks, like Washington, and make it easy on their backs. Our scheme makes the back read all the way. No one's better at it than Joe.

I thought we'd eventually get him back but I didn't know when. Joe did return for the last pre-season game but the drama continued until kickoff of the regular season opener, when he finally signed, averting a boycott. Before it was finally over, the situation would put a lot of strain on everybody, but it never got to the point where it hurt the team.

In the middle of the whole controversy, trade rumors started to swirl. With Adams hurting and Lee Rouson still green, it looked as if Parcells might have to pick up another back. With the three rookies in camp—and especially before Curtis went down—we had an overabundance of defensive linemen. Something had to give and I even considered myself vulnerable. As it turned out, Dee Hardison was waived and Casey Merrill—talk about a wild character—was traded to the Browns.

The other big media issue in camp revolved around Lawrence Taylor. In February, news broke that L.T. was enrolled at a drug rehab center near Houston. A month later, he confirmed that he was undergoing treatment for substance abuse. That really shocked me because I know L.T.—and basically I thought he was just crazy like the rest of us. He just seemed to live life a little closer to the edge.

Parcells didn't want the issue hanging over training camp so he tried to protect Taylor from the public eye as much as he could. Taylor wouldn't give any interviews and was trying to remain low-key. I felt bad for Lawrence because he couldn't be himself; he had to sit back and say to himself and his teammates, I'm going to show them this year.

People who are with Lawrence every day and know him have a different perception of him than the people he just meets at an autograph session. Deep down, he's a very good person. It's harder for him to show his true colors in public because he's always under a critical eye. The reason why he would be so successful this year was because he relied on his friends and teammates more than he had in the past. He became less of a loner.

Lawrence and I have gotten into many arguments and have even come close to a fistfight or two on and off the field. Still, I regard him as a very good friend because I know when it's time to battle, he'll be behind me.

There've been a couple of times in the middle of the game where we've been toe-to-toe because we have the same competitive feeling about what we're attacking. Those emotions can sometimes overflow in different directions. He and I are both people who can go to extremes.

But at this training camp, L.T.'s self-control was remarkable. A few beers, some fast drives in his new Porsche (which would get stolen outside a bowling alley), but that was about it. It wasn't a new Lawrence, just one with clearly defined priorities. It was as if he was turning this thing into a challenge, which meant—watch out.

At the same time, our defensive coordinator, Bill Belichick, was working on schemes to make better use of Lawrence as a pass rusher. Outside linebacker is a hybrid position and Taylor had coverage responsibilities too. If he was unleashed all the time, he'd be ineffective, because if a team really wants to shut one guy off, they can overcommit and do it. Belichick was finding better ways to avoid involving Lawrence in double-team situations.

Naturally, with all the back-breaking that goes on at camp, you've got to break things up with a little ball-busting. Phil Simms and I are kind of like the main event.

The dorms at Pace are up on the hillside. The parking lots surrounding the dorms are empty but we're supposed to park down below. Hey, that's college, right? Stupid-ass rules. One day, Parcells made a point of telling us that any unauthorized cars parked in the upper lot would be towed. Naturally, since Parcells had just thrown down the gauntlet, I *had* to park there.

Simms was parking there, too. Why not? Break as many rules as you can. Well, someone told me Simms was going to have my car towed away that night. I had to act fast. This was the first day Phil had his brand-new, charcoal-gray Corvette and he was beaming as he showed it off to everybody. I waited for him to go into the bathroom to brush his teeth that night. Conveniently—why do they make it so easy for me?—he left his door open, so I grabbed his car keys and moved the shiny 'Vette to the other side of the campus.

When I got back, I distracted him and got one of our wide receivers, Bobby Johnson—he can slither real well—to sneak into Phil's room and put the keys back on the dresser. Then I got another guy to knock on Phil's door.

"Hey Phil, didn't you just get a new Corvette?"

"Yeah, I did," Simms said proudly.

"Gray?"

"Yep."

"Well, I just saw three strange characters hitching it up to a tow truck and hauling it away."

Phil immediately ran to see if his car was in the spot where he'd left it. When he saw it wasn't there, he screamed, "Ahhhhhhh!" and then "Buuuuuurt!"

I arrived innocently enough, even though my stomach was killing me from laughing so hard. "I haven't paid for the car yet," Phil said, looking hard at me. He knew that if three low-lifes hooked it up to a tow truck, it would be destroyed or at least scratched. "That's your car," he told me. "You've got yourself a 'Vette. You're paying for it and I'm getting a new one."

I said, "Uh-uh. I've got nothing to do with it."

"Bullshit." He was starting to panic. I allowed him to rant and rave for a couple of hours, then I told him what I had done. But in the meantime, thinking Conrad Goode, one of our linemen, had something to do with it, Phil let the air out of all four tires of his car. Eventually, I had a couple of kids retrieve Phil's car—tires fully inflated, I might add.

Well, that started a war for the next few days. We went back and forth. Nothing major—maybe a few grapes stuffed into each other's shoes—until I really outdid myself.

It was about 11:15, after lights-out. We were just working in shorts the next day so I didn't care about curfews. I was wide-awake and in the mood for some horsing around.

I took the fire extinguisher off the wall and slipped down the hall to Phil's room. My idea was to stick the hose under his door (as a quarterback he doesn't have a roommate—and I know he sleeps with his head next to the door) and scare him a little. I had no idea that I'd give this thing one pop and have it virtually explode with sticky, white powdery foam.

As soon as I stuck the nozzle under his door and pushed the trigger, I heard this sleepy belch, followed by a bloodcurdling scream: "Agggggghhhhhh!" I thought, *Holy shit, I killed him.* I got scared as hell, threw that damn thing on the floor and ran for the stairs. Then I heard him open the door so I knew he was okay.

He must have heard me cackling. Then—I've heard this before—he screamed, "Buuuuuuuuurt!"

I was running my ass off up the stairs and laughing. Then when I came back down, a big crowd was gathered around his room—equipment managers, players, everybody. Phil was pacing back and forth in a rage, covered with the white stuff and looking like the Abominable Snowman. Some of the gunk was hanging out his mouth and some was clinging to his eyebrows (which are blond anyway). Later, he'd have to take two showers just to get the smell off him.

He saw me. "Burt, you asshole," he screamed. "Payback's a bitch." He was not amused.

I acted innocent.

"What do you mean?" I said, teary-eyed with laughter.

"Look what you *did*," he said, pointing at what used to pass for his room.

I walked in to survey the damage. White paste was everywhere—all over the expensive suits hanging in the closet, inside and outside his shoes, covering the furniture, and the rest was caked on the walls.

"I've got a sixty-dollar belt here and you're paying for it," he informed me.

"Why the hell did you pay sixty dollars for a belt?" I said. "That's *your* fault."

He wasn't listening.

"These are two-hundred-dollar shoes," he carried on.

"That's your fault too," I said. "Why would you bring two-hundred-dollar shoes to this place?"

He paid two of the equipment guys fifty dollars to clean up the room. I didn't pay for anything. I knew he would try to pay me back, one way or another.

Now you know why I never had a chance. That's me, John, Sally, and Kathy.

Mom, John, and me. Nice legs, huh?

The face of an angel.

Dad with his game face on.

Now, this was a team. That's me in the front row, fourth from the left.

Scoring with my left hand.

Slugging with my right.

Bill Parcells displaying one of his many
moods. *(Ira N. Golden)*

Bill Belichick at his chalkboard. *(Blair Holley)*

Here's my line coach, Lamar Leachman. It's like they invented the word *redneck* to fit Lamar. *(Jim Turner)*

Johnny Parker must be asking Kenny Hill for a dollar. *(Blair Holley)*

My roommate, Billy Ard. (*Jerry Pinkus*)

George Martin, our leader. (*Jerry Pinkus*)

A day or two later, my roomie, Billy Ard, japped me and behind my back let the hell-bent-for-revenge Phil into my room. I had been telling everybody about the fire extinguisher incident and naturally Phil was forced to make his move. It was a feeble effort.

When he got into my room, he emptied a couple of tubes of toothpaste and shampoo under the sheets at the bottom of my bed so that when I got in, my feet would get covered in slop. Even if he had succeeded with this amateurish prank, it was nothing compared to my roomful of white foam.

Anyway, just before I was about to slip under the sheets, Ard was hit with pangs of conscience and whispered to me what Simms had done. Of course, Phil was standing outside the door, listening anxiously for my reaction. So I immediately launched into an Academy Award-winning performance. "Oh, shit, that f——ing Simms," I snarled loudly. "That SOB got me back. He *always* gets me back." Meanwhile, I'm jabbing Billy with my elbow and we're trying not to laugh.

Phil ran down the hall, laughing, convinced that he had gotten even. Yeah, right.

I told Ard, "You japped me by letting him in." "No, no," he denied. "I've got a feeling you did," I said. "And if I find out you told the guys I put my feet in there, then I know you're involved in this." He never said a word about it. Phil still thinks he got even.

Of course, Phil will never get even. The only time he really scored against me was after the '84 season. It was his first great season. He threw for over four thousand yards and revitalized our offense. We made the playoffs after a 3–12–1 record in '83. That was the season when Bill picked Scott Brunner over Phil to start the year—probably one of the worst mistakes Bill has made as coach of the Giants. Phil knew it then and Bill knows it now.

Phil and I both have the same agent, David Fishof, who was

enlisted by Simms for this one. When I called David, he asked me if I had heard the news that Simms had been traded to the Rams.

A few days later, I saw Bill in the weight room at Giants Stadium. "Bill," I said, "I can't believe you're going to trade Phil. That's the craziest thing I ever heard. The guy throws for four thousand yards, brings us into the playoffs, we beat the Rams, and we probably should have gone to the Super Bowl."

I had six or seven more reasons for him why it was so dumb. Before I could say another word, he said, "Whoa, whoa. What have you been smoking lately? Burt, what the hell are you talking about? I'm not trading Simms. You're crazy."

I knew right then and there that they got me. I didn't want Bill to know what a sucker I was, so I said nonchalantly, "Just testing you. I was only kidding."

Heat balm in the jock is an old trick but a good one. Once you start sweating, it sets you on fire. Phil tried it on me once, but I was able to detect it before I got dressed. When I tried it on Phil, I made sure I got to the locker room early so that the balm would dry out and become odorless.

The reaction was delayed, but by the time we started running, Phil started itching. In a few minutes, his ass was on fire.

Once in a while, we sting offensive tackle Brad Benson just for practice. Our strength coach, Johnny Parker, loves sticking it to him, too. Brad's been around for ten seasons, third longest on the team, but he's still too easy a mark, sort of like playing chess against your son. He's full of bullshit about everything he says. He's got the best dogs, the most high-tech car, and he's an expert on home improvement. This characteristic tends to make him vulnerable. With Brad, you don't even have to bait the hook and throw it in the water. He'll jump in the boat after it. And he's so sensitive, you can really hit home. We actually feel sorry for him after it's over.

Brad's also a hard worker and he hates to make mistakes and get chewed out by the coaches. That's why a sting devised by Phil one day in training camp worked so well. In the huddle, Simms called the count "on one," but he had told everybody but Brad to go "on two." *Hut, hut,* and Brad's already across the line of scrimmage. Ron Erhardt, who was in on the gag, growled, "What the hell's wrong with you, Benson?"

Then they got back to the huddle and Simms said "on two," which of course meant "on one" to the rest of the offense. Brad was left in his stance at the snap of the ball and his guy blew by him.

"Benson, not again," Erhardt barked. Three days later he still hadn't figured it out. See what I mean? Too easy. That's Bebo.

Brad's not very good at carrying out scams, either. He really gave away a good one I had going after our rookie linemen reported to camp last July. I told a couple of them—John Washington and Stanley Scott, a free agent—that there was one thing in particular they'd have to watch for.

"The coach. Lamar Leachman," I said. "He's gay. You have to watch the guy, especially when he tries to get friendly. He's always trying to put his arm around the players to get a quick feel."

John and Stanley were alarmed but grateful for the tip. For the next few weeks, they avoided getting anywhere near Lamar, which is sometimes difficult because he's always on top of the rookies—especially during last camp, with so many new linemen in his charge. Lamar would come over, real friendly like, and they would promptly scoot. "Good thing you told us about Coach Leachman," they'd whisper to me. "Don't mention it," I'd reply.

What a scam! My only mistake was to let Brad in on it. I wanted him to reinforce it for me, but that's just not him. He's a lousy liar. Guilt complex, I suppose. Finally, after a few weeks of this, he blabbed. *This* year I might tell the rookies to watch themselves when they're in the shower with Brad. Brad's already convinced Curtis McGriff that he's gay. It started out as a prank but Curtis still hasn't caught on. He's so afraid Brad might grab him in the shower, in fact, that he's stopped taking showers. He changes from practice clothes to street clothes at his locker, when Brad's not looking. He doesn't care if he smells.

I suppose that Brad conforms pretty well to the nickname Parcells gave the offensive line. The Suburbanites. If not for football, it would be easy to picture any of them easing into a yuppie lifestyle. Brad sells Jaguars in the off-season. Billy Ard is a stockbroker and Bart Oates attends law school. Chris Godfrey says that *his* idea of a good time is to trim the hedges and take out the garbage. Karl Nelson is a farm boy from Iowa but he's certainly boring and nondescript enough to be a Suburbanite.

Funny thing, though. They sure don't play like the suburbanites I was used to in Orchard Park. I don't think it will be long before Billy, Bart, and Chris follow Brad's footsteps to the Pro Bowl. It wasn't too long ago that the offensive line was the weakest part of the team. Now it's the foundation of our offense.

I've been going up against Bart Oates in practice and at camp for two seasons now, ever since he came over from the USFL to fill a big hole left by an unfortunate accident involving Kevin Belcher. Kevin started at center in 1984 and had a promising career in front of him before his jeep collided with a truck on a Pennsylvania highway. Kevin was lucky to escape with his life but his football career ended due to a nerve injury in his leg. Bart, however, really bailed us out of a tight spot in 1985.

He's an excellent center, especially as a pass blocker. We get along extremely well because of a mutual respect; we help each other out instead of battling. At training camp, where jobs are won and lost, some guys can resort to cheap stuff in order to gain an edge and impress the coaching staff—always at the expense of the other player. That has never happened between Bart and me and it's the biggest reason why I'm not involved in as many training-camp brawls as I used to be.

It wasn't that way with Rich Umphrey, a center who hung on with the team for a few years. Umphrey was the type of guy who did an extraordinary amount of holding, liked to hit after the whistle and cut below the knees, which you don't do against teammates.

The worst part was that he'd wait for his other teammates to come break it up, then act as if he wanted to fight you when really he couldn't punch his way out of a wet paper bag. He'd pull this act, mind his p's and q's for a couple of days while I calmed down, and then he'd start the same old nonsense. This continued for two seasons.

Our third year together, things came to a head on a hot humid day in camp. Same as usual. He pushed after the whistle and waited for his teammates. But I'd had enough.

I just took my helmet and started windmilling it so no one could get close. When everyone had backed off, I grabbed hold of his face mask and started hammering him with my helmet while I started to pull his off. He backtracked at full speed and I threw both helmets at him before everyone managed to break it up.

Parcells came waddling over. "That was stupid, throwing your helmet at him. You could have hurt him."

My answer: "Aw, he's an asshole."

"Oh yeah?" Parcells said. "Well, maybe *you're* the asshole."

"Oh yeah?" I said. "Well, maybe . . ."

My next words were either going to be the old point-of-no-return, or reconciliation. With everyone circled around, I knew I was in dangerous waters. I caught myself.

"Well maybe . . ." I continued, "I *am*."

# 5

---

## DALLAS


## The Family

Lamar Leachman, as you know, is my defensive line coach. It's a good thing, because if he were the head coach, none of us would ever have survived a single training camp. Or so Lamar says.

It's like they invented the word "redneck" to fit Lamar. He's a strange-looking character bearing an uncanny resemblance to Popeye. We call him "Knock-Knee." He's got a barrel chest left over from his playing days but his legs are real skinny at the bottom and seem to be screwed on the wrong way, as if the left one got attached to the right side. He struts around almost as if he has to twist his torso to move, and he has a vocabulary all his own. For instance, he'll say, "Boy, your titties are gonna get moldy if you don't start liftin' some of those weights. Ya know what I mean, boy?"

Lamar himself had quite a high school career as a tailback in Cartersville, Georgia, back in the early fifties. In fact, when Herschel Walker was setting all those schoolboy records down there, those were records that Lamar once held. In college at Tennessee, Lamar played linebacker and a position called bubble back, a precursor to nose tackle because it put him up on the center.

These days, he spends a lot of time up on *our* backs. When things are going well, Lamar can come off as your best friend. But when they're not, Dr. Jekyll turns into Mr. Hyde. If we were his kids, he'd probably lock us in his basement.

When Leonard Marshall came into the league as a second-round pick in '83, that's just what Lamar wanted to do with him. Leonard will admit it. He wasn't ready for the NFL then. He was overweight and spent more energy on Big Macs than on sacks. Lamar had been friends with Leonard's coach at LSU and it was he who recommended Leonard to the Giants. Seeing Leonard out of shape at camp, Lamar kept saying, "Boy, when I get time, I'm gonna call that coach up and ask him what the hell was he talkin' about. He sent me a *dawg* down here." He got on Leonard so hard even the veterans felt bad for him.

Still, as much as I hate to admit it, Lamar's a great coach. He took Leonard, who they thought was a wasted second-round draft choice, and helped him become an All Pro; he took Curtis McGriff, a free agent, and turned him into a five-year starter; he took over George Martin, an eighth-round draft choice. . . . Let me rephrase that. George took *him* over.

You see, George seems to be the only person on the whole team that Lamar will listen to. But on the other hand, George uses *me* to stir things up with Lamar.

When I first came into the league as a rookie, Lamar didn't bother me because I thought his behavior was normal for a coach in the pros. Then I started talking to guys from other teams who couldn't believe my horror stories. They were telling me, "No, our guy's not like that at all. He's real nice." Then I knew I was just stuck with Lamar.

To give you an idea of how things had gone in the 1986 pre-season, Lamar was in a good mood during the entire camp. He was treating us relatively nicely. He was a little tough on the three new guys, but it was nothing compared to when I was a rookie. Little wonder. It just so happened Lamar was in the last year of his contract and he needed all the friends he could get. I'm sure he'll be back to his old self this year.

Lamar kept repeating all through training camp, "This is the best we've ever been. The best we've ever been." And at our position meetings he'd say, "This is a family in here. Whatever happens, we stick together. We're a family."

George Martin and I were cackling over that one. "Just wait until he japs us," George whispered to me.

So the "family" bundled up its things and headed for its semiannual feud with the Cowboys, our opening-week opponent on Monday Night Football. When you're a Giant, it's easy to hate the Cowboys and the "America's Team" image that TV gave them. One of our sweetest wins ever occurred at Texas Stadium in 1984, when they had the nerve to schedule us for their homecoming game, as if we were chumps or an easy mark. At halftime, they introduced their "all-time" team, including a few current players, and put them up on big pedestals all around the field.

We watched all this from the tunnel, and did it ever fire us up. We put on a second half that blew them away, 19–7, and we swept the season series that year for the first time since 1963. In our 1985 game in Dallas, the one we lost to blow first place, I was so mad that I chased away their cowboy-suited mascot, Whistling Ray, from behind our bench, where he'd been stirring up the crowd. When he saw the crazed look on my face, he got out of there pronto.

On our first flight to Dallas this time, I felt good about our team and about our prospects for this season. The night before, my attorney, Paul Rotella, was at my house and I dragged him across the street to the schoolyard, where I went wild doing chin-ups on the playground equipment, yelling, "We're gonna smoke 'em, we're gonna smoke 'em." Later, I woke up at 1 A.M., went outside and started sprinting around the neighborhood. I was suitably psyched.

Personally, I was happy to get out of the pre-season; after a
3 – 1 record in the summer, we thought we had no reason to
question our press clippings. We knew we were a better team
than the Cowboys, even though they pulled a horseshoe out
of their rear ends to win both games the year before. Then
again, this was the opening game on a Monday night in Dallas,
and a lot of strange things can happen. Sure enough, they
happened early.

Joe Morris was on the plane with us but he was still un-
signed, and there were stories all week that he might boycott
the game. When we got to our hotel off the expressway in
Irving, we were mobbed by what seemed like a thousand Giant
fans who were staying in the same hotel with us on some travel
junket. There were more of them there than would be in California when we landed for the Super Bowl. After games I
don't mind the hoopla, but before a game this kind of thing is
a pain in the ass.

So there they were, telling us what we didn't need to hear—
a constant chant of "Super Bowl, Super Bowl." Smart fans,
huh? But at the time, I freaked out. We were trying to look
five miles down the road at the Cowboys. We had sixteen regular season games in front of us and *they* were yelling about
the Super Bowl.

We had a walk-through practice at the stadium on Sunday
evening and Joe made the front office sweat by staying in his
room to let them know how serious he was. Parcells and the
coaching staff were serious, too. They were seriously blowing
a fuse. They'd put in a game plan with Morris in mind and
now there was a chance he wouldn't play. We couldn't really
comment, but ninety percent of the team was behind him all
the way, because we know what kind of person Joe is.

I figured it four to one that he wouldn't play. I knew Joe
wasn't balking and the only way he was going to play was if

the Giants made the move. If I were to have bet on it, I would have said no to that possibility: that just doesn't happen with the Giants. Wrong again.

Somebody said that what Joe did was like holding a gun to the Giants' head—but if that's what it took, it worked. Harry Hulmes negotiated with Joe's agent all day Monday so that when Joe walked into the pre-game meal, he was ninety percent sure he was going to play.

The deal wasn't wrapped up until the team was getting dressed in the locker room. Joe got the news on the pay phone: $2.24 million over four years. That took a load off of the offensive guys' minds. But for those of us on defense, we would have had to play the same way with or without Joe.

As for Joe, he played pretty well that night. Even though he thought he might have run out of gas in the fourth quarter, he gained eighty-seven yards on twenty carries and the offense certainly didn't suffer. Phil was hot, as he usually is against the Cowboys. He loves to attack the Cowboys' man-to-man defense and can always hit big plays against their blitz. Simms finished with three hundred yards, Bobby Johnson had eight catches and Mark Bavaro, our indestructible stud of a tight end, caught seven.

Johnson, the kind of receiver who gets better nearer the end zone, had two TD catches, Morris had a TD and Stacy Robinson another. Hey, when our offense scores twenty-eight points, there is no way we should lose a game.

But we did. And you can blame it all on us, the defense. We missed tackles all over the field and we made Herschel Walker look like all-world in his NFL debut. It was truly our worst performance of the year and possibly over the last three years.

Coming into the game, we had a lot of respect for Walker and not only because he kicked our pal Lamar out of the Georgia record books. The guy was unstoppable in the USFL, and even if those defenses didn't compare to ours, we knew he was a powerful runner. Of course, we've shut down plenty of powerful runners before.

Herschel's one of those players who try to nice-guy you to death before games with that humble-pie drawl of his: "I just think the world of the New York Giants defense. I'm just honored to be playing against them. I reckon this and I reckon that." Yeah, sure. Then he steps on the field and starts running over people.

Like any other great back, you've got to wrap Herschel up. You can't just hit him high and expect him to go down, especially with those tree-trunk legs of his. He's built low to the ground. Once he hits that open field, there aren't too many backs who can pull away from DBs like he can. And he's just so big that he terrorizes them. I think he's going to be a great one.

This was his first game and even the Cowboys weren't sure how they were going to use him. They couldn't split the ball in half for him and Tony Dorsett. But after Dorsett twisted his ankle while planting his foot in the first half, it was Herschel's show—six catches for thirty-two yards, sixty-four yards running on ten carries, including the winning touchdown.

For a while, we were playing okay on defense. We gave up a cheap field goal with twenty-two seconds left in the half. Still, after three quarters, they had only seventeen points. If that's how the game ended, it would have been an average night. We usually outlast teams in the fourth quarter, but on this night, they just snuck up on us. Somehow, we lost our intensity, even though we didn't know it. Maybe we thought we were too good—but if we had realized we were playing flat, we would have done something to get it back. If you have to smack somebody in the head to get something started, you smack somebody in the head.

This time, we just lulled ourselves to sleep.

When we got into the fourth quarter, we were kind of tired and not really concentrating. Meanwhile, Herschel was in there fresh. Twice in the quarter we led by four points and both times we let them back in front. They drove seventy-four yards by using ten plays and taking up 6:05, and that's unheard-of against our attrition-oriented defense. Herschel got ten yards running a reverse and on the next play, Danny White threw a one-yard pass to Thornton Chandler to put them in the lead, 24–21.

It didn't last long. Phil quickly got it back. Even though we lost a 52-yard pass to Stacy Robinson because of a clip, Simms got us in the end zone by reading a blitz and hitting Bobby Johnson against Ron Fellows. Bobby made the play by tipping the ball in the air at the 20 and taking it in for the touchdown that should have won the game for us.

The Cowboys were at their 28. I looked up at the clock and it showed 2:10 left in the game. They had one last chance but they'd have to march the full seventy-two yards against our defense. A field goal would have left them short. We'd given them one long drive already, and I thought there was no way they'd do it again. It was our chance to stop them cold.

Instead, Herschel got things started by taking a middle screen pass from White against our nickel defense—the formation we use in obvious passing situations where we take out a line-backer, usually Harry Carson, and replace him with a fifth defensive back. I leave, too, for Jerome Sally. But the nickel didn't stop Herschel, who bounced off six of our blue shirts before he went down on our 49.

Harry stuffed Walker for a two-yard loss on a screen pass but Tony Hill spun Elvis Patterson around and caught a pass at our 16.

Now it was third and five from our 10 with 1:20 left. All we had to do was keep them out of the end zone. They lined up in a shotgun and ran what we call a 43–I–trap. In layman's terms, that's a draw play—to Herschel Walker in this case. The Cowboy line pulled back to give the impression they were pass-blocking to sucker us into rushing. Then they fired out on us, hoping to trap someone upfield and give Herschel the running lane he'd need to get at least the first down.

The way the play's drawn up, their center hits me and their left guard blocks down on me with his arms and tries to turn me. Meanwhile, their right guard pulls and trap-blocks Leonard, who has started to pass-rush. Harry Carson is supposed to scrape behind me to fill that hole, and when that happens, the guard chips off me and onto him, which allows me to get the center out of the way.

But it didn't happen that way. Harry gambled when the guard pulled—you've got to do that sometimes. Instead of scraping behind me, he shot underneath for a clear shot at Herschel, but bounced off his legs at the line of scrimmage. When Harry shot the gap, the guard stayed on me. Shielded by two guys, I had no chance to make the play.

Once Leonard sees the play, he's supposed to double back like an SOB and make the hole smaller. Instead, he got upfield too far and couldn't make it back. There was a gaping hole. And our other inside backer, Gary Reasons, had no chance at Walker either because the lane was so huge.

Herschel rolled into the end zone as if the play had come straight off their chalkboard. The Cowboys had just demonstrated the anatomy of a screwed-up defense. The play was totally contrary to philosophy—which always gives a number of guys a chance to make the play. Harry took a gamble, Leonard didn't turn it down enough, and I couldn't fight off the double-team.

We lost, 31–28, and our defense came off the field stunned by what had happened to us in the final quarter. We'd been given the credit for a lot of wins. Now, we were the reason why we lost. Our offense had played well and if it hadn't been for us, we would have won. It was our worst defensive effort in a long time. The locker room was like a morgue. "Too big for our britches," I told reporters. Some Super Bowl express.

What was I supposed to tell the press? We lost the game because we took them too lightly? Who gives a shit? We lost the game. If we were going to be a championship team like I thought we were going to be, you just don't do that, because that's what the Giants had been doing for years—losing the games they're supposed to win. We took the Cowboys lightly and we had no reason to take anyone lightly because we hadn't done anything yet. Any excuses you make up are pure bullshit.

What really ticked me off was that we played badly against a team that wasn't that good. At the time, everybody thought Dallas' offense was pretty potent, but *I* didn't think so. And now we were looking down the barrel of the San Diego attack, which had just scored fifty points against Miami.

I used the loss to the Cowboys as a tool for the rest of the season. I hate to admit this, because the following week was pure hell, but the loss served its purpose very well. It jolted us into preparing as hard as we could for every game. When things get bad like that, I generally think back to the 1983 season, when we were 3–12–1 and things couldn't get any worse. This one game, I thought, was as close to that miserable season as we could get. Things had fallen apart on us, just like in '83. Things were threatening to snowball, just like '83.

Everyone on defense felt responsible for the loss and it banded us together to play our best defense ever the rest of the year. Amazing. After our worst game ever, our defense played its best football ever for the remainder of 1986. We were giving up yardage but it was just garbage stuff. In pressure situations, we came through.

As for Lamar, he was trying to control himself after the Dallas loss, which was pretty difficult for him. Usually, whatever's in his way, he says Screw 'em all: I've got my wife and kids and if these guys can't win for me I'm gonna stick it up their you-know-whats. I couldn't blame him this time. We were awful.

But at our first meeting after Dallas, he kept things cool. He pointed out some no-hustles and short arms, which means you turn down hits. He told me I was "average," which was more than a fair assessment. He re-emphasized that family thing about sticking together. Then on Thursday, the press got around to asking Lamar about the "family's" problems. So he laid out the dirty laundry.

"That was the worst performance by a defensive line in the seven years I've been here," he said. "I thought we were mentally and physically ready to play Monday night in Dallas. I thought the enthusiasm factor would be there but it wasn't." Then he admitted: "I must have done a poor job in preparing them." How about that? But he quickly shifted the onus to us.

"As far as lack of execution is concerned, I think that's their fault. As far as hustling is concerned, I think that's also their fault. We had more no-hustles, more poor efforts, more L.G.s [that's lying on the ground after being blocked] . . ."

And on and on. He even said that with this kind of production from us, it wouldn't be long before the three rookies would start rotating in more often.

When the reporters got their hands on that stuff, they rushed into the locker room to get our reactions. I seemed to be the only lineman there. My reaction? "F—— Lamar," I said. I can't say I'm surprised that nobody printed it. The time came for our next meeting. George and I are the spokesmen for our group. We're like a law firm. George handles the misdemeanors and I handle the felonies. This was my case.

"Lamar?" I said. "We're a family?"

"That's right, we're family," he said.

"Well, how come you just went to the press and said all this bad stuff about us?"

"Well, we all make mistakes, don't we?" he stammered, taking the defensive. "That was a mistake. I've got to retract that statement."

By the end of the meeting, we were all so ticked off that no one was talking to him. It turned out that Lamar went over to the press room and told the beat writers he didn't mean what he said and could they please not quote him? The reporters said, "Hell no, this is the best story we've had in years."

In one story, I even came off as being the worst of the bunch. The reporter had looked at the stat sheet handed out at the game, and saw I was credited for no tackles (it was wrong—I had four). His creative mind went to work and he concocted "sources" close to the Giants organization revealing that my "bad" performance was back-related. Bullshit. The only "source" was himself. Even Lamar had nothing to do with it.

The one good thing about the many battles I've had with Lamar is that Parcells doesn't intervene, even after a stool or two has been thrown across the locker room. He knows Lamar gives us a lot of crap; so he also knows that whatever Lamar gets in return, he deserves. Like the time in the film room last year.

He'd been getting my blood pressure up (not an unusual occurrence) and I wanted to return the favor. I reached across George Martin, who was sitting next to the light switch, and clicked on the light.

"Turn the light off, George," Lamar said.

George obeyed.

"George, you've got no guts," I said.

"Okay," George replied. "If you turn the light on again, I won't shut it off."

Thrilled that he was going along with me, I turned it on again.

"Turn the light off, George," Lamar said. Nothing. "I said, George, turn the light off. C'mon George."

George just sat there.

"George, turn . . . turn . . . turn the light *off*." Lamar was stammering now. "Hey, now boy, turn the f——ing light off!"

Finally he got so burned up, he walked over to us, where he knew I was instigating George, grabbed five canisters of film, and slam-dunked them into the floor.

"Just get the f—— out of here, there'll be no meeting," he yelled.

Just another routine incident in the meeting room. Family, you know.

# 6

---

# EAST RUTHERFORD


## Doom's Day

Gary Anderson's body was twisting in midair. Saturday's meal was turning cartwheels in my stomach. This was our final film session of the week at our home before home games, the Woodcliffe Lake Hilton in New Jersey, and we were nauseous over the San Diego offense that awaited us the next day at Giants Stadium.

We had already studied reels of videotape offering us brutal evidence of San Diego's 50–28 Week 1 rubout of the Dolphins. By the time Dan Fouts, Gary Anderson, Kellen Winslow and the others had called off the dogs against Miami, they had run up five hundred yards of insufferable offense. Five hundred yards look like more when they are being crammed into your memory banks at every chance the coaches get.

Our defensive coordinator, Bill Belichick, wanted us to know what we were up against. By Saturday night, we knew. There was no way of telling that the Dolphin defense was that bad— but after all, our defense had just made Supermen out of the Cowboys and now we were looking down the barrel of a gun with a speeding bullet.

Belichick had taken the loss in Dallas just as miserably as his players had—maybe more so. We gave him the nickname

"Doom," as in gloom and doom. He's an eternal pessimist, always worried, always fretting. While we blamed ourselves, he blamed his preparation, thinking that he had done a poor job of selling us the Cowboys. Each week, a coach has to convince his players of two things: that the upcoming opponent is dangerous enough to respect and mortal enough to beat. We usually have problems with the first part, though we always play better when we're scared.

Belichick felt that the films we had watched before Dallas had lulled us into a false sense of security about the Cowboys. That attitude can show up pretty fast on the field.

Because Assistant Coach Paul Hackett arrived in Dallas from San Francisco to help run their offense, we expected the Cowboys to look more like the 49ers. Therefore, Belichick thought that last year's films would have been of little help, and mostly we saw their pre-season games. There was nothing in those films that made us think the game was going to be anything more than a Texas stroll. The Cowboys had been atrocious. They lost all five exhibition games, and, as it turned out, Tom Landry scrapped most of the new elements anyway. What we saw on opening night was pure Cowboys, the same spaghetti-western things we'd been facing twice a year, every year. I didn't buy it as an excuse but he felt we had been flimflammed by the films.

This week, then, Belichick was determined to turn our film sessions into Chiller Theatre. Conveniently, the Chargers played well the week before; their fireworks display was the next best thing to *Friday the 13th* as far as Bill was concerned, so he kept a heavy hand on the tape machine.

We were getting one last look at Jason, alias Gary Anderson, as he executed the most incredible play any of us had ever seen. At the tail end of a run, Anderson reached the Dolphins' five-yard line, launched himself into the air and performed a double twist over a dumbfounded Dolphin into a perfect stand-up, landing two yards inside the end zone. Hell, he looked like Mary Lou Retton.

The room was dead silent. A number of playbooks had already been closed with a thud, a message to Belichick that we'd had enough, and a few restless catcalls had already bounced off the walls. Lawrence and I were in the chairs we traditionally occupy in the front of the room alongside the projector, closest to Bill. We both got up at the same time.

"Enough," I said. "We've had enough of this shit." I told Bill to turn the damn projector off. We had seen all we wanted to see, and we all left the room at once. Believe me, we were never as terrified of an offense and never so determined to stop one.

I walked out into the parking lot, got into my car, and started driving around. I felt the top of my head turn red. Then I suddenly realized I didn't know where I was going. I went home on automatic pilot and when I walked through the door I noticed that my clothes were drenched from the sweat. It was that kind of week for me—the most humbling one of my career.

Each day at the stadium I'd be tormented by Lamar's lip and the Chargers' films. When I got home later than usual after practice, I made life just as miserable for Colleen. Football season is a lonely time for players' wives. Our routine points us from one game to the next. We can get so caught up in what's in front of us on the schedule that we ignore what's in front of us at home. Winning changes that to a degree, but losing, especially the way we did in Dallas, can make domestic life unbearably tense. I tried to spend my time with Jimmy but that's about all I was up for that week.

Colleen has always felt that the most important thing isn't winning but seeing me come home uninjured. Of course, I'd probably get myself hurt if it meant winning; anything else is a waste of the effort you put in.

It was a rough week. I wasn't taking any phone calls, even from friends and family, and I wasn't entertaining Jimmy. All I did was eat and sleep, or try to sleep anyway. The first night, I kept Colleen awake by flopping around and yelling out football terminology in my dreams. For the pounding she took, she should have come to bed wearing a helmet.

From the second night on, I chose—or was it Colleen who chose?—the solitary confinement of the rec room sofa downstairs. I studied endlessly in my sanctuary, watching films over and over until two in the morning, searching for weaknesses, looking for positive ways we could beat them. I got about five hours of fitful sleep each night but my mind never rested. By seven the next morning, I was up and headed back to the stadium in a state of nervous exhaustion.

Colleen, who found I would snap at anything she said, tried leaning on our neighbor Maureen for comfort: "I can't take it any more," Colleen complained. "He's like a time bomb waiting to explode."

As I ticked away toward Sunday, my thoughts were simple, as well as exasperating. Throw in terrifying, too. *This is it, Burt,* I told myself. *If we don't win this one, it's '83 all over again.*

I was rehashing my career and I was afraid this was going to ruin everything. We'd gone through the pre-season so confidently and maybe we were about to blow it right here: blow everything we'd worked for, everything we'd built. I thought back to that nightmare 3 – 12 – 1 '83 season. We had to take control *now,* because once the defense falls apart, it's a case of "See you next year."

We knew we wouldn't win a shoot-out. We tried that with the Chargers in '83, but we still lost, 41 – 34. Now we were scared shitless. Yet in the middle of all those fears, I knew there wasn't any way we were going to lose. At least I can say that now. There is a special confidence that anxiety sometimes breeds. It was an all-or-nothing situation, and we were tired of the nothing part. The paranoid Parcells, who'd been setting up the press by going ga-ga over the Chargers, was now telling them he wasn't "completely confident" we could get everything straightened out by Sunday.

Bill takes one of two approaches the week before a big game. He either goes all-out crazy and yells at every turn or he doesn't say anything and lets things take care of themselves. It's the same way at training camp. If he bitches at a guy every day, you know he likes him and that the player has potential. When he stops talking to a player, you know that player is gone. Maybe it's the next day, maybe the next year, but he's always gone. I see it all the time.

This week, Bill was stone silent. That meant he was worried but it also meant he knew what he was doing. He said only a few words to me all week: "You've got to do better than that." I think he knew what was going to happen.

For one thing, Belichick had us super-prepared for this game. If there's a better defensive coordinator than Belichick out there, you'll have to show me. In fact, while Lamar may be in his own solar system on Planet Redneck, I think our entire coaching staff is built the way Bill Parcells wants it—hardworking guys who won't take the credit they deserve. We don't have any Buddy Ryans or Bud Carsons on our staff and that's certainly true of Belichick.

He did a lot of work with the linebackers while Parcells was running the defense and when Tuna got the head coaching job following Ray Perkins' departure, Belichick stepped up as defensive coordinator, younger than a good many guys on that team. Last season, at thirty-four though he looks even younger, Belichick was only a year older than George Martin and Harry Carson.

Bill looks more like a stockbroker than a football coach and he is extremely intelligent. He has come up with new ways to use our personnel so that offenses are always guessing. He doesn't get carried away with a lot of fronts and looks, but his subtleties work. He's able to control a lot of different person-alities—renegades such as L.T. and myself—and make us all function within a team concept.

No one in the organization outworks Belichick. He prepares with the same intensity each week. He leaves his house at four-thirty in the morning and doesn't come home until midnight. Colleen would *love* that. Other guys work those hours and get nothing accomplished but Bill will present us with three dif-ferent game plans each week, and they change once we start working them out on the practice field.

Bill does everything right down to the last detail—and I'm a stickler for getting as much information as I can. Usually, Belichick will run the first play on a reel of film and I'm al-ready asking him to run it back again, sometimes above the moans of the other guys. I don't know of anyone else who could possibly cover any more than Bill Belichick—even Par-cells, as meticulous as he is.

Doom's preparation for San Diego had started months ear-lier. Since we had problems with unfamiliar teams from the AFC Central the year before, Parcells sent Belichick and the staff out to Denver for a mutual exchange of information with the Broncos, of all people, back in March. The Bronco coaches helped orient our staff with the AFC West. We did the same for them with the NFC East.

As we got ready for the onslaught of the Chargers, Bill pro-vided us with information about every player on their offen-sive team, from the line to the wide receivers to the quarterback. Strengths and weaknesses alike were pointed out so that by the time we took the field we were aware of every technicality, from what kind of moves Gary Anderson favored to what kind of toughness he had. We knew exactly what plays the Chargers ran, why they ran them and where they ran them.

Our keys as pass rushers would be to push the pocket back into Fouts' face and to tag him every chance we had. We knew we wouldn't pick up a lot of sacks because he takes a short two-step drop and releases the ball so quickly. But it doesn't matter who the quarterback is: if you keep hitting him, you're going to get to him. Meanwhile, our cornerbacks were ready to jam their receivers at the line. Fouts likes to use a lot of pop passes and hitch patterns to isolate Anderson and Winslow. If you take that away from Fouts, he looks downfield, where we would be sitting in a two-deep zone.

The pre-game locker room was quieter than usual as we re-hashed all of this one final time. Keyed-up, the defense was even happy when we got to kick off and face their offense first.

Fouts' first play was a little out-pass to Anderson but L.T. smothered the dangerous little back, who we felt was the best athlete we faced all season. Then Lionel James tried our left side and got just two yards. That's how it continued. We wanted to see how the Chargers would respond to our physical brand of defense. We wanted to put footsteps in their ears along with helmets in their chests. Our mad-dog aggressiveness, as it usu-ally does, was paying off with drops, messed-up timing and hasty decisions by the Chargers.

The same Charger offense that piled up twenty first downs against Miami went three downs and out the first two times they had the ball. On their third possession, they ran just one play. James fumbled after Lawrence nailed him from the back side.

Every time a Charger caught the ball, there was a conversion of angry Giants. You could *hear* how we were playing. Not all games sound the same, but that day we were just flying around and helmets were popping. The tune we were playing was forcing their heads onto swivels. It seemed as though we were playing for our lives. After their first five possessions, they had managed to squeeze out only twenty net yards.

Unfortunately, our offense wasn't having one of its more productive days. Though we were able to move the ball, we bogged down close to the goal line. The Chargers, who always played defense like World War II Italy, actually stopped Joe Morris seven times inside their two-yard line. Despite the pounding we were giving the Chargers, we had only a 10–7 lead to show for it at the end of both the second and third quarters.

Before we went in the locker room at halftime, however, a funny thing happened. We got a break that didn't seem that significant at the time—but as the season wore on, other plays like it formed a pattern for our success. Fouts had just struck quickly for a big-play TD to that Anderson character and with less than a minute remaining in the half, they had one last chance to gain at least a tie.

But the Chargers screwed up. Their sideline staff sent out their field goal team too early, with their regular offense still on the field, and the mix-up caused them to run out of time on our 12-yard line, unable to get off a last play or even to throw an incomplete pass to stop the clock. Don Coryell was left screaming at his coaches as the Chargers headed for the lockers. It was a blunder that might have happened to us in the past. But for once, we were the beneficiaries of fate's kindness.

San Diego never recovered from the mistake. The way our defense was playing, the Chargers had to take what they could get when they could get it. Instead, it was our defense that did the taking. The next six times the Chargers had the ball, they gave it up with turnovers. Fouts wasn't at his best, throwing five interceptions on the day, but I know our pressure had something to do with his strangely frantic right arm. Our free safety, Terry Kinard, picked off a pair of passes—he'd be voted defensive player of the week—and our strong safety, Kenny Hill, got another two, including the one that finally got our offense going again.

As I said, the offense was having its problems. The game should have been a blowout, although San Diego's defense, more aggressive than in the past under a new coordinator, was getting in a few good shots too. The most frustrating failure came after George forced and Leonard recovered a fumble in the third quarter. The offense had a first and goal opportunity at San Diego's two-yard line but Joe was stopped three straight times up the middle. When Bill opted against a field goal, Joe was stopped again on fourth down.

At one point in the game, we were lining up third-string quarterback Jeff Hostetler as a wide receiver because of injuries to our regulars. Earlier, while trying to make a backward diving catch in the end zone, Stacy Robinson landed flush on his tailbone. After a scary five minutes on the ground, Stacy left the field on a stretcher. In an amazing display of toughness—people are always underestimating our receivers that way—Stacy returned to the game in the third quarter and made two big catches down the stretch.

With his wideouts hurting, Phil Simms was looking more and more toward Bavaro, who caught five more passes, high for the day. As the season went on, Mark would become an ultimate weapon for us. Perhaps no other tight end in history has combined the many different aspects of the position in one package. Bavaro can block you off your ass, he can run crisp routes, and he's alert enough to feel things and make adjustments as a play develops. His hands are like flypaper and once he catches the ball, he becomes a bull. As Billy Ard said, defenders bounce off him like rubber bullets. It's not uncommon to see five or six guys trying to drag him down. I love him.

We named him "Rambo" during his rookie camp and the press picked up on it. He doesn't like the nickname but you can see the connection. He's a real jungle fighter on the field, but he's a sincere, good-hearted person off of it. That's why he hates the nickname. Mark had an uncle who fought in Vietnam and he feels that the Rambo image is an exploitation of our veterans.

Right now, all he was exploiting was the Charger defense.

Behind his blocking, we got the running game in gear after Hill's interception stopped a Charger threat at our 31. Joe broke off a 17-yard run, Stacy went over the middle for twelve and Tony Galbreath, our special third-down back, went thirteen yards with a screen pass against their blitz—a great call. Finally, we got a payoff as Phil drilled a 12-yard touchdown pass to Lionel Manuel.

Three plays into the next Charger possession, Kinard got his second interception and with 3:12 left in the game, we turned it into a safe 20–7 lead on a field goal by Joe Cooper.

Now that's a name for the trivia books. By this game, our placekicking saga had reached ridiculous extremes. We'd been going through kickers faster than jocks. Haji-Sheikh. Schubert. Atkinson. Thomas. Even Gary Reasons, our starting inside linebacker. Cooper was our third in three weeks and our fifth in seventeen games.

We opened camp with Ali Haji-Sheikh and Eric Schubert going toe-to-toe, so to speak. The Sheikh, of course, had that great rookie season in 1983 when the rest of the team was horrendous. Since our offense kept sputtering short of the end zone that year, he had opportunities for a bunch of short field goals. But he also seemed to automatically succeed on longer tries, too. The next year, it turned around. Ali battled through a sophomore jinx and in 1985, he missed all but two games because of a hamstring injury. We finished that season with Jess Atkinson and Schubert. When camp started in 1986, Parcells was set to give the shattered Sheikh one more chance to hold the job in training camp.

His competition was Schubert, a pal of mine since training camp the previous year. Eric wasn't like most kickers. He was a real beer-drinking guy with more of a football mentality. Problem was, he went into a tailspin during the '85 playoffs and seemed to be in camp more to keep the Sheikh company.

Both kicked in Atlanta when the pre-season opened. Then

in Milwaukee, the Sheikh hurt himself again. This time it was a pulled groin during pre-game warm-ups. When the team got back to camp, Schubert was the only healthy kicker and he appeared headed for the opening-day start. He was the story of the day as far as the papers were concerned and, for some reason, he said he was happy that Sheikh was injured because it meant he had won the job.

When Parcells read that in the *Post* the next day—he knows what's in all the newspapers even though he says he doesn't read them—he was furious and he called Eric into his office and onto the carpet where he blasted him for several minutes. The next day, Schubie was cut. To be honest, I think it was just coincidence. I've said worse things than that about Parcells and *I'm* still here, so I've got to think that Parcells just wasn't happy with Eric and he wanted to start fresh again.

Fresh was old in this case. In came Bob Thomas, the former Bear and Charger. But Thomas didn't last long. Parcells still wanted to give the Sheikh every opportunity to prove himself healthy, and Thomas was cut once Parcells was satisfied Ali could kick in our final pre-season game. Wrong. The snake would bite again. Ali injured his back by favoring the groin in pre-game warm-ups, and Thomas was our kicker the next week with the Sheikh put down on injured reserve. Thomas kicked well enough against the Cowboys but early in the week, his hamstring unstrung. Parcells, who already had enough on his mind, searched for a possible replacement. Carl Banks asked Bill if he was hiding these guys in airports.

We all thought the next kicker was going to be Raul Allegre. He'd been in for a tryout on Thursday and he was kicking the hell out of the ball. Parcells loved him. It seemed he was cut by the Colts for reasons that had little to do with his ability. Everything seemed great until Raul was called up to the front office to settle his contract. At first, his agent suggested the Giants simply pick up the one he had with the Colts.

Fat chance George Young was going to buy that. When the Giants saw that the Colts' contract called for cash bonuses for each field goal, extra point, and touchback, they wanted no part of it. Raul really didn't expect that they would, but as he got on the phone with his agent, Parcells wanted an answer. Parcells had an afternoon deadline for adding new players, you see, and he was anxious to get this thing settled. He hit the roof when he learned that Raul, innocently enough, was talking to his agent.

"Get him a plane ticket and get me Cooper," Parcells ordered. Adios, Raul, at least for the time being.

For now, Joe Cooper was one of the happy Giants celebrating our first win of the season. Harry Carson, as usual, was celebrating by dousing Bill with the Gatorade bucket.

A lot of people don't realize that I started the tradition. I just didn't want to make it into such a ritual. I wanted to reserve the baths for special wins.

I'll tell you why. Back in 1984, we were hosting the Redskins, the defending NFC champs at the time. We were 4–4 and Parcells felt he had to spark the team somehow. As usual, he got to everybody else through me. Jeff Bostic, their regular center, wasn't going to play and Parcells felt that if I could manhandle his inexperienced replacement, Rick Donnalley, we would shut down John Riggins and their power running game, which at the time was at its peak.

Man, Parcells was on my ass, literally. At practice he was right behind me, screaming. During my usual break when the offensive practice was going on, he had me going one-on-one with some of the rookies. Then, three days before the game on Thursday, he took me back into the weight room and told me to get down in my stance. He handed me a twenty-pound dumbbell for each hand. Every ten seconds, I had to snap up and pound the dumbbells against the wall. Forty-five minutes later, the ordeal ended with my arms on fire.

He said it was to improve my technique. Bullshit. I've been

told my technique is the best on the team. It was his way of pissing me off. But it didn't stop there. The morning of the game I picked up the paper and started reading about my "pivotal" matchup with Donnalley. Parcells was quoted as saying, "We're going to see if Donnalley can play now. He's going against Burt." I threw the paper down, thinking, *This SOB gets on me all week and then he's going to fire up my guy at game time. What the hell is going on?*

I could see the future. I could tell that it wouldn't matter what else happened, that if Riggins got close to a hundred yards it was going to be my fault. It was now a personal challenge; I kept thinking, *I've got to stop him, I've got to stop him.*

When Riggo was held to forty some-odd yards, Parcells felt somewhat responsible. We blew them out—a real landmark win for us—37–13. Near the end of that game, Bill flashed me this funny kind of smile. "I got you ready for the game, didn't I?" he asked. I didn't say anything but I had to get back at him. It was another situation in which I didn't think about the consequences. I just looked for the Gatorade bucket and dumped it over his head. The guys on the sidelines weren't laughing. They couldn't believe what I had just done. The fans went crazy. Bill didn't say anything. He just smiled; he was so happy about the win.

A week after that first bath, Harry said, "C'mon, let's get him again," so we both dumped him. Then I got sick of doing it. Once we started doing it after every win, it wasn't that special. It became a media thing that was expected, not spontaneous, and that wasn't my intention. It didn't mean that much to me anymore. It became Harry's thing.

When I appeared on the Joan Rivers show during Super Bowl week, she asked me about the Gatorade tradition. "It's like when you were in school and always used to pick on the chubby guys," I told her. "That was sort of what we were doing, picking on the chubby guy."

The chubby guy was pretty happy and very wet after we

beat the Chargers. The usual routine is for us to follow him into the big meeting room where he says a few words, then we disperse to our lockers before the press is allowed in. But this time, just before Bill was ready to speak, I told him to wait a minute, that I had something to say. I was so relieved that I didn't want to let the moment go without expressing myself.

"I know all you guys were feeling the same way I was feeling," I said. "We really got ourselves in a hole, and I never want to experience that feeling again. We can't ever take anyone lightly any more. I did, and I promise you I never will again."

It was the first time I ever went in front of a group and blamed myself. It was hard to do but it was the truth and I was relieved after I said it.

Bill's speech was brief after that. "This was Giants football. This is how it should be played. Now that you guys know what you can do, we've got to keep it going."

Then there was Lamar, meanwhile, straining his arms to pat himself on the back: "Boy, that helped us. It really helped us," he chattered. "The guys that had the pride came through."

Thanks, Lamar.

# 7

## LOS ANGELES

## Going Up, Coming Down

**N**ose tackle isn't the sexiest position in football. It's not like quarterback—not that Phil Simms is that sexy. Nose tackle is a little like being a fire hydrant at the Westminster Dog Show. You've got all these pedigrees around you, and all you do is get pissed on. It helps if you've got the attitude of one of Brad Benson's pit bulls.

I was over at Brad's place once when he took out his "pet" pit bull and sicced him on the branch of a tree. The dog hung there for five minutes trying to tear through the branch with his teeth. That's a nose tackle. Tenacious. Vicious. Ugly. And sacrificial.

Tenacious because you can never rest during a play. You're involved with every snap regardless of whether the play is run right at you, on the outside, or whether it's a pass. All the blocking schemes are centered around you. If you're a defensive end on the right side and they run the other way, basically you're out of the play. You hustle a little bit, but you're usually standing on your feet. Nose tackles see a lot of the ground and bounce right up again. And we always have to keep our intensity because with all the bodies flying around, there's a greater chance we'll be injured.

125

Vicious? That's self-explanatory. I've got to do anything I can to beat the guy in front of me. We're not playing patty-cake out there.

Ugly? Have you ever gotten a look at my uniform? Well, there's a good reason why my jersey looks like I just stepped out of a vat of Shrinko. You can never tell me by the scorecard because it's impossible to read my number 64. It all started my rookie year, when in my fourth pre-season game, I went up against the great Steeler center Mike Webster, who had always been one of my idols.

Here I was a green rookie, playing against a guy who had already been to four or five Pro Bowls, and every time I tried to grab him, Webster slid away, leaving me with a handful of grease that he had smeared all around his arms. "Shit, what do you put on your jersey?" I asked him. "Elbow grease," he said. He was also grabbing *me,* clawing me and coming up with fistfuls of my jersey. Whenever I tried to run off to make a play, he'd just yank me back. And did it so that the official was directly in back of me and unable to see well enough to make the call.

Enough of *that.* I wasn't going to give anybody that advantage again, least of all an All Pro like Webster. Ever since, I've had our equipment manager, Eddie Wagner, cut out the side panels of a regular jersey, then sew it back together again. Then I put two-way tape inside the shoulders so that when I pull the jersey over my shoulder pads, it's nice and tight. I've started a lot of teammates using the two-way tape.

As for sacrificial, let me just say that there are nose tackles and then there are nose tackles. In the two-gapping technique the Giants use, the nose tackle has little chance of making a big play. In two-gapping, the defensive linemen are straight up on the men in front of them, responsible for both gaps on either side. I'm right on the center, reading both guards.

All running backs key off the nose. My responsibility is to

stand up the center so I can make the tackle should the back choose either gap. That's harder than it sounds, because a nose tackle is hardly ever blocked one-on-one by the center. I can get double-teamed, split-blocked, or chopped by the guards. I can get blocked down and around. It helps to be a contortionist because a nose tackle's body is going to end up in a lot of unnatural positions. And with so many different blocks to look for, I've got to sit back, read, then react. That's probably the toughest thing to do. It takes a lot of concentration. As soon as the ball is snapped it's instant reaction. You hesitate for a second, the center has you hooked.

At the other end of the nose tackle spectrum is Joe Klecko of the Jets, a great nose in a different system. Joe is able to slant and pick gaps. He doesn't have to read blocks in the Jets' scheme of defense. He just fires out and puts himself in the backfield quickly. It's possible for me to make plays along the line of scrimmage, but hardly ever in the backfield. Sometimes I wish I could play the way Joe does, but I do feel that our defense, when played the right way, is the most sound because it's so very basic. We start in the middle and try to funnel everything out so that our linebackers can make the play. If I can stand up the center and play either gap, we can stop a running game. Two-gapping just can't be played by any team, however. It takes discipline to play it well.

So why do I like playing nose tackle? Probably because I'm crazy and you've got to be crazy to play nose. I also don't know any better. I came to the pros at nose tackle and I just take it as my job. Playing tackle in a four-man line would be easier, but I like the responsibility.

That's why I don't know if I'm that good. I really *don't* know.

I've worked hard and I've got a lot of pride in my job, and I know one thing's for sure. Talent is a lot of bullshit. When you hear somebody ask, "What kind of football player is he?" and the answer is "Well, he has talent," what they're really saying is he isn't worth a crap yet. He'll be good someday . . . maybe.

When they talk about me, talent is never mentioned. I don't have size and I'm not what they call a great athlete. Who knows? If some of the guys who are bigger than I am worked harder than I do, they'd probably be better than I am. But they don't. I'm not going to tell them to stretch two hours a day or to go lift weights. Why should I? If everybody did that I wouldn't be in the league. I really believe that.

Still, I'd like to see someone come in, play our defense, and not have more than five minutes in one game like me. Look at Tony Casillas, the Falcons' top draft pick last year. He was great in college, but in the pros, he found it tough to excel in a read-oriented defense like ours. And still he was slanting one-third of the time. No one else really plays nose like we do.

One of the toughest things I have to do is prepare for a center I've never faced—and that was the case with Don Mosebar of the Raiders, our next opponent after San Diego. Not knowing what to expect, I tend to practice a little harder and concentrate a little more than I usually do. Most of the time I end up playing better because I've worked so hard. Mosebar presented a unique problem because as a converted tackle, he stands six-feet-six. Centers are usually shorter and stockier. Mosebar's good. Once he gets his legs underneath him, he can really drive you. I decided to play more on top of the ball, to take his momentum away.

Meanwhile, the team wanted to keep our own momentum headed in the right direction. Having just won as big a game as possible in the second week of the season, we were able to head into Los Angeles with more confidence. The pressure was off and now we could get back to playing our kind of football. But if we were relieved, the Raiders were desperate. The "Pride and Poise" boys had lost their first two games to Denver and Washington and this was their home opener. They'd be mean. Not many fans or sportswriters thought we could win this one.

What they didn't know was that we carried just as much motivation with us to Los Angeles. It was the first of three West Coast games on our schedule—Seattle and San Francisco were to follow. Football players are so routine-oriented, it's not easy to go three thousand miles and play in another time zone, sometimes in completely different weather than you've trained in. It's a combination of things. A combination of excuses. So it became another barrier for us to crash through this season, one more set of odds we had to beat. Champions win on both coasts.

Champions also don't ride roller coasters. In '85, we could turn on the horses one week and play like horseshit the next. It had become our trademark. After practice on the Wednesday before the Raider game, Bill called the team together on the field. The great teams, Bill emphasized, are the consistent teams. We had to keep going what we started against the Chargers. A loss here would put us in a 1–2 hole and in our division, with the Redskins and Cowboys already 2–0, we couldn't afford to lose ground.

Bill had his own motivation as well. He's always been close to the Raiders' maverick owner, Al Davis. Al helped him with his career a number of times. Now Bill had a chance to be the first Giant coach ever to beat the Raiders and he wanted to show off for one of his mentors. He had already been reading Davis' mind on the Raiders' choice of quarterbacks. They didn't announce until Thursday that Jim Plunkett, the thirty-eight-year-old plowhorse who Coach Tom Flores said had more comebacks in him than Rocky Balboa, would start instead of Marc Wilson, who had supposedly injured his shoulder in Washington the week before.

Who knew if he was really injured? But the move didn't surprise us at all. Bill had been getting us ready for Plunkett all along, figuring that with the Raiders being 0–2, they had to do something. I would rather have seen Wilson, anyway. Plunkett may be old, but he's still cagey. And although everyone says he's slow, he can still move around pretty well and step up in the pocket, always looking for Todd Christensen or Marcus Allen when he gets into trouble.

We worked hard that week, especially on the details. Ex-Raider Kenny Hill even tutored our defensive backs in how to taunt and harass our receivers in practice, so they'd be ready for similar tactics by Lester Hayes and Mike Haynes, the Raiders' not-so-friendly cornerbacks. Meanwhile, our defense concentrated on Allen and Christensen, who up to that point had accounted for sixty-five percent of the Raiders' offensive production. We had special incentive where Allen was concerned. We had a chance to snap his NFL record of eleven straight 100-yard rushing games. Our defense hadn't given up a 100-yard game since Eric Dickerson gained 104 yards in the tenth game of the 1985 season. That still stands.

Something had to give—and it was Allen, who sprained his ankle in the third quarter after gaining only forty yards on fifteen carries. My opinion of Marcus didn't change, however. I thought Allen was awesome coming into the game and I felt he was even better when it was over. He's tremendously quick and what impressed me most of all was his ability as a receiver. He went up for one pass in the back of the end zone and snared it with one hand like the tongue of a frog—an unbelievable catch. Lucky for us, he landed out of bounds. Another time, he took a quick pass and blew by Andy Headen, one of our fastest linebackers, who has 4.5 speed. And they say Allen is slow? He caught that ball and exploded for an extra thirty yards on speed alone.

Obviously, we were up against it, yet we responded with another of those character-building victories that required sixty minutes of sheer effort. This was textbook Giant defense. Go ahead, take the short stuff, but you're not going to be able to drive it in on us. For example, on their first drive, the Raiders used up 7:15 and went seventy-five yards. But after Allen's near-miss in the end zone, they settled for a harmless field goal. Then, later in the quarter, we stopped them for another field goal after an interception in our end. We squelched yet a third opportunity by the Raiders when Headen sacked Plunkett from the blind side and forced a fumble that Leonard recovered at our 32.

At halftime, it was still 6 – 0. The game was being played on terms both of our teams liked. Defense. This was a find-a-way-to-win game. The kind the Raiders throughout history had pulled out. The kind the Giants of 1986 would become famous for: when one part stopped working, another would pick up. And by the end of the season, everyone on the team had made a big contribution in one way or another.

That was especially true of our punter, Sean Landeta, who thought he'd never stop hearing about his whiff in Chicago. People may still never forget that mistake, but in 1986, Landeta proved that he was the best punter in the NFL. He never seemed to make a bad punt, regardless of the circumstances. If we needed Sean to kick us out of a deep hole, he did. If we needed him to stick one close to their goal line, he responded—and that included a few games played in some tough wind.

The weather was perfect in Los Angeles when Landeta changed the flow of the game. In dog fights like those, field position is critical and after we stalled a foot short of a first down at our 40, Landeta got off a 54-yard bomb that set the Raiders back at their 10. Once we stopped the Raiders on three downs, our offense got the ball back at midfield. It took Phil three completions to get us into the end zone for the go-ahead touchdown.

The next series by Los Angeles was probably the turning

point of the game. First, Allen twisted his ankle as the Raiders were moving all the way to our 12. Then, Terry Kinard blind-sided Plunkett on a safety blitz and knocked the ball loose, right in front of me. I dove on it and when none of the black shirts dove on me, I took off, with nothing but eighty yards of Bermuda grass in front of me. I tucked the ball under my shoulder, fullback style, just like at Orchard Park.

*My God, a touchdown,* I thought, if I could make it that far. As I kept running, the distance only seemed longer, as if I had lead in my ass. I started to weave, just in case anyone was close to me. And when I reached the end zone, I put my arms over my head to signal my first NFL touchdown. Except it wasn't. The officials had ruled that while I was on the ground, a Raider's foot was touching me, though I didn't feel it. By the time I walked back to our bench, our offense had already run off a couple of plays. I was tired during the next series because of that run.

Touchdown or not, we went on to win the game. Joe Morris broke off a 53-yard run to set up Lionel Manuel's second touchdown catch of the game and we stopped them twice in the fourth quarter, once at our 16, and then in the final 1:41 of the game against their hurry-up offense. That has to be one of the most tiring parts of the game for a defensive player, because you're making a play, getting up, running downfield and setting up again without a break.

I was on the field the entire series and when the game ended, I was bushed. Bill Parcells, who's usually pretty tight, even after wins, was elated as a little kid on Christmas morning, having just beaten Al Davis. I guess I happened to be the closest man available, because suddenly I felt my helmet being ripped off from behind, nearly breaking my nose. I thought it was Lawrence or some fan and if I hadn't been so dog-tired I might have reacted by taking a swipe. Good thing I didn't, because it was Parcells. He had ambushed me with a flying headlock—in full view of the CBS cameras. I looked at him like *What the f*——? and he backed off, blinking sheepishly at me. He composed himself and waddled off into a locker room that was as filled with excitement as I've ever seen it, even more so than in the playoffs. We were finished with a tough part of our schedule and we were out of the hole we had dug in Dallas. Of course, we still trailed the Redskins by a game—they had just pulled another one out down the road in San Diego—but we were back for good.

The game had been a perfect example of sixty-minute football and was another credit to Johnny Parker, our strength and conditioning coach. Johnny came to the Giants before the 1984 season as the product of a widespread search by Bill to upgrade our weight program. Johnny had worked at the University of Indiana, where another of Bill's cronies, Bobby Knight, recommended him, telling Bill that Johnny wasn't happy until he could get his players shooting jumpers from thirty feet out instead of just twenty.

What clinched it was when Bill talked to Steve Sloan, who'd worked with Johnny at the University of Mississippi, Johnny's home state. Steve told Bill that there was only one thing wrong with Johnny. He was a little weird. All he liked was weights. As far as Bill was concerned, he had his man.

Since then, Johnny—we call him "Hillbilly" since he's from Mississippi—has had a big impact on our team He's turned around the confidence of certain players a hundred and eighty degrees, because he individualizes programs and stays on guys to follow them properly. He can really stay on a guy's ass, but you don't mind it when you can see the results.

Phil Simms was already a hard worker but until Johnny got hold of him, he didn't have much direction in his training. Now Phil's got to be the strongest quarterback in the league and I'm sure the most avid weight lifter among quarterbacks. Karl Nelson, our right tackle, is the biggest man on our team at 6-6, 285, but he lacked strength when he first got here. One year in Johnny's program and he became a starter in 1984.

Leonard's a totally different player now because of him, and Brad has really become a believer. He credits Johnny with saving his career. I'm not talking about a little bit of improvement now. I'm talking about turning guys around.

Johnny had to work a little harder to sell *me* on his methods, mainly because I'm so stubborn. I had my own ways of training that always seemed to work for me. I believed that the harder you worked, the better you got. I'd hit the weight room in the spirit of the Spanish Inquisition, and that would really get under Johnny's skin. He insisted that I was overtraining, because instead of doing four or five sets, I'd do ten or twelve. I was going full tilt all day, burning myself out in racquetball when I wasn't lifting, which I was doing six days a week instead of the four days I work out now.

I didn't want to change but one day I came home and said to Colleen, "I'll do it his way for one month and that's it. I'll give him one month." In reality, I was heading to a local gym after his workouts and doing my own workouts on top of his. Finally, Johnny found out about it. But eventually I came around.

I don't want to give the impression that Johnny's program is a picnic. He devised something special for me we call "comedowns." We do them in the off-season and it draws quite a crowd in the weight room. Everybody wants to see me doing it. Not many guys want to go through it themselves. Only two other players on the team even attempt it. Phil's one of them but he does it at a much lower weight.

Comedowns involve my favorite lift, squats—I've squatted up to about seven hundred pounds—arranged in a test of endurance, desire, and will. Comedowns are the toughest things I've ever attempted in my life.

In squats you take the weight off the bar, and just as the name suggests, you squat with it and stand back up again. The back and thigh muscles are key. In comedowns, we start at one weight, do ten repetitions and "come down" twenty pounds, resting only for the thirty-five seconds it takes to change the weight. We come down four times and do forty reps in all.

It's the thirty-five seconds that kills you. If I had two or three minutes between sets I could probably run off about fifty of them. But the thirty-five seconds work against you. Blood rushes into your thighs and makes it difficult to breathe. In squats, you hold your breath going down and breathe out while going up. In comedowns, my legs are so pumped I can't catch my breath.

When I started doing comedowns last off-season, I began at 215 and built my way up to 425, with successive sets at 405, 385, and 365. The first set was a snap but fatigue starts in quickly and the mind starts fighting. The second set was the toughest because I knew I still had two more to go. The third set was the hump set and the fourth was all blood and guts. My legs shook like rubber. I couldn't breathe. But I had to get through it because I couldn't quit.

When I finished, I just collapsed on the floor and left a wet spot on our Astroturf carpeting. I got sick to my stomach. My legs and ass were burning as if someone doused them with lighter fluid and lit a match. Worst of all, I had the biggest headache. I stayed there for two hours trying to work it off.

That's exactly how comedowns help you in a game. They make you so strong mentally that you can overpower anything in your mind. Whenever I reach a point where I'm not sure I can go on, I continue—regardless of how hot it is or how tired I am in a game, I can never get to that point of exhaustion I reach while fighting through those comedowns. Never, not even one-third of the way. I can get through anything on a football field because I've already been through something that's harder. If you don't push yourself, you're never going to get the most out of yourself.

For me, getting the most of myself means just that. Me, on my own. Without anabolic steroids.

First off, let me say that there is a difference between the use of steroids to enhance performance or to gain strength and the use of steroids strictly for medical reasons, which was why they were developed in the first place.

Under a doctor's supervision, for a limited time, steroids can be helpful in cutting down rehab time following an injury. For a professional athlete, the difference between a season-long rehab and eight weeks could mean a career. Under those strictly controlled circumstances, steroids shouldn't be condemned. However, those are the only conditions where steroids should have a place in football.

I realize the steroid decision is something even high school players are faced with these days. I confronted the issue sometime in college. I chose no and that's my advice to anyone. I believe that a player can get strong enough on his own without exposing himself to the side effects and unknown dangers that steroids pose. All it takes is dedication. I think that as a team, we've proven that out.

# 8

## EAST RUTHERFORD

## Pre-Game Tension

We're supposed to be in the locker room at Giants Stadium ninety minutes before kickoff. That's 11:30 for one o'clock starts. If I'm lucky, I get there at 11:45. It's just for one reason. Brad Benson.

I used to get to the locker room very early to relax, go over my playbook, and watch some last-minute films. But Brad was driving me crazy. He was always there by 8:30 and by 9:15, he was in full uniform, meditating on his stool with a chaw of tobacco imbedded deep in his cheek and a paper cup nearby for spitting. Always in the same place.

Brad is one of the nicest guys you could ever want to meet. I love him, I really do. But he's an absolute head-case when it comes to routine and superstition. Before a game, Brad is a bundle of nerves. And I'm the lucky guy who has occupied the locker next to his for the last six years.

If anyone passes by, Brad starts asking stupid questions. Say it's Billy Ard. He'll say, "Billy, what do we do on Flow 36?" He already knows by heart what he does on Flow 36, but he's got to ask these stupid questions just the same.

When he's not bothering people, Brad stares at the floor, looking for the loose pieces of adhesive tape that are fixtures on locker room carpets. If he sees any, he picks it up and throws it in the trash bin. Sometimes the tape gets stuck to the bottoms of players' shoes or socks. For some reason, that bothers Brad. Brad wants everybody to look their best.

"Hey, you got tape on your shoe. Hey, there's tape on your sock," he says. The same thing. Every week. No wonder he gets there so early. His wife probably kicks him out of the house because he wants to vacuum all morning.

Then there's the blue tape Brad wraps around his socks to keep them in place. He won't touch the roll until I get there. Then he says, "Here Jim," and hands the thing to me. One time I told him to toss it to me. "No, no," he said. He walked over and placed it in my hand. And I don't even use the tape anymore since my knee protectors hold up my socks.

You can imagine. I'm jumpy enough before a game and this SOB is making me even more nervous. Finally, during the last pre-season, I said, "I can't take this anymore," and I moved my locker clear across to the other side of the room. Now Parcells, Mr. Superstition himself, yelled at me: "You've been there for five years. You can't move!"

I stayed there anyway. Brad was pathetic. He'd come over and start begging, "I can't take this anymore. You've got to come back." He badgered me every day. On the Tuesday after our first pre-season home game, he practically got on his knees: "You gotta come back, you just gotta." This was worse than putting up with Brad the other way. Finally, I told Eddie Wagner to move my gear back, that I couldn't take it.

But at least I didn't have to put up with it for three hours before games.

My new routine begins with breakfast at least four hours before a game. For a normal one o'clock start, Colleen fixes me a big bowl of spaghetti—Ronzoni, the breakfast of champions—at 8:30 and I'll wash that down with a quart of orange juice and some fruit.

I don't talk at all before games. It's the only time I won't even deal with Jimmy. When he was younger I would tell him, "I can't talk to you because if I do, it'll take my concentration off the game and Daddy will get hurt." This past season, he got so good at the routine, he was protecting me. He just took control of the house. He'd tell Colleen, "Mom, don't bother Dad" and he made sure the door was shut for me once I went down to the rec room to study tapes. We'd get a bunch of friends gathered at my place for the game, and he'd tell them to be quiet so Daddy could rest for the game. I could hear him scoot down the stairs when someone came to the front door. "No one's allowed in the room," he'd inform them. "Daddy's studying film."

I usually watch just a few tapes—inside running, outside running and passing—before I start to get wired. I'll go up to the bedroom and just lay there and imagine myself making tackles. I'll get up about 11:15, fifteen minutes from when I'm supposed to be at the stadium, a normal half-hour's drive away, forty minutes with game-day traffic. Which means I'm late.

That's great because by now I'm fired up. I'll walk down the stairs with my game face on, which means a grungy beard, and I won't say anything to the people downstairs. Or if I'm in a good mood, I might give out a few high-fives.

Then it's into the car, where I turn the radio on full blast. If it's the fall, I'll roll down the window. With the regulars outside my house watching, I slam the car into reverse and peel out into the street, screeching to a halt. Then I throw it in first, burning rubber and spinning my wheels. When I get to the end of the block, I peek in the rearview mirror to see if they're looking and I just skid into my left-hand turn.

Once I get on Route 17, a two- to three-lane highway lined with shopping malls and pockmarked with construction work, I'm rolling. I'm in and out of traffic and probably on the shoulder half the time. In the twenty minutes it takes me to get to Giants Stadium, I've got myself wired to the hilt.

I enter through the Giants offices, not the players' entrance, because I don't want to talk to anybody and I don't want to disappoint any kids who might ask for autographs. I'm usually downstairs by 11:45 and we've got to be out on the field in twenty minutes. Excellent. No time for Brad to get me nervous. I take his damn tape and he helps me on with my jersey but mostly I don't notice because I'm in a rush.

When I'm done, there's still time to talk to Brad for a minute or two. We tell each other how nervous we are, then, without fail, he says to me, "I don't know how many more of these we've got to go through. Boy, I tell you, this is killing me."

And I say, consoling him, "Yeah, me too, Brad. It gets to me too."

On this particular afternoon of Brad's impending death, we were hosting the New Orleans Saints, the beginning of what people were calling a three-game "soft spot" on our schedule. Compared to our first three games, I guess it was. Neither the Saints, the Cardinals (in St. Louis), nor the Eagles (back home) were thought of as contenders. Still, the old Giants inevitably lost a game or two to underdog teams like those, especially after big wins such as the one we had in Los Angeles. The saying that you can never take anyone lightly has always been true in our case.

Three weeks later, however, we found ourselves with three more wins and five straight on the season. We took it as a sign of maturity. Our team grew in many ways those three weeks, and those wins were part of the bonding process that would turn us into Super Bowl champs. More and more of our team character began to emerge and we found that when pushed back against a wall, we fought our way out.

We became a bottom-line team for the time being, but all that counted was that we were winning. When you win games when only half your cylinders are functioning, then you know you've got something great in the works. We won a lot of games when we didn't have all our components together, yet one phase picked up the other. We were scratching and crawling and starting to roll.

The New Orleans game was a perfect example of our new-found tenacity. We battled back against illness, injury, a pair of bum calls by the officiating crew, two cheap shots from the Saints, and a 17–0 deficit on the scoreboard early in the second quarter. Everything short of storm and pestilence.

First, we played without Joe Morris. Earlier in the week, he was hospitalized because of a bad reaction to a combination of two separate medications he was taking. Throughout the week, we weren't sure whether he would play, and as it turned out, he missed the game as a precautionary step.

But that was only the beginning. The game was just six minutes old when Mark Bavaro, fighting off a host of tacklers, caught a forearm underneath his face mask, cracking his jaw. But Mark, who doesn't have much use for his jaw anyway, wasn't about to be stopped. Spitting blood and in obvious pain, he missed only a quarter's worth of playing time and returned to be a major factor in our win, including a touchdown catch with the Saints' Antonio Gibson clinging to his jersey. Mark's toughness was inspirational and there were other things that fired us up too. Nothing enrages us more than cheap shots and that day, the Saints hit us with two beauts.

Midway through the second quarter, our No. 1 receiver, Lionel Manuel, was lowbridged at the knees in what we all felt was a blatant cheap shot from Gibson. Lionel was two feet in the air at the back of the end zone, defenseless as he reached for a pass that was well overthrown. While that might be a receiver's occupational hazard, there was no excuse for Gibson, who threw himself at Lionel's knees well after the ball sailed out of the end zone, leaving Lionel on the ground with a badly strained left knee.

As it turned out, Lionel didn't return until the playoffs. Gibson, who should have been suspended, didn't even draw a penalty. Later, he maintained that he was unsure whether Lionel could make the catch or not. But in my opinion, going for the knees is inexcusable. It's one thing to cut a guy legally, when you're in front of him, and it's quite another to cut someone from the side, where he can't see you.

Violence is a natural part of the game, but there's a not-so-fine line that exists between hitting hard and hitting to hurt. The way I see it, there are no excuses for late hits unless you happen to be pushed into someone. There's a point where you go over the edge and if you've been playing football long enough, you can tell in your mind when it's time to pull up. You can feel it, even when you're overexcited.

That's why the second cheap shot by New Orleans had us ticked off like never before. Our rookie cornerback Mark Collins was returning a punt when his helmet rode up on his head. In attempting to pull it back down, he knocked it off. The danger should have passed once Mark was stood up by three or four players, stopping his momentum. Players from both teams were trying to shield and protect him when a certain Saint came in late and actually rammed Mark's head with his helmet, a deadly weapon in that situation.

Mark crumpled to the turf immediately. We got him to the sidelines where he passed out and had to be taken away by an ambulance. We played the rest of that game not knowing his condition, which fortunately amounted to just a minor concussion. We played, quite naturally, with a vengeance.

Usually, we have our own answer to those situations. Kenny Hill, our strong safety, has a Raider mentality to go along with the two Super Bowl rings he won there. I feel the Giants have a good reputation as one of the cleanest teams in the league, but Kenny is our enforcer, as unlikely as that might seem if you just met him on the street. We call him "Psycho" in the locker room and he really is. Kenny is super-intelligent, a Yale graduate who majored in molecular biophysics. He uses words in everyday speech some of us have never heard of before, and he's got a soft voice that makes him sound like Clark Kent.

Once he hits the field, however, Kenny is transformed into a maniac. He is a hitter—Bill demands that of all his defensive backs—and he's the first guy to come to the aid of a team-mate.

If someone cheap-shots one of us, Kenny will retaliate in the flick of a 15-yard penalty flag. I'm not saying I *want* him to do it, but at least you know he'll be there if you're backed into a corner. If Kenny retaliated this time, the officials didn't call it.

In my opinion, they had called plenty already. In my opinion, the officials, not the Saints, scored the second touchdown of the game. It came following an interception, thanks to two bullshit calls, both on third down to keep the drive alive. On the first one, our free safety, Terry Kinard, was called for interference. I had a good look at the play because once the ball is thrown, it's my responsibility to do a one-eighty and run downfield. From my angle, the pass was five yards over the receiver's head and clearly uncatchable. Interference should have been waved off in that case. Instead, they were given a first down at our 11.

Three plays later, on third and goal from the two, their quarterback Dave Wilson took off on a rollout to his left. He was already out of the pocket and running. Harry Carson, meanwhile, was within five yards of the line of scrimmage, where chucking is permitted. Yet when Harry tossed aside his blocker to take off after Wilson, he was called for holding. It was totally ridiculous, especially since the guy who made the call was clear on the other side of the field. And instead of fourth down and a field goal, the Saints had first down at the one and soon after, a touchdown.

To tell the truth, those are the times I start thinking, *Something's up here*. Of course, there's nothing much you can do at the time except try to set up the next call, like basketball coaches do. I've been held many times when the official has missed and I've told officials, "You want this to be a fair game. This guy is holding me. You can call it if you want to." I don't want to make a scene. I just want to get their attention.

Sometimes they can key on one spot and not see the overall picture. Like the time when I was actually tackled and nothing was called. "Hell, didn't you just see him tackle me?" I called out to the ref. Then on the next play the guy held me, and I just screamed out like I was being murdered. That got the ref's attention and when he saw me on the ground, that's when he called it. I don't ask them to make any calls they don't see. I just want them to be aware.

Of course, in spite of the officials, we rallied to beat the Saints. Would we have lost this game in 1983? We wouldn't only have lost it, we'd have lost it big. In 1984? We might have made it close, then lost. But 1986? I wasn't worried when we fell behind like that, and sure enough, we rallied, hung on, and won it, 20–17. Our defense held New Orleans to one first down and thirteen yards of total offense in the second half and even though Phil was intercepted three times in the game, he hit Zeke Mowatt with the game-winning touchdown pass in the fourth quarter. And sandwiched around Phil's first touchdown throw to Bavaro were a pair of field goals by . . .

Raul Allegre. That's right. Raul was back. He had sent a letter to Bill explaining his side of the mixed-up contract story; being no fool, Bill signed him and cut Joe Cooper. That was the final touch of irony, because when Bill waived Ali Haji-Sheikh and Bob Thomas off the injured reserve list the previous week, he said it was to let Cooper know that the job was his. We were lucky that Raul was still available. The Redskins had given him a close look, too.

Kickers, of course, aren't really football players per se. They're always a little different. On our team, they seem to disappear for the longest times during practice. Who knows what they do? Maybe they listen to music or something, then it seems that they're back just before the end of practice still fresh and clean while the rest of us are sweating like pigs.

But I like kickers. Especially ours. Raul is a funny guy, especially since Landeta got hold of him. And Landeta keeps us loose in the locker room with the stories of his conquests. I've never seen anyone like Sean. He's kind of on the pudgy side but he's always walking around the locker room bare-assed. The first thing he does is take off his pants. Then he'll walk around. Usually, he keeps his shirt and shoes on. But his ass is always bare. All day. It's the weirdest thing.

With Sean, it's always can you top this? Two things are important to Sean: women and money.

Just before our playoff game two years ago, Sean was charged by the Division of Consumer Affairs with scalping tickets in the parking lot. The next day, we built a miniature ticket booth around his locker.

As for the women part, all that needs to be said is that he dates the runner-up *Penthouse* Pet of the Year. Sean's no Joe Namath when it comes to nightlife. He doesn't drink, not at all, but boy is he an operator. The guy has balls. He uses the direct approach. He just goes for it and most of the time he gets it.

He's no bullshitter, either. His stories are all true. I know because I've seen him in action. I once went into the city with him on a speaking engagement and before long, he was with four women in the corner of the room. Last training camp, he came up to me on the field and said he had just gotten a little action. I looked at him like "C'mon, Sean," but he insisted, "Yeah, just ten seconds ago." I won't tell you how he proved it to me but he did. The girl was still in her car in the parking lot—in broad daylight. I just wish I'd have known while it was going on. I would've sneaked up on them and done something to distract them.

Sean does one other thing extremely well. He can punt the hell out of the football. In our next game in St. Louis, he had as much to do with the win as anybody. The game, a defensive struggle that neither side seemed willing to take control of, was another example of us doing whatever we needed to do in order to win. And it marked the return of a player who exemplifies that attitude. We had cut wide receiver Phil McConkey at the end of training camp so that we could keep two rookie draft picks, Solomon Miller and Vince Warren. But with Lionel gone and Bobby Johnson hobbling on a sore ankle, Bill needed an experienced receiver. Mark Collins was woozy, so he needed a punt returner. Phil fit both descriptions, plus he knew the system. So, after spending four weeks of exile in Green Bay, where he hardly played a down, Phil was a Giant again and just about the happiest guy in the world. I was thrilled to see him back. I've always liked him because he's a tough little guy and a real competitor. Besides, Phil's from Buffalo.

Phil celebrated in St. Louis by returning seven punts for eighty-two yards, more yards than the return team had produced in the first four games. With Landeta out-punting Evan Araposthatis by an average of nine yards a kick, we controlled field position, which was of the utmost importance in that game. Our offense was listless and accounted for just 144 net yards. As our receivers coach Pat Hodgson said afterwards, "We were just standing around, waiting for somebody to make a play."

Perhaps the Cardinals could say the same thing about their offense, which only two seasons earlier had been making big plays as a matter of routine. In the pre-season of 1985, they were being touted as a Super Bowl contender. Now they were a classic example of a franchise gone to seed. In fact, we were using their decline as a reminder of what can happen when you're picked—like we were—to win the Super Bowl back in training camp.

What exactly happened to the Cardinals? There have been

all sorts of rumors, some drug-related, but I've got my own theory. I think a lot had to do with their losing to the Redskins in the final game of the 1984 season. They certainly had the talent that year. Lomax was hot, Roy Green was healthy and burning DBs deep, and Pat Tilley was just about the best possession receiver in the league. Ottis Anderson, Stump Mitchell and Earl Ferrell gave them a triple threat in the backfield and their entire offensive line was outstanding. To me, they were the best offense in the league.

We went into St. Louis that year in the next-to-last week of the season knowing that if we won our last two games, we would win the division. But the Cardinals had turned things around on us. They beat us with a late rally that put them in command of the situation. Now, while we watched the game on TV, the Cardinals played the Redskins, needing a win to give them the division title and eliminate us from playoff contention. As we held our breath, Neil O'Donoghue missed a do-or-die field goal in the closing seconds. We were in. The Cardinals were down and out, never quite the same team again.

Had they won that game, who knows what they would have done in the playoffs. Had they gotten over that hump, they might have started playing over their heads and by doing that, they could have lifted their potential even higher. I really think that one game, that one kick, killed them.

Certainly in 1986 their offense wasn't what it used to be. Our defense was dominant in that game in St. Louis as we chased Lomax around, sacked him five times, and held their running game to under three yards a carry.

Still, football can sometimes be unfair. As it turned out, one play could have turned our great defensive effort into an afterthought. With just over 2:00 remaining in the game, time stood still on us. Leading 13–6, we were holding off a final Cardinal rally when Collins tipped a ball into the hands of their receiver, J.T. Smith, who bobbled it near the back corner of the end zone. We knew he was out of bounds. The official ruled him out of bounds. But 1986 was the year of the instant replay, and the eye in the sky took a second look . . . and a third . . . and a fourth. We stood around on the field sure it would go our way but as time went on, we began to think that we might be getting screwed. Finally, about five nervous minutes later, the replay official upheld the field crew. Incomplete.

That one incident told me exactly what's wrong with instant replay. I agree it should be given a chance, because certain mistakes are so obvious that they should be corrected. But it has to be revised so that the process takes no longer than the length of an average time-out. If it lasts five or six minutes, it breaks up the continuity of the game. If that kind of thing keeps happening, I'd rather see them just get rid of instant replay entirely.

After the ruling, the Cardinal drive fizzled with a dropped pass, a penalty, and a Carl Banks sack. We won another close one. As I walked off the field I saw O.J. Anderson, my teammate for two years at Miami, where he was just incredible. I still remember watching him return two kickoffs more than a hundred yards each for touchdowns against Tulane. After our win, he looked dejected. It was the then-winless Cardinals' fifth straight loss and his relationship with their new coach, Gene Stallings, wasn't the best. I'm sure I shocked O.J. when I told him, "Don't worry. I think you might be coming to the Giants."

I'd already been questioned by Bill as to what kind of person O.J. was, and I knew we were interested in a running back as insurance for Joe. By this time, also, the team was almost certain that George Adams would not be returning before the end of the season. A few days after I spoke with O.J., he was a Giant, in exchange for two 1987 draft picks. O.J. joined us just in time for the Eagles. Although he didn't see much action—in fact, he aggravated a hamstring injury—O.J. must have appreciated the feeling of winning again. The game ended in a 35–3 rout, our first blowout.

We didn't expect it to be that easy. The Eagles, it seemed, were going up against an undefeated team every week but they were playing them tough. We also didn't know what to expect with Buddy Ryan running the show. Buddy, who predicted before the season started that his Eagles would win the division, said that he was coming after us. "I don't know what we're going to do, but we're going to play some physical football," he said.

It didn't work out that way, although the Eagles played hard. We sacked Ron Jaworski and Randall Cunningham three times each and turned a 13–3 game at halftime into a rout. We even added a little razzle-dazzle with a fake field goal, Jeff Rutledge passing to Harry for a touchdown. Rutledge laid it up for Harry like a loaf of bread. Harry, with those brick-oven hands of his, almost dropped it. In fact, he'd been dropping it all week long in practice.

As for the Eagles, they're going to improve under Ryan, I'm sure of that. I like his philosophy. He talks up his team until he's got them believing him. It was the same thing he did in Chicago, getting the Bears thinking that no one could beat them. I see he's already planting that seed in Philly. He's got some players too. Reggie White is awesome, and just may be the best defensive lineman in the league. And I think Cunningham is going to be a great quarterback, just as soon as he can discipline himself a little more; know when to scramble and when not to. These days, with the pressure that defenses put on, a quarterback has to be mobile. Cunningham can run as well as any quarterback and he's got an arm like a cannon. When he gets a better offensive line in front of him, watch out.

But not last year. Not the way our defense was playing. Needless to say, Lawrence was a big part of it and in those three games, it was obvious. The Saints tried to run away from him to the right side but he chased them down. He added two sacks and a forced fumble against the Cardinals, and he picked up four more sacks against the Eagles. A new Lawrence? Not on game days. But during the week, yes.

He was more involved in both the locker room and the meeting room. In '85, Lawrence would roll in at the last minute and actually fall asleep in team meetings. But in 1986, I think Lawrence realized that giving one hundred percent only on game day wouldn't do any more. He badly needed the support of his teammates—and he got it. With that, he became the team player he had been in previous years.

Naturally, Lawrence's dominating play was drawing all sorts of attention from the press. After his four-sack game against the Eagles, I thought I would add a little more drama to the story. You know, spice it up.

The first reporter at my locker was Judson Hand, who works for the *Asbury Park Press*. Judson got there quickly so that he could get my reaction to Lawrence's big day.

"Judson," I said without blinking an eye, "I tell you what. That's a hell of a job for a guy that was hurt."

Old Judson was intrigued. He thought he had a story. I knew I had him.

I acted as though I was leaving him out on a limb and started walking away toward our shower room. "Hey, c'mon," he said, running after me. I stopped and turned around, just before I headed into the shower.

"Didn't you know the guy was injured?"

"No," he said, swallowing the bait.

"He's got bad, bad hemorrhoids," I said.

"You're kidding."

"I'm telling you. His hemorrhoids are bothering him so much, they're bleeding. He could hardly move all week."

Judson wrote it all down. When I took off, he ran into Johnny Parker.

"Johnny, has L.T. been doing much lifting?" he asked, looking for evidence. Of course, Lawrence *never* does much lifting.

"Why no," answered Johnny. "He hasn't been doing much lifting at all."

Said Judson, "What about the hemorrhoid problem he's got?"

Johnny couldn't believe it. "Who told you that? Burt?"

Too bad I hadn't gotten to Johnny first. The next day's paper could have had the exclusive on L.T.'s hemorrhoids, according to a source close to Taylor. Real close to Taylor.

# 9

---

## SEATTLE


## Pass the Cotton

I've been around Bill Parcells long enough to know to expect almost anything. He's an absolute psycho. He'll do anything to get us ready for a game and when combined with some of his superstitions, things can get pretty bizarre. For instance, we no longer practice at the site of a road game the day before the game, because the two times we did it last year, we lost. When Super Bowl week came, Bill wanted to hire the same pilot and crew that had flown out a couple of previous Super Bowl winners. The pilot, Augie from the Bronx, had taken us to San Francisco and was a big Giants fan, so Bill made sure that he would fly us to Pasadena. The only problem was that the team had chartered a DC-10; Augie only flew DC-8's. Bill had the club rent a different plane.

Bill also has this thing about elephant trunks and pennies lying tails-up. He doesn't dare pick them up. Ten of them still remain on the coaching room floor. He's also napped on some locker room floors while on the road, because he did it once and we won. Sometimes we can make Bill's superstitions work to our benefit. For instance, if there's something new on the practice schedule that we don't like, we just tell Bill that we didn't do it the week before when we won, and he'll take it off immediately. At the Super Bowl, do you think we didn't want to practice at the Rose Bowl that Saturday because we were frightened of some silly hex? Hell no, we just didn't want to take the long bus ride out there.

Then there are times when we become the victims of Bill's idiosyncrasies. Nothing surprises me with Bill but when we walked outside Giants Stadium to our grass practice field the Thursday before our game with Seattle, even I did a double take.

Our closed-in little field looked more suitable for a Bruce Springsteen concert than it did for football. Bill "The Genius" had set up four huge sound speakers in each corner and they were blaring the most horrendous noise known to eardrums. McConkey said it took him back to the flight deck of the aircraft carriers he served on in the Navy. Phil replied that the only difference was that if you made a mistake on the field, it might mean a five-yard penalty. If you made it on the flight line, it might mean decapitation by a helicopter rotor.

Here, all I knew was that it was loud. *What the hell is he doing now?* I thought. Bill, of course, was trying to prepare us for the infamous crowd noise that we'd face that Sunday in the Kingdome, allegedly the loudest and toughest stadium for an opponent to play in. Bill had been planning this for a while but never let on to the players. Our film coordinator, Tony Ceglio, rented sound equipment and arranged for the shipment of a special tape put together by the Broncos, who play in Seattle annually. The crowd was taped at Mile High Stadium and the volume was being turned to the max by Eddie Wagner.

"That sounds almost as bad as that soul music they play in the locker room," I yelled within earshot of Parcells. Then I turned and teased him. "Way to be a genius," I said.

"Pretty good, huh?" he said, all proud and patting himself on the back.

I asked the trainers for some cotton and shoved it into my ears. I tried whenever possible to stand behind the speakers, and since the noise was more for the benefit of the offense, I was able to catch several breaks that way. Harry even sneaked over behind a speaker and pulled its plug. I also couldn't help but wonder what Wellington Mara was thinking about the racket. Wellington uses our practice time to get in his exercise, walking laps around the field as he watches us. I knew it was screwing up his walk. And I was hoping Seattle's fans wouldn't get wind of this because if they did, they'd only get louder.

The trip to Seattle was like every other road trip. They can blend into each other and get pretty tedious. We're on a regular, strict routine, with a 9 P.M. film meeting and a curfew to follow. Film sessions, with the exception of the one before the Charger game, can last a long time, mainly because of me. I'm always asking Bill to run back certain plays, even if the other guys gripe about it. Then, once everyone else leaves, I stay longer to watch film on my own.

I know this is going to surprise some people but the most important thing to me on the road is sleep. My roommate, Billy Ard, and I have a code. We don't disturb the other's sack time. If one guy wants to sleep, the other has to agree to it, or get out of the room. We've got all sorts of little rules like that. We're great for each other that way. There have been only a couple of times when the code's been broken. But the problem with Ard as a roommate is that he likes it cold. I mean air-conditioning, full blast. It got to a point where he was sleeping like a baby—without a shirt, with just the sheet pulled over him—while I was shivering, wearing my sweats to bed with the hood pulled over my head.

On one trip in the dead of winter, Billy even sneaked a few windows open on me after I went to sleep. Other than that, he's a great roommate. He may be one of the all-time instigators of mischief but he helps supply me with some of my ammunition, especially with Brad. He's only one of my spies in the offensive line meeting room.

One thing about road trips, though. You get to know your teammates and coaches pretty well. As Lamar would say, like a family.

And one thing about *this* family. They're some of the tightest people on Earth. Those people who keep insisting the Giants are cheap must be talking about the players and coaches. Eric Dorsey for instance. As the first-round draft choice, he became instantly rich with a $500,000 signing bonus. Know what he does? He lifts six-packs of soda out of the refrigerator in the locker room and takes them home.

Then there's our tradition that the top draft pick has to buy doughnuts for Saturday practices. George Adams did a great job with that in 1985 but the first time Dorsey bought, he went to the day-old thrift store. And all he got was two dozen. Landeta alone eats that many. He's another one. Always looking to make a buck, that's Sean. And he knows every salary on the team right down to the fine print.

Karl Nelson's another penny-pincher. Every time you go to a restaurant on the road with Karl, he has to check every item on the bill to the penny, to make sure he's not being overcharged.

But the two cheapest guys on the Giants are Lamar and Johnny Parker. Neither of them eats out on the road because they'd rather save the $22 meal money we get each trip. Monday night games are really tough on them because the last meal they have is on the plane, then they've got to wait all that time until the pre-game meal. And it really hurt them when the Giants discontinued the 5:30 Club on Saturday evenings on the road. The team used to put out a big spread each week and invite the press, coaches, and friends of the team. George Young stopped it because the team was making too many friends and it started costing something astronomical.

Lamar and Johnny suffered the most from that austerity cut. But do you think they got hungry enough to eat out? No way. They starved instead. At the end of the year, Johnny told me that with all the meal money he had put aside, he was able to buy half a fur coat for his wife.

"Johnny," I said, "that's twenty dollars a week for ten weeks. That must have been a hell of a fur coat." A full-length skin-flint, I bet.

At least Johnny doesn't go around stealing stuff, like Lamar does. I remember in my rookie year, Bill Neill and I were coming out of our hotel room when we saw this figure at the other end of the hallway, jamming all sorts of soaps and shampoo into his bag from the maid's cart. "Lamar!" we yelled, startling him.

"Y'all got me, baby, y'all got me," Lamar said, strutting away.

Well, we thought we'd really get him. So we told all the players to bring all the soaps and shampoos they could find to the meeting that night. Just before Bill started his talk, we bombarded Lamar with the stuff. You know what he did? He picked it all up and put it into his bag. I swear, Lamar's house looks like a *museum* of our hotels on the road. Towels, plates, spoons, soap—you name it. He takes it. Even hangers. He gets those from our locker room. One day when Dave Jennings was still on the team, he saw Lamar sneaking around in a suspicious-looking way, with a big bulge under his jacket.

"Lamar, what do you got?" Dave asked him. Lamar opened up his coat and he had about fifty metal hangers inside. He'd gone around clearing everyone's locker of their hangers. Amazing.

Once, about two years ago, we got Lamar good. He kept sneaking into Brad's locker for snuff, so we doctored a can by mixing in a little horse manure. Sure enough, Lamar grabbed the bait. When he stuck that little pinch between his cheek and gum, what he tasted wasn't the pleasant Happy Days flavor that Walt Garrison raves about in his commercials. It tasted more like Garrison's horse. "This stuff tastes like shit," Lamar cried. He didn't know how right he was.

Then there was the time last year when Lamar and Johnny roomed together during our four days in Atlanta. A couple of Lamar's good-ol'-boy friends dropped by and when Lamar left them with Johnny for a few minutes, they got the itch to go through his drawers for a few souvenirs.

"You won't find anything in there that'll fit you," Johnny told Lamar's pals.

"Wait a minute," said one. "Here's a T-shirt that's just fine."

But when Johnny took a closer look, he saw the initials J.P. on the shirt. Lamar had stolen it from him!

I don't what mementos Lamar brought back from the Great Northwest. But none of them brought back a win.

When we got to the Kingdome, it was loud, though not as loud as those damn speakers. I actually found it fun to play there, outside of the fact that we lost. The fans are close to you and that creates an exciting atmosphere. As far as I'm concerned, they can yell all they want. That wasn't why we lost the game.

In fact, when the game was over, I couldn't believe we had lost. We had played well again on defense and held another great back, Curt Warner, to under a hundred yards (fifty-six on nineteen carries). We controlled the yardage (307 to 218, which was 130 yards below Seattle's average) and the clock, by over ten minutes. But it was a game of what-ifs, a game in limbo the whole time. They just made more of their "ifs" happen.

We didn't take control. They didn't take control. We left it hanging there for them and they didn't take it. Then *we* didn't take it. Then, *boom*, they took it and that was it. That's what left us scratching our heads, our five-game winning streak snapped, 17–12.

It was another game with our offense at less than one hundred percent. Stacy Robinson had joined Lionel Manuel on injured reserve after our win over the Eagles, and Mark Bavaro hardly played at all because of a bruised foot suffered in Philadelphia. Because of the crippled state of our receiving corps, our offense looked more and more to Joe Morris to carry the load, which he did twenty-four times for 116 yards. At the same time, Phil was finding it difficult to establish any kind of rhythm. By his own admission, the Seattle game was the worst of his season. He threw four interceptions and was sacked six times, partly because he refused to get rid of the ball quickly enough. He later told reporters, "I sucked." He was caught in a trap of being too tentative, and it would take three weeks before he realized it and snapped out of it.

Actually, most of the offensive problems came once we got inside the 20, what we call the red zone. On five penetrations inside Seattle's 22-yard line, we came up empty three times and settled for field goals the other two. We truly had the opportunities to win the game. We just didn't capitalize.

Seattle scored first after an interception. A Dave-Krieg-to-Gordon-Hudson TD pass was the first touchdown we had allowed in eleven straight quarters. But we came back when rookie Solomon Miller made a nice tiptoe move up the sidelines to complete a 32-yard touchdown pass. We took a 9–7 halftime lead on Raul's 23-yard field goal.

Norm Johnson retaliated for Seattle with a 25-yard field goal to regain the lead in the third quarter. And that's when things really started to work against us. On our next drive, we moved as far as Seattle's 15, where Phil took a sack. A third-down handoff to Tony Galbreath lost four yards and Raul came on to miss a 42-yard field goal that would show up big when we needed a touchdown on our last drive of the game. Had we been three points closer, we would have needed only to kick another field goal to win.

The big mistake of the game occurred on our next offensive possession, when Phil's pass deflected off Maurice Carthon's hands for an interception at our 19-yard line. Those are the ones that really kill you. Those are the ones championship teams don't allow to happen, late in the game, deep in your own territory. Instead, you have to force a team to drive on you to beat you. But Maurice had broken his thumb earlier in the game, yet another bruise in our offensive armor, and he couldn't hang on.

Now it was up to us, the defense. But we didn't do our jobs either. We made a critical mistake as well. On a third and eight play from the 17-yard line, we flushed Krieg out of the pocket. George Martin had contain responsibility on that side, which means he couldn't allow Krieg to get too far outside, where he could turn the corner or make a play. George, however, was forced inside instead and that allowed Krieg the room and time to find Warner underneath our linebackers. Curt made a slick move on Andy Headen and got all the way to the five. Two plays later, he went in.

Warner, by the way, is an amazing runner, who fought his way back from knee surgery. It's remarkable how he is still able to make such sharp, crisp cuts after he sees a hole. Sometimes he'll be running a sweep off left tackle and he'll cut it back to the other tackle's side. If there's a weak link in a defense, if for instance a guy on the defensive line is getting hooked, Warner not only recognizes it but is able to change direction and get there. The only other guy I remember making cuts as well as Warner was Billy Sims of the Lions. Warner is probably second to Sims, although Billy never did make it back after major surgery on his knee.

We, however, would never make it back after the Warner touchdown that made it 17–9, even though our offense had two more opportunities deep in Seattle territory. Yet another sack by Jacob Green forced us to settle for a field goal after we reached their seven. We were down by five at the time, needing a touchdown on our final possession. Phil, the competitor that he is, drove us from our 34 to the Seattle 22 after hooking up with McConkey for a 31-yard gain. On first down, he sent Solomon Miller on a little in cut and threw the ball well enough to lead the receiver into the end zone. But the rookie made a rookie mistake and allowed the ball to ricochet off his chest. A sack, an incompletion and an interception later, we experienced our second, and as it turned out, last loss of the season.

Who knew at that time what kind of team we would become? That those same opportunities we squandered in Seattle, we would use as our tickets to the Super Bowl? We knew for sure that the Washington Redskins, with whom we had been running neck and neck all year, were next on a Monday night at our place. Our loss in Seattle dropped us one game behind the Skins but we also had two games remaining with them.

We'd have to take it home ourselves.

# 10

## EAST RUTHERFORD

## Big G, Little Joe

I'm often asked what made the Giants tick in 1986, as if the answer's a deep, dark mystery. Actually, the answer isn't complicated. It's because of the people who made up our team. The 1986 Giants were a team of high-caliber individuals who were willing to work and willing to believe. You combine that with ability, and you have a winner.

That's all Bill Parcells asks from his players, that when you play for the Giants, you accept a certain responsibility, that you are as prepared as possible for each Sunday. Bill tolerates physical errors but loathes mental mistakes. If someone persists in making them, he isn't a Giant for very long.

By the time we faced the Redskins and Cowboys in back-to-back divisional showdowns at Giants Stadium, games that would bridge the two halves of the season, we were ready to assert ourselves as the premier team in the NFC East. And in both those games, we fell back on a couple of those high-caliber people I've been talking about: Joe Morris and George Martin. They were the stars of the next two weeks, so much so that we probably wouldn't have won either game without them. Yet each of their performances occurred within a team concept— and that's what was so impressive about our team. We were

169

consistent; someone would always pick up the slack when necessary.

Joe had been doing more than just picking up slack. He'd become the workhorse of our offense, a contradiction in itself since most people thought Joe—5-7, 195—was too small to take that kind of pounding every week. They were wrong, but that only put them at the end of a long line, which started with the Giants' management itself. The Giants blew it concerning Joe. What Joe did these last two years, the two most productive seasons ever by a Giant running back, he could have done as soon as he came into the league—except that he came into the league in Butch Woolfolk's shadow.

I played against Joe in college when he ran out of the I–formation at Syracuse. He ran up and through there as hard as anyone we ever played. When Joe came to the Giants as a second-round draft pick in 1982, I really and truly felt that he was a better back than Butch. But Butch was a first-round draft choice and that was the unfair predicament that Joe faced for the next three years.

The media put pressure on management. Why did they draft running backs consecutively? How would it work? And if Joe won the job over Butch, wouldn't that mean that the Giants, with a history of ridiculous drafting in previous regimes, would have blown a first-round pick? Management, in turn, transferred that pressure to the coaching staff, which stuck with Woolfolk too long, only to undermine Joe's confidence. Joe would not have been beaten out by Butch unless it was political. And that's what it was, political.

While Joe, who was close to Butch, constantly had to wrestle with the "who is better?" question, I already knew. On the first day of his rookie camp, Joe was zipping through the holes, real low, the same way he did in college, and I remember saying to teammates, "This guy's gonna be good. He's the guy." But they kept pushing Butch and playing Butch, even when

Butch just didn't get it done. As a runner, Butch didn't have it. He always zigzagged and made cuts he shouldn't have made. There were holes that sometimes were unbelievable but he didn't find them because he was jitterbugging.

Now Joe's not the type of guy who's going to get in there and do things immediately. He's got to get enough work to build a rhythm and establish some confidence. Instead, he'd make a mistake, fumble, and get yanked. It wasn't until the end of the 1984 season that Joe finally became the No. 1 back with time enough to prove himself.

That following off-season, Butch was traded to Houston, where they used him the way we should have used him, as a pass receiver. I always thought he had a great ability to catch the ball, and that's where he made his biggest plays with us. In any case, once Butch was out of the picture, it took Joe about half a season in '85 to get rolling. From then on, he's been remarkable.

Joe's nickname is "World," not as in all-world, but after World B. Free, the basketball star. Mark Haynes gave it to him after playing with Joe on the Giants' off-season basketball team. Joe takes his hoops very seriously, and he likes to shoot, just like World. He's such a little tank that when he drives to the basket, it's always straight ahead without any moves.

He's the same way on the football field. He explodes through holes, keeps those powerful legs driving, and once he gets up a head of steam, he can break off some big ones. He's saved some of his bigger games for the Washington Redskins, who can't stop him even when they know he's coming.

We knew we'd need a big game from Joe against the Redskins when we hosted Washington in a Monday night game the eighth week of the season. Our games with the Redskins are always physical and are usually decided by the success of each team's running game. When Washington had John Riggins on a roll, we had a hard time beating them, but ever since

'85, we've been able to clamp down on their running game and turn the series our way.

This game just so happened to be played on the same night that the Mets, make that *my* Mets, were playing the Red Sox in the seventh game of the World Series at Shea Stadium. For us, our little football game was almost as important. The Redskins and the Giants had been watching each other's results all season, and it seemed as though we couldn't count on anyone else to beat each other. If we didn't beat them that night in the Meadowlands, that rematch at RFK Stadium the fourteenth week of the season was going to be extra tough.

My blood was boiling for this one. I really enjoy playing against the Redskins for a number of reasons. First, because they run a certain sweep we call the "counter tray," we slant our line against them, so that I play more like Joe Klecko and I'm able to penetrate into the backfield. And even though the Redskins' rivalry is among our fiercest, I respect Washington more than any other club in the league. They just line up against you and dare you to beat them. There's no bullshit, no cheap stuff. If they cut you, they do it legally. You have to respect a team that doesn't come out to maim you, that just tries to knock you on your butt. As a matter of fact, I wouldn't mind playing for the Redskins. They're my kind of team.

Of course, that doesn't mean there aren't any words that go back and forth between us. Yes, fans, there really is a bulletin board. Before a game, our public relations man, Ed Croke, gathers the out-of-town newspapers together just looking for a hint of anything inflammatory. Before this particular game, Bill Belichick read aloud a clipping at a defensive team meeting.

The story quoted Washington's general manager, Bobby Beathard, being critical of our draft. Beathard said they didn't think it was a great draft for defense and that they were excited when the Giants picked Eric Dorsey and five other defensive players. He said that they really felt as though they got a better deal in the draft. So what, you might say. But it's all part of the game and it can get you pumped up if it hits the right nerve.

I know we came out smoking. Joe got going early and we scored the first ten points of the game. At halftime, we held a 13–3 lead. The crowd was only half-interested, however, because of what was going on at Shea. There were portable TVs all over the place and there was cheering at every move the Mets made. At first, I didn't know what was going on when one of their outbursts forced Redskins tackle Joe Jacoby to jump offside. Actually, I was thinking about the loud crowd in the Kingdome and that maybe our fans were taking a cue from them by making noise to disrupt the Redskins' offense. *Pretty neat*, I thought. But that theory went out the window when the crowd went wild following a 49-yard completion by the Redskins. *Pretty dumb*, I thought.

By the time we came out for the second half, the Mets had things under control. So did we, we thought. It's not easy to come back from ten points down against our defense, especially the way we had been playing for so many weeks. But if there was one thing the Redskins did all year, it was to come from behind on the arm of Jay Schroeder, and did we ever make it easy for him. Our secondary gave up 260 yards on five passes alone—five mistakes, actually. By night's end, Schroeder piled up 421 yards passing with eleven completions for 260 yards to the Smurf-sized Gary Clark.

I told you how Bill feels about mental errors. We just had some serious breakdowns and at least one instance where each half of the secondary was playing a different coverage. People were wide open and Clark ate us up. It wasn't as if he was burning people. He was getting turned loose, and with about 4:00 left in the game, we were suddenly tied, 20–20.

If not for Joe, the Redskins would probably have taken all

that momentum and moved for a game-winning touchdown. But with 3:58 remaining, Joe took over. He had already gained 115 yards rushing and caught five passes for an additional fifty-nine yards. Now he started off the drive with a 10-yard gain to help us reach our 44-yard line. From there, Joe exploded through the middle of the Redskins' line and cut sharply to his left, sprinting thirty-four yards to the Redskins' 22. With 2:00 left, we pounded Joe at their line again, hoping to eat up as much of the clock as possible. World got five yards, four yards, and then broke two tackles to get us in the end zone on a 13-yard run, giving him 181 yards for the game. The key block came from our fullback, Maurice Carthon, Joe's favorite escort.

Mo could probably play defense. He's the one guy on our offense with that mentality. I wouldn't even say that Bavaro has it. Mo really goes after guys and just bangs them. There are players who hit hard and there are other guys who hit hard and heavy. When Mo makes a block, you can hear the shoulder pads popping. People do not want to hit him. Bill Bates of the Cowboys hates him. Ronnie Lott of the 49ers hates him. They won't take him on. And Maurice isn't a big weight lifter. He just flat out knocks the crap out of you.

Joe's touchdown behind Maurice's block gave us a 27-20 lead. The problem was that Schroeder and Clark still had 1:32 to tie it up. A 16-yard completion, a 17-yard completion and a 12-yard completion gave them hope and pushed our defense to the brink. With twenty-one seconds left, the Skins had a fourth down on our 35 with a light rain wetting the field. Clark got open across the middle, but slipped on the Astroturf, the pass incomplete, the game ours.

Whew. After that game, I was sure that the Redskins would remain our biggest threat to a divisional title. There was little doubt that two championship clubs were going at it that night. We had now thrown the NFC East into a three-way tie along with Dallas, and the Cowboys were coming in next. After what happened the first week of the season and with so much at stake now, I certainly didn't need any incentive to play well against Dallas. Bill Parcells thought otherwise. He had already let us have it after the Redskins game, so much so that the next day, he felt apologetic and told the press he had "acted like a jerk" in the post-game locker room.

We realized more than anyone that after winning a big game like we did, it's possible to come out flat the next week. I was sure that Bill was making sure we wouldn't.

On Wednesday, our first full practice of the week, I was certain that Bill had told the offensive linemen to step it up and go full speed in the drills. He sometimes does that to stir things up. Fine. I knew what was up. The next thing I knew, however, Brian Johnston, our backup center, made a wisecrack to me. When I looked at Bill, he had a half-smirk on his face, as if he was enjoying what he had set up. *Okay,* I thought. *We'll play that way if you want.*

I threw a punch on the next play, and the next. On the third play, things were out of control. Dorsey coldcocked Damian Johnson with a sucker punch out of nowhere. Helmets were flying. The practice field was mayhem, and that's when Bill tried to stop it for good by threatening thousand-dollar fines. "I don't care," I told him. "Fine me two thousand dollars if you want."

Later, he took me aside and chewed me out. Then he figured things were cool. But things weren't settled as far as I was concerned. First of all, Johnston was only in his second year. Why did he have to start in with me? Second, I didn't feel that justice was served to me. Bill had gotten his cackles but I needed to finish things for myself. In my mind, I was convinced Bill was behind it, even though to this day, Brian Johnston says he wasn't. Later, in one of the back rooms at the stadium, I confronted Johnston and challenged him to square things. But he wouldn't fight, which only frustrated me more.

I started to lift weights, then got so pissed off just thinking about it that I grabbed my stuff and finished my workout at a gym near my home. Thursday, it was the same thing. I had a bad chip on my shoulder. I didn't talk to anybody the rest of the week. On Sunday, I was ready to play, and not because of Parcells.

You see, I really believed that we had given Dallas life by losing to them on opening day. That win lifted and carried them. But never, never, did I think that they were better than we were. This one was to even the score. Better yet, this one was to bury them for the season. When we did beat them, I was sure we had put them behind us. As it turned out, they never did recover from that loss, and went into a tailspin that left them short of the playoffs.

In Dallas, they trace their downfall to one series and one man, Phil Pozderac, a heretofore unknown offensive tackle whose moment of infamy arrived when he lined up against George Martin with 3:33 left in the game. We led, 17–14, thanks to a second straight 181-yard game by World, though our lead had been 17–7 earlier in the fourth quarter. Steve Pelluer was in at quarterback (Carl Banks had sent Danny White to the sidelines for the season with a broken wrist), and he was threatening to reprise our old backup quarterback jinx as he moved the Cowboys surely up the field.

The clock ticked down to 1:15. Pelluer flicked a screen pass to Tony Dorsett, who carried it thirty yards to our six. But as we turned to take the long walk downfield, there was a yellow flag lying on the ground. Holding, Pozderac on Martin. With fifty seconds left, George exploded past Pozderac to sack Pelluer for a 15-yard loss. On the very next play, George rose in the air above Pozderac to bat away a pass intended for a wide-open receiver.

Thirty-three seconds remained now and it was third and 25 for the Cowboys. The crowd was Kingdome-loud and George was twelve-year-veteran smart. George knew two things: Pozderac would have a hair-trigger after being beaten for a sack;

and Pozderac could not possibly hear the snap count above the roar of the crowd and would have to start on motion. George provided that motion by lifting his hand just before the snap. It was perfectly legal and exquisitely sly. Pozderac jumped early and the flag went up just as Pelluer's pass was being delivered to Timmy Newsome for what should have been a killer first down at our 11-yard line. The play was brought back. The Cowboys were forced to try a 63-yard field goal, the NFL record, in order to tie the game. It was short and we had another win, leaving us in a two-way tie with Washington, a deadlock that wouldn't be decided until the fourteenth week of the season.

For George Martin, it was quite a day in what would be the season of his life. George is a unique individual and a father figure to many of the younger players. Players use his shoulder to lean on when they can't go to the coaches. The coaches use his understanding when they can't go to the players. He is a veritable rock in the locker room, and he does his work quietly and behind the scenes. He's respected so highly because he doesn't just talk about values, he lives them. Everything you see in George is genuine. He is one hundred percent class.

Bill recognized these qualities in George when he first came to the team, and I think by putting him into a position of leadership, Bill propelled George's career. Those two have a unique relationship that's based on respect; and I think that's the reason that George has wanted to win more these last few years than ever before in his career. In the past, George may have been getting a little too accustomed to losing. He even thought about retirement for three straight years. After last year's draft, he asked Bill if he still needed him. George didn't want to be "excess baggage," as he put it. Need him? George made some of our biggest plays all year. As Bill says, the ball just has a way of finding him. He's scored more touchdowns than any other defensive player in the history of the game.

Bill's relationship with George is unlike the one he has with me. Here's one example. Even after we beat the Cowboys, I was still steaming about the fight at practice the week before. The day after the game, Bill approached me in the weight room and started some small talk, but I ignored him because I was still ticked off at what had happened in practice.

The next day, our day off, I got a call from Bill at seven in the morning, asking me to come down to his office to straighten everything out. So I went in. "Jim, I can only take so much," he said. "You know the problem with you? What makes you a good player is the same thing that brings you down. You are so freaking stubborn."

"Bill," I answered, "that sounds like someone else I know." Maybe that's why we like each other so much.

Anyway, I had other problems that week as we got ready for our second game with the Eagles, to be played at the Vet in Philadelphia. On Monday, I found an unlabeled brown bottle of multivitamins that Colleen was keeping fresh in the refrigerator. I took one with my cereal in the morning and one again at night. That day at the stadium, the vitamins gave me a real case of get up and go. That is, I was hit with the runs. I thought nothing of it, but as the week wore on, I was in the toilet eight or nine times a day. Lamar thought I was pulling his chain because I was running out of our defensive line meetings so many times. A couple of times, I even left the practice field to go. It got so bad that my rear end was on fire and I had to keep showering to relieve it. *Holy shit*, I thought. *Literally.*

Now, I'm not the kind of guy who complains. If I get sick, I don't even tell Colleen. I don't like to be a hypochondriac. I just blow it off, even if I'm excreting my brains out, like I was that week. I'm talking about forty-five sittings in five days. At that rate, I would have looked like Phil McConkey in no time.

Finally on Friday night, Colleen saw me go to the refrigerator and take another pill.

"What the hell are you doing?" she asked me.

"Just taking one of these vitamins," I said.

She burst out laughing. "Those aren't vitamins," she said. "Those are laxatives."

"What?" I couldn't believe it. "What the hell are they doing in here? No wonder I've been shitting my brains out." I glared at her. "I can't believe it, Colleen. My ass is raw and you're feeding me *laxatives.*"

Colleen didn't answer me. She was too busy rolling around on the floor.

# II

---

# MINNESOTA

# Fourth and 17

Fourth and 17. Say those words and any Giant fan knows exactly what you're talking about. One play that changed the course of our franchise, that made people stop thinking in terms of history and start thinking in terms of destiny. If "The Fumble," that infamous turnover against the Eagles in 1978, was so responsible for sinking the Giants, "Fourth and 17" should be given as much credit for resurrecting us.

When Phil Simms, facing a final fourth and 17 situation late in our game with Minnesota, found Bobby Johnson for the first down, it not only made the difference in winning or losing that one game but it let us know what we were capable of doing from that point on. It was a lightning-bolt message that told us our team was something special. Not just "good" or "full of potential" or even the "odds-on favorite." But "something special." Hard to describe, maybe, but easy to feel once you've got it.

If we already "had it" after our back-to-back wins over the Redskins and Cowboys, we still weren't sure. The following week, we went into Philadelphia and beat the Eagles, 17–14. We had a 17–0 lead until the fourth quarter when we gave up two meaningless touchdowns. The game was never in doubt

183

although we should have really put them away. At that point, we still had to fight through a "Murphy's Law" stigma that was even more pronounced in the minds of our fans and the media. And of course, who could blame them?

At the same time, all the mistakes and frustrations of the past were being deposited as sludge on one man's shoulders. It's tough enough being a quarterback. It's even tougher being a quarterback in New York. It's murder when all the fans remember a quarterback named Y.A. Tittle and some championship game twenty-five or thirty years in the past. Phil Simms was supposed to be some sort of savior when the new Young-Perkins regime selected him as their first-draft pick in 1979. Whenever he wasn't perfection in shoulder pads, the more ignorant Giant fans dwelled on his every mistake, even when he wasn't exactly surrounded by the best weapons available. Phil *had* to take chances. In fact, that's what our offense has been based upon for three straight playoff years. Yet Phil played to a symphony of boos at home games and was called the guy "who could never win the Big One."

Even as we compiled an 8 – 2 record coming into the Minnesota game, Phil couldn't escape the criticism. The day we beat Dallas, Phil completed only six out of eighteen passes and the fans were brutal. No less of a self-proclaimed authority than Howard Cosell wrote in the *New York Daily News,* "It's unfortunate for a player with his ability, but the man's trademark has become the critical mistake at the critical time, the fumble, the interception."

How do you like that? This bitter old man hadn't been to a game or practice for years and *he* was calling Phil gutless in the clutch—ignoring the times, such as in Dallas the year before, when Phil would have won the game if not for someone else making the critical drop or failing to get both feet in bounds. Of course, Cosell and I go way back, to a Buffalo Bills game when I was a freshman in high school. ABC was filming a feature on Howard so I made my way up to the press box, pointed at the cameras and screamed, "Cosell's a bum."

Years later, my opinion of Howard still holds true, as does my long-standing opinion of Phil, that he is a competitor and a winner. I have first-hand experience. Phil, you see, is my best friend on the team. We went through a lot together in '82 and '83. It was a time when our careers paralleled each other, and I'm talking low. We were both trying to save our careers from injuries, me with my back, Phil with a shoulder and then a knee. We started rehabbing together at the beginning of January when we were practically the only players at the stadium. Those are the times when a player can feel like an outsider, not really a part of any team, but Phil and I relied on each other for support. We drove in together and drove back home together. We played cards together. We dreamed together. We did a *lot* of talking.

I remember Phil saying, "If I ever get a shot, I'm gonna light them up." And I'd tell him, "Phil, I know you will. Things have to happen. You're just having bad luck."

That's what it was. Bad luck. He's always been a well-conditioned athlete. He was just a victim of freak injuries, like his last one, the dislocated thumb he suffered when he hit a helmet with his follow-through, just as he was regaining the starting job from Scott Brunner. And hell, the way they were blocking for him back then, what quarterback wouldn't have been injured?

All I know is, no quarterback works harder than Phil does. No quarterback I've ever seen has been in the weight room until eight at night. No quarterback ever wanted to win more. I know because when we compete against each other, it's cutthroat. Golf, basketball, cards, even pitching pennies. It's the same way with the jokes we pull on each other and it's why we'll strike whenever there's an opening. For instance, there was the time last year when Phil was on the cover of *Gentle-*

*man's Quarterly,* the men's fashion magazine. Tony Galbreath brought it in and we pinned it up on the bulletin board. They had his hair all moussed up and he was wearing eyeliner and makeup. I couldn't stop laughing.

"You gotta be kidding me," I yelled over to Phil. "Eyeliner? I hope you made a ton of money for this, because you look queer. You must have gotten a lot of money."

"I did," Phil said, not blinking. "And f—— you, Burt."

As for what kind of guy Phil is, I'll never forget when I was a rookie, and Phil, who was already an established quarterback, was signed to do an engagement in the Catskills, for a thousand-dollar appearance fee. Well, he called those people and insisted that I come along too. Then he split the money with me. He didn't have to do that. He just wanted to help me out. That's how he is.

That's why when Phil was catching all that flack from the fans and when he went through a rough couple of games, I never stopped believing in him. The same could be said of Bill. The first practice after the Dallas game, Bill took Phil aside and told him to go back to being himself. He told him that he had to be aggressive, that he couldn't play as if he was afraid to make a mistake, and, more than anything, that he still was his quarterback.

Although Phil didn't have a spectacular game statistically against the Eagles that week (8-for-18 for 130 yards), he proved a few things to himself concerning how he threw the ball and when he threw it. Then came our trip to the Metrodome in Minneapolis—and Fourth and 17.

We all knew it was a big week for us and the start of a potentially murderous stretch of games. It started with Minnesota, and then home for Denver, which had been playing for a while like the best team in football. A Monday night game at Candlestick Park, where we had been winless, would follow, before we arrived at our rematch in Washington. Bill's message to us that week was: "The race starts here."

Race? It had been more like a decathlon. The Redskins were hanging with us the whole way, playing the same exact schedule of teams. I had a feeling we'd beat the Redskins again but I wanted to go into that game at least even, so that if we won there, we'd be assured of winning the division. The Redskins had already beaten the Vikings. But we had the Vikes on the road and they were emerging as a playoff contender, behind an explosive offense run by the veteran quarterback Tommy Kramer, who was having a Pro-Bowl season. They needed to win our game to stay in the NFC Central Division hunt with the Bears and to boost their wild-card hopes in general. They were up for us as much as for any opponent of theirs all year.

At the same time, Bill and Ron Erhardt were intent on mixing in more of the pass with the run, especially with Stacy Robinson back off injured reserve to replenish our receiving corps, which had been in mothballs. Meanwhile, Joe had rushed for over a hundred yards in four straight games. We knew there would be a day when he'd be stopped—and the Vikings, by stacking their line against the run, dared our offense to beat them in the air.

Besides incentive, the Vikings came into the game with a solid game plan based on misdirection, play-action, draws, and one-step drops and quick passes by Kramer, all to take away our natural aggressiveness. Their running back, Darren Nelson, is built for that kind of offense. He's a scaled-down, shiftier Joe Morris, and he concerned us as a pass catcher.

At the same time, Bill and Ron Erhardt were intent on mixing in more of the pass with the run, especially with Stacy Robinson back off injured reserve to replenish our receiving corps, which had been in mothballs. Meanwhile, Joe had rushed for over a hundred yards in four straight games. We knew there would be a day when he'd be stopped—and the Vikings, by stacking their line against the run, dared our offense to beat them in the air.

In the first half both offenses moved well in between the 20-yard lines but neither team managed a touchdown. Phil ran into some tough luck on the first series when Joe was unable to make a catch in the end zone. Instead, Raul kicked the first of his five field goals that day, beginning a battle with Chuck Nelson. For the rest of the half we traded field goals, three by Raul to two by Nelson. Both missed field goals late in the half, Nelson from thirty-four yards, Raul from sixty as time ran out.

Our 9–6 lead was hardly comfortable, but the game had

settled into our kind of pattern with our defense getting stingy once they reached the red zone. Sure enough, as the third quarter began, the Vikings were at our doorstep one more time. It was first and 10 from our 11 when I read the play, side-stepped the center and came in clean to nail the runner, Alfred Anderson, for a one-yard loss. When a Nelson draw play was stuffed by Lawrence and Dorsey on third down, we thought we had held them to another field goal, but the play was nullified by an offsides call. Jerome, who comes in for me on certain third-down plays, jumped the snap. The Vikings made the most of their second chance as Allen Rice caught a touchdown pass out of the backfield from Kramer. The lead switched hands again. It was 13 – 9, Minnesota.

Raul got us within one point again with a 37-yard field goal late in the third quarter, and it looked as though things were swinging against the Vikings when Kramer caught his hand on a helmet and was forced to leave the game, to be replaced by Wade Wilson, an experienced backup quarterback. Before Wilson entered the game, however, we regained the lead with two big plays in a row. Bobby Johnson got twenty-two yards by running a reverse. On the next play, he got behind their secondary and caught a 25-yard touchdown pass from Phil.

We led, 19 – 13. Now it was up to Wilson to bring back the Vikings and up to our defense to put the clamps on him. Wilson shocked us. On his first three plays off the bench, he threw passes for 13-, 18-, and 16-yard gains. Then he completed the drive in the face of an all-out blitz by recognizing single coverage on Anthony Carter, their speed receiver. Carter got behind Perry Williams and we were behind the Vikings again, 20 – 19.

At this point, I wasn't willing to accept what was happening, because it seemed like the same old stuff all over again. We had a chance to put the game away and they beat us with a big play. Now, with 3:53 left in the game, it was Vikings' ball again, and if they could control it and pick up a few first downs, we'd be sunk. On first down, they ran Nelson on a delay up the middle. Gary Reasons, one of our fastest-thinking line-backers, got him by the ankles and I came in to finish him off after a two-yard gain. On second down, they tried a little swing pass to Nelson. I was able to skate along the line with their center, Dennis Swilley, fight him off and chase down Nelson for a one-yard gain. On third down, I was in on the play again, tackling Wilson after he rolled out and scrambled for five yards, two yards short of the first down.

They punted and our offense got it back at our 41-yard line with 2:14 left. This was one of those situations I had talked to reporters about during the pre-season. I'd been telling them that we were a good team but that to become a great team, we would have to make critical plays at critical times of the game. *C'mon, Phil,* I thought as I walked off to the sidelines. *Yes, Phil,* I thought as he faded back and threw one deep. "Yeah," I was about to yell as the ball settled into Stacy Robinson's out-stretched hands, a game-winning touchdown in sight. Except Stacy dropped it. Nothing against Stacy, mind you, but that had to be one of the most frustrating moments of the season right there, and I took out my frustrations by kicking over a wooden bench, Gatorade and all.

Phil, however, kept his cool. You talk about guts in the face of pressure? On the next play, Minnesota sent linebacker Scott Studwell in on a blitz but Phil shook him off and spotted Bobby dragging across the middle for a 14-yard gain and a first down. Two plays after that, it was third and eight at the Viking 43. The pocket collapsed around Phil, and George Martin watched his younger brother, Doug, sack Phil for a nine-yard loss.

There was 1:12 left in the game when we called time-out to talk it over. It was fourth and 17. I stood on the sidelines, ready to get back on the field to play defense.

Pat Hodgson, our receivers coach, suggested the play, called half-right – 74, a pattern the offense had yet to run all year. The Vikings would be playing a loose zone with just a three-man rush, eight men in coverage. We sent three receivers into patterns. McConkey went in motion and ran a go-pattern up the right seam of the zone. Stacy ran a 20-yard out, enough for the first down on the left side, and Bobby ran a fade pattern toward the first-down marker on the right sideline. The idea was to force their safety into a quick decision: either he covers McConkey or slides over to get Bobby. By putting their man into a bind like that, it would hopefully create enough room to complete the pass.

When Phil stepped over the center, his thought process was McConkey first, then Stacy, then back to Bobby as his third option. He never had the time to go through all that as Mike Stensrud put on quick pressure right in his face. Looking at McConkey first, Phil noticed the top of Bobby's helmet on the same side and in an instantaneous decision, he let the ball go just as Stensrud was hitting him. My thought at the time was *Oh, no, he's just throwing it up.*

But Bobby had worked his way wide open into a big open area behind their nickel back, Issiac Holt, and had the good sense to stop his pattern short. The pass had to be perfectly air-lifted. Phil himself said that he gets that pass over the top maybe five or six times out of a hundred. This was one of those times. He threw it softly, just as he wanted to, and it hung in the air like a marshmallow for Bobby, who made the grab for a 22-yard gain at the 30 and the biggest first down of our season.

The Vikings could feel their doom, I'm sure, and anyone who had played for the Giants long enough knew what they were going through. The energy passed in a whoosh from one sideline to another. An offsides penalty on Doug Martin, and three carries by Joe Morris got us to the 15, where we called time with fifteen seconds left. Raul, as he always does, said a quick "Our Father" in Spanish and trotted onto the field to make history. His 33-yard field goal capped one of the Giants' greatest victories ever, and everyone went wild, mobbing our amigo on the field. Well, almost everyone.

Lamar had been standing on one of the benches I hadn't knocked down so that he could see the winning field goal. He ran along and along and must have forgotten he was on a bench, so that he just went flying off, landing in a heap. He sat crumpled on the ground, his ankle sprained, crying for help, but no one came.

For about ten seconds he whined, "Ronnie, Ronnie, I'm hurt. Ronnie Barnes, I'm hurt. Come get me. Get me, Ronnie, I'm hurt, I'm hurt."

Pepper Johnson did a wounded-Lamar imitation all the way home. It was our most excited locker room and plane ride all year.

I know that I kept thinking about the Mets after that game and how they seemed to pull out games like this on the way to the World Series title. And I was happy for Phil, who had the guts to bring us back. I'd known all along that you can have the best defense in the world, but you also need that leader on offense. I think what that fourth and 17 play did more than anything else was to rally our offense around Phil. During the tough times, nothing much was said, but the questions from the media and fan reaction had created a sense of controversy in the locker room.

But after fourth and 17, I felt that if Phil had been having any problems, they were over at that point. Absolutely. Everybody realized that if we were going to make it to the Super Bowl, we had to have Phil. He had to be the catalyst. Once Phil felt that support, it was all he needed and his confidence began to filter down to everyone else. My roommate, Billy Ard, was one good example of a guy who rallied around Phil. Each night before a game, I always asked how he thought we'd do the next day. It was usually, Well, I think we can win if we do this, this and this. From that point on, Billy's answer was always, "We're gonna kick ass." That reflected the attitude of the entire offense right there.

As for me, I was convinced after that play that we were going all the way. I mean it. Things weren't going well, then all of a sudden, *boom*, we hit that fourth and 17 and pulled out the game. Hell, the Giants had never done anything like that before. When we came back like that, I said to myself, *This is destiny. We're gonna win this thing.*

The problem was that even the press, which had a right to have a negative attitude after they saw so many negative things happen, started getting on our side. That bugged the hell out of me. I liked it when the reporters went against us—we didn't have as much pressure on us. In fact, I checked the predictions of our regular beat guys every week. Before that Minnesota game, we were picked to lose by every reporter who covers us. That was our history. But after that game, they started switching over. When they did that I said, "Oh no, pressure."

Suddenly, we were expected to win games, and our postgame locker rooms began to reflect that. Our celebration in Minnesota was the last time we really showed a lot of emotion. All hell broke loose coming down that tunnel. Lawrence kept screaming, "F——, I can't believe it. I can't believe it." McConkey, who had this thing about the receivers getting a bum rap, ripped the adhesive tape off his wrists and began hurling it at the crowd of reporters. Raul, who the day before told a few guys he didn't yet feel like he was part of the team, was mobbed, and Bill was off in a corner telling the press, "Anyone who doesn't think that Phil Simms is a good quarterback should go cover another sport." Of course, Howard Cosell wasn't there.

Like I said, I kept thinking about the Mets and destiny and ticker tape. Little did I know that I would have other worries first.

# 12

## EAST RUTHERFORD

## My Aching Back

"Super Bowl preview?" I was asked. *Sure*, I thought. "No," I snarled. "Too much ahead of us to think about that."

Nevertheless, here we were, fresh off our miracle in Minneapolis, feeling as good about our 9–2 record as ever, bracing for the invasion of another 9–2 team that had started the season playing better football than anybody. The Denver Broncos. Funny we should have met in the middle of the season, because it said a lot about the development of our team. On November 24, we beat the Broncos because of a few plays that we made and they didn't. When we met again in Super Bowl XXI, we beat them because we were the far superior team. In our first game with Denver, though, we were just beginning to pull things together.

The problems were the same. John Elway is a scrambler and improviser. Their defense has a multiple-front scheme with excellent quickness. And their center is Billy Bryan. Boy, did I ever remember him. The only other time we played against each other was in a pre-season game in 1984. Parcells had me prepare as hard as I would for a regular season game, simply because I had never gone up against Bryan before.

It's always a battle against him and it was no different in this game. It was clear that the defense would have to play at what Bill Parcells calls "our optimum level." Our offense wasn't able to dent the end zone all day against Denver's sometimes confusing defense but that was okay, because although Elway threw for over three hundred yards and scrambled for fifty-one, we held him pretty much in check.

They led, 6–3, after recovering a fumble and moving in for a second Rich Karlis field goal. Our points were made possible on a fourth-and-four gamble that Bill had conceived in September and was just waiting to use. Our special teams coach, Romeo Crennel, "RAC" for short, named it ARAPAHOE, meaning A Run, A Pass, A Hit On the Enemy. Jeff Hostetler, our third-string quarterback, went out on the field with the punting unit; then, with the Broncos back in return formation, Hostetler ducked under the center and handed off to Lee Rouson, who gained eight yards for a first down. It was just another example of how Bill has come of age as an offensive coach. When he first started, all he knew about offense was that you run and you pass. But last year, Bill had enough confidence in his offense and enough courage within himself to make calls like that.

Late in the first half, they recovered another fumble at our 41-yard line and Elway had them on the move. With a first down at our 13-yard line, the Broncos had the potential to take a 13–3 halftime lead, and considering how our offense was playing, that might have stood up. What happened instead was another one of those special plays that made this a special season.

I came in on Elway and was about to hit him when he released a screen pass meant for Gerald Willhite. Remarkably, George Martin had gotten by their tackle, Ken Lanier, and now Pops was high in the air with basketball-like skill. He reached behind him with his right hand and simply snared the ball out of the air, then began a fourteen-second trip toward his seventh career touchdown, an NFL record for defensive players. I had a good view but to tell the truth, I didn't think George was going to make it. He's not as swift as he used to be. It was almost suspended animation as he hurdled one Bronco, then actually showed the ball to Elway, who was in pursuit and made the mistake of trying to tackle George high instead of by the legs. George shrugged him off, faked a lateral to Lawrence and kept going. It seemed like tomorrow when he finally got into the end zone. I swan-dived into the pile of blue jerseys already on top of George.

George was out of breath but loving it and I'm sure it's one of the moments he treasures most from our season. At thirty-four, he may have lost a step or two but he's still a great athlete and it took a great athlete to make that play. George has the strongest arm on the team. Lawrence can throw farther than Simms, but George can throw farther than Lawrence, about seventy-five or eighty yards. That day, he also out-scored Phil by turning a potential ten-point deficit into a four-point lead.

As it was, the game was still far from over. After two more field goals by Raul and one by Karlis, we held a 16–9 lead with just under 10:00 left in the game. That's where I got off. On Denver's next play from scrimmage, I was practically tackled by Bryan, but I bounced off the ground to chase Elway, who was headed on a rollout around his right side. As he was going out of bounds, I felt it. My back. Again. Without warning.

I thought it was just a twinge, or more accurately, I *hoped* it was just a twinge. I stayed in for another play then took myself out on a short-yardage situation. I went back in one more time. I halfheartedly rushed the passer and tried to jump up to block a pass. It just didn't work and I watched the remaining five minutes of the game from the sidelines. In pain.

It turned out to be a hell of a game to watch. Elway led the Broncos to a touchdown to tie it, 16–16, with less than 2:00

remaining. Our ball at our 18. Third and 18—sound somewhat familiar? And Phil did it again, spotting Bobby for a 24-yard completion. A couple of runs by Tony Galbreath kept us going but a holding call against Karl Nelson set us back to the 39 with a second and 12, just over thirty seconds left. Yep, Phil did it again.

It was something our offense worked on in practice all week. The Bronco defense plays a lot of cute tricks. In one of them they line up in what looks to be a blitz formation, just to sucker our receivers into making a sight adjustment. In other words, an alternate pattern designed so that Phil can hit them with a quick pass. Instead, the Broncos really don't blitz at all, and the quarterback is left throwing into a deep zone with little chance of making the play.

It was McConkey who read the smoke screen correctly and stayed with his original route deep down the seam. With Bavaro running a shorter route down the same seam, we turned the tables on the Broncos. Now they had to play a guessing game and their safety, Tony Lilly, guessed wrong by picking Bavaro. Simms, who was reading McConkey's mind, found McConkey wide open for a 46-yard pass play, our longest of the season. Two plays later, Raul won it with a 34-yard field goal with just six seconds left.

Incredible. For the second straight week, we made the impossible happen. But while most of the guys went off to celebrate, I headed off in an ambulance. There we were, 10–2, and steamrolling toward the Super Bowl. There I was, flat on my aching back in traction at the New York Hospital for Special Surgery. That I was pissed off is putting it mildly. Not only was I having a good game against Bryan, who's a hell of a center, but I thought I was having one hell of a year. And now this. All over again. You certainly have time to think when you're in traction and the memories I was recalling weren't pleasant.

In 1982, my second season, the Players Association struck the NFL in a six-week walkout. I'd been doing all I could to stay in shape. The word was that we'd be settling the strike on a night I happened to be working out at a local gym. (As it turned out, the strike was settled the next day.) I was trying to be safe and I didn't squat. Instead, I worked on a leg-press machine one leg at a time. Suddenly, I felt my back go on me.

I hadn't had any back problems before. I didn't even know what it felt like and so I really didn't know what was going on. I was a scared kid, still far from established as a player, and to me, the injury didn't seem to be that bad. I thought it was something I could just work through. The last thing I wanted was to be put on injured reserve, where I could really get lost. So I continued to push myself and when it hurt I pushed harder. All the while, our orthopedic surgeon was bewildered. He took countless CAT scans and turned up nothing.

Something was there. I knew it. And finally, I pushed myself to the point where my left leg went numb. There was one game near the end of the 1982 season when I came straight up the middle on Joe Thiesmann. He made a move to my left and when I tried to react, my leg simply collapsed. I went straight down like a sack of potatoes. I had no strength and no balance. I knew then that I was in real trouble.

Yet it continued that way for me until the end of the 1983 season—a year and a half of agony. I struggled. I had to. I had a family and I had to take care of them. The more it hurt, the more I fought against it, because I knew I had to do what I had to do to stay on the team and make a living. Even walking would produce shooting pains from my back through my leg. Getting hit on top of the head was the worst. Every single time that happened, it felt as though voltage was being passed through from my hip to my toes. I got to a point where I actually got used to that feeling and just started to live with it.

Finally, in the middle of the 1983 season, I couldn't play

another down. Pain wasn't a factor anymore. My body just stopped. My left leg had atrophied six inches and lost seventy percent of its strength. My quadricep was pathetic and my left leg was so numb that someone could have stuck a pin into it and I wouldn't have felt it. And you know what the doctor said? Nothing. He couldn't find anything wrong.

My career was almost over when the Giants hired Dr. Russell Warren. The first time Dr. Warren took a look at my X-rays and test results, he said, "These films are worthless." He told me that I had the classic symptoms of a two-three disc problem. The more common disc problem is lower, at the four-five level, and that is where our previous orthopedic surgeon had concentrated exclusively. He had never bothered to check higher up, where the disc was suffocating the nerve to my left leg.

I was praying that Dr. Warren was right, because there was no way I could have continued to play football otherwise. Sure enough, he located the problem at the two-three level, then presented my options to me. He told me I had a fifty-fifty chance of recovery if I was willing to try an enzyme injection treatment that had been developed in Canada. It had been used there for ten years but it was still new in the United States. Otherwise, I would have to undergo surgery for the removal of the disc. My choice wasn't as easy as it sounds. If the enzymes failed, I could still have had the operation. But it would have been too late for me. I couldn't have missed another season.

In the end I decided on the enzymes. I didn't want to have surgery because I knew that scar tissue can create even more problems in the back. In December, I was given the enzyme injection. By March, I was feeling like a new man. The enzyme shrunk the disc and alleviated the pressure on the nerve root. I was lucky, too, because that disc had been sitting on the nerve for a year and a half; when it's on there that long, the nerve doesn't always come back. If that had been the case, I would not have had the use of my quadricep.

So ended the most frustrating part of my life, frustrating because I knew I could play well, even though the people around me probably thought I was horseshit. Even hurt and struggling, I was playing okay. I knew I could excel and be a real good nose guard, maybe one of the best. They probably thought I was an average nose guard just plugging away. But I knew I could be more than that.

I'll admit that I was bitter because I felt that the '83 season was taken away from me. I didn't say much, though, even to Colleen, because you can talk about what you're going to do but if you don't do it, it means nothing. Finally, when I felt healthy again, I said to her, "Colleen, I'm not saying anything to anyone else, but I'm going to kick ass this year. I feel like I've been given another life. I'm healthy now for the first time since I've been a rookie, and I know so much more now that I'm going to surprise the shit out of them."

I said the same to thing to Bill Parcells, more or less. "I'm gonna kick ass this year. I'm gonna be a starter and I'm going to kick ass."

"You really think so?" he replied.

"Hell yes," I answered. "You'll see."

I was like a boxer from day one of mini-camp all the way through. I had a chip on my shoulder for other reasons, too. I found myself third on the depth chart behind Jerome, who had finished the season for me after they picked him up as a free agent, and Bill Neill, who had missed the entire year and still was No. 2. That chip didn't come off until I won the starting job.

And now, here I was again three years later, with the same type of obstacle in front of me, just as I was having the season of my life. To be honest, I didn't feel as though this injury was anywhere near the severity of the disc problem I had in '82 and '83. I was also going to be smarter this time. Rest is the only thing that makes it better. I wasn't going to push it, or at least I was going to try not to push it.

For the time being, I was a lousy patient. I hate hospitals, particularly when I'm in a bad mood. They want your temperature, then they want your blood, then they want something else. I wasn't in the mood. I growled at the nurse, "I'm not giving you any blood and you can take my temperature once a day, not every three or four hours. Nobody's waking me up in the middle of the night."

I was a bitch. I had Colleen smuggle in some decent food because I wasn't going to touch the shit they gave me. All I wanted to do was get out. On Tuesday night, I called my attorney and friend Paul Rotella and we escaped in his Lincoln. I was home, where at least I could relax.

Just from the rest, I started to feel better. In fact, I was feeling pretty decent. I was really encouraged that I was going to play on Monday night in San Francisco, especially since I had an extra day to recover. Though the Giants didn't know it, I was seeing a chiropractor, Dr. Albert Wolanese, twice a day and he was helping me. Thursday came and I decided against practicing. Friday, the same thing. But on Saturday, I knew I couldn't wait one more day to try it. I said to myself if I could just go out there and get through practice by going through the motions, I would still have two full days for those spasms to go away.

I never should have done it. I did it. I was so hyper that I didn't give the back the rest it needed. After I tried it on Saturday, I just went backwards. For the next two days, instead of healing, it only got worse. On Monday it was as bad as it had been after the Denver game.

Now Bill Parcells had to make a choice. He didn't want to go with just one healthy nose tackle on his roster, Jerome Sally. Erik Howard was on the injured reserve list since the St. Louis game and he was ready to play again. Unless someone else was injured, his only option was to place me on injured reserve, where I would have to remain inactive for four weeks—in other words, the remainder of the regular season. He had until noon Monday to make a move or not.

After our team meeting Monday morning, Bill approached me and we went out to the terrace to talk. He asked me if I could play. Right there, I felt the threat of IR laying over my head. I knew Bill wanted to give me every shot to recover without going on IR, but I also knew that if it came to a choice between me and the good of the team, Bill would have to IR me. Hell, I agreed with him.

"Bill," I said, "this is a weird situation you're putting me in. If I tell you I'm not playing, you may put me on IR. If I tell you I can play, then you're not going to put me on IR. This is how I feel," I told him. "If I play tonight, I probably won't play the rest of the season. If I don't play, I'll have a chance of playing again this year." I looked him straight in the eye. "Bill, I can't. I can't even walk. But if you really need me, I'll play."

"All right," he said. "Be ready." He kept me on the active roster, anyway, taking the chance that something else might happen to open up a roster spot by next week, because he sure wasn't going to go up against the Redskins and their inside running game with only one nose. As it turned out, Jeff Hostetler, our third-string quarterback, fractured a bone in his leg on special teams that night, freeing up the roster spot for Howard.

I put on the equipment that night but didn't even go through warm-ups. I was just trying to cool out. Once the game started, I found it increasingly difficult to relax. Our defense looked like Zombie U and Joe Montana was slicing us up with a clinical demonstration of how the 49ers had won two Super Bowls. *Zing, zing, zing.* His two-step drop and quick release enabled him to routinely find open receivers. And they were running the ball just as successfully, up the middle and around the ends. We were missing tackles in the secondary and allowing the 49ers to do just about anything they wanted.

A 30-yard field goal by Max Runager, a 16-yard timing pass from Montana to Jerry Rice and a one-yard end around by Rice completed drives of twelve, eleven and fourteen plays. The troubles even spread to Raul Allegre, who missed two field goals for us. At halftime, we trailed, 17–0, and appeared to be headed for the wrong end of a blowout.

I could no longer remain calm. I went berserk in the locker room. I told people to get their heads out of their asses and I was going to make sure they didn't forget that the rest of the game. As we were coming out on the field for the second half, I charged Phil Simms from behind and slammed him across the back. Startled but psyched, he screamed, "Just stop those f——ers, will you, so we can get it going." Honest.

Well, if Phil was getting that excited you could imagine *me*. As our kickoff team lined up, I lined up with them on the sidelines and, honest to God, I sprinted down the field step for step with them, bad back and all. Through that whole second half I was running up and down the sidelines, pounding my hands, screaming constantly, sometimes right in front of the coaches. I was a total psycho.

And it started for us right on that first kickoff, when Pepper Johnson raced downfield to make a big hit. Backed up at their eight-yard line by an offensive pass interference, the Niners stalled and had to punt. Our offense took over at the San Francisco 49. Phil flipped a short one eight yards over the middle to Bavaro, who turned the momentum of the game around with one relentless effort. Six 49ers hit him at one time or another but Mark wouldn't go down. He simply turned into a human tank. With Ronnie Lott, Keena Turner, Riki Ellison and Tom McKyer all hanging on his back, Bavaro carried them twenty-three extra yards to the 49er 18.

Meanwhile, I was screaming on the sidelines, "See, I told you we could do it." And when Mark came off the field I greeted him. "Mark," I said, "that was f——ing unbelievable. You are the biggest f——ing stud." Mark smiled back and nodded his head up and down. Then he let out with a loud "Yeah."

*Holy shit,* I thought. I even got *him* excited. I must be doing something right. So was our offense. Two plays later, Phil hit Joe on a post pattern in the end zone and we were on the board, 17 – 7. Three plays and out went the 49er offense. Phil started at our 29. A quick twelve to Ottis Anderson, before Joe lost three. Then, Bavaro again, this time for an 11-yard gain, dragging 49ers again. This time, however, they stopped Mark two yards shy of the first down, leaving us with a third down.

Here was the situation. The 49ers had been stacking their defense to stop Joe and, with the help of Candlestick's mushy turf, they were doing the job. On third down, Joe took off on a flow play to the right, but the 49ers penetrated and got to him at the line of scrimmage, still two yards behind the first-down marker. At that point, fourth and two from our 49-yard line, Joe had gained just eight yards the whole night.

Maybe it was a carryover from Fourth and 17 and from what we had done the week before against the Broncos, but Bill, who for the previous three years would have punted the football in that situation, decided to go for it—with the same play that had failed on third down. Fans watching at home on TV must have been knocked off their seats by our bravado. Certainly, the 49er defense was knocked off theirs. Our offensive line executed their blocks perfectly and with Maurice Carthon leading the way, Joe sliced through for not only the first-down yardage but a 17-yard gain. With the 49er defense in a state of shock, Phil struck quickly to Stacy Robinson, who got behind their rookie cornerback, Tim McKyer, for a 34-yard touchdown that brought us within three points before the third quarter was even half over.

Now we became unstoppable. Once the 49ers surrendered

the ball after three plays, we took the lead, set up by a juggling 49-yard catch by Stacy at the 49er one-yard line. Ottis went over on the next play to make it 21 – 17. More than a quarter remained but there was no way we were going to lose it now. Montana took one final shot at us late in the fourth quarter when he got them as far as our 17-yard line with 1:00 to go. But on a third-and-four play, Carl Banks and Gary Reasons burst through to drop Wendell Tyler for a three-yard loss, separating him from the ball, only to have it ruled no fumble. Luckily, it didn't matter. When Montana's fourth-down pass, with a blitzing Andy Headen in his face, was deflected incomplete by Perry Williams, we owned our biggest comeback victory ever. I'm sure it gave the Redskins something to think about as they watched the game—not that it mattered, either. For the seed of confidence that we planted in Minnesota and nurtured against Denver was now fully grown. For the rest of the season, our offense and defense clicked together so well that no one was going to beat us.

I couldn't believe how happy I could be after not playing, but I felt as much satisfaction from that game as any I've ever played in. When I came off the field I was covered in sweat and my voice was gone. But I paid for my exuberance with my back.

After the game, I just lay in the back of the bus in pain. I wasn't supposed to run. It was the one thing that really harmed my back, yet I ran more during that game than if I had played. I *really* screwed up my back that night. I was in so much pain on the plane, I could hardly move. I lay across a few seats thinking, *What the hell did I do to myself?* And when I got up after that five-hour plane ride, I felt as though my back had just come apart.

I could hardly carry my bag, let alone walk to my car. But since I didn't want Bill or the coaches to see me, I tried not to limp. The biggest game of my life was six days away and I was worse than ever.

# 13

## WASHINGTON

## What About Brad?

"**W**on't hurt bit," said Dr. Chu.

Of course, Dr. Chu wasn't the one getting four five-inch needles pushed into the top of his head. Dr. Chu was doing the pushing.

It was just another example of the extremes I went to in order to play against the Redskins. Our biggest game of the regular season—another do-or-die battle for the NFC East title we coveted so much—was only two days away and my back, I felt, would need a miracle cure if I was to play. It was 8 P.M. Friday night and we were leaving for Washington the next day.

I called Paul Rotella, my man in charge of impossible tasks.

"Paulie, how you doing?"

"Good, Jim. What's up?"

"Listen, I want to go see an acupuncturist. I gotta play. I've tried everything. You know any acupuncturists?"

"Jimmy," Paul said. "It's Friday night. It's eight o'clock. What if I know ten of them? How am I gonna get one at eight o'clock on a Friday night?"

"Please," I begged. Paul never lets me down.

"Jimmy, I'll see what I can do."

Paul remembered that his grandfather had seen an acupuncturist, so he called him and got the name. He had an office in Paramus, which happened to be where Paul once sat on the city council. So Paul called his men at the police station. "Get me Dr. Chu, *stat.* It's an emergency." Soon he was on the phone with the good doctor, laying on the line.

"Dr. Chu. Hi. This is Paul Rotella. You know Jim Burt of the New York Giants? I'm his attorney. We have an emergency here. He needs your professional assistance. This is vital to the NFL."

"I no watch football," said Dr. Chu, who didn't know the NFL from an IRA.

"Any price, whatever it takes," Paul pleaded. That Dr. Chu understood.

"I call you back," said Dr. Chu. He called back a few minutes later and agreed to meet us in his office at ten o'clock.

"Jimmy," Paul told me on the phone, "I got you your acupuncturist."

"I knew you'd come through," I said. Soon, Paul was picking me up in his Lincoln, which I could barely lower myself into, and we were racing down Route 17 to face the needle man and his bag of tricks.

Dr. Chu let us in. "I come here because my wife big sports fan. Said you very important. Must play."

So I sat on his table. "Just do what you have to do to me, Doc."

Dr. Chu took out his charts and started feeling my head. "Ah, pressure point," he said as though he had made an amazing discovery. Then he took hold of a handful of long, thin needles.

"Doc," I said, "my back hurts, not my head."

"No, no," said Dr. Chu. "Head secret. Is key."

*Oh shit.*

"Won't hurt bit," he said as he started to jam the needles into my head. After inserting four of them, he stopped. "All better."

I looked at him like he was crazy.

"How feel?" said the intense Dr. Chu.

And to tell the truth, I felt pretty good. "Is key," said Dr. Chu. "You have it now." Hey, if this helped, I would have told Eddie Wagner to cut holes in my helmet so the needles could stick out on Sunday. I looked at myself in the mirror. I looked like My Favorite Martian.

Dr. Chu massaged my back a little and then I was anxious to test it out, so we cleared the furniture out of the doctor's hallway to give me ten or fifteen feet of running room and I went charging up and down the corridor. Pretty good. But I wanted to really let it out. So out I went into the chilly parking lot at 11 P.M., with four needles sticking out of my head. I started to run sprints, as hard as I could. If any nosy neighbor happened to peer out of the window, he or she would have sworn we were being invaded by creatures from outer space.

So much for acupuncture. The pain pierced my back again. Ten minutes later, I reported back to Paul. "Feels good," I told him, "but I think I overdid it."

We went back inside, where Dr. Chu went to work on my back as I lay across his table. Every time he stuck in another needle, he said, "It better now, right?" But it wasn't. After my back looked like a pincushion, I just said, "Thanks, Doc," and I pulled the needles out of my head. Paul couldn't believe it. "Send us the bill," he told Dr. Chu.

When I got home, I told Colleen I didn't think I'd be playing on Sunday.

I had done all I could to be ready to play. On Wednesday, the day we held our first practice, the pain was so bad that I had tears in my eyes. "I can't practice," I told Bill. "I can't run."

There wasn't much improvement on Thursday and although I tried to convince people I was okay, I knew better. All the while, I kept telling myself that if I was able to play that game, I didn't care if I played the rest of the season. When we got to Washington on Saturday, I tried to loosen it up in the hotel pool, but it didn't improve. I couldn't play and I had to tell Bill the truth. "But if you need me . . ."

I was totally depressed. This was Washington, the game we had been waiting for. We were both 11–2, and the winner of this game was going to win the division. And I was going to have nothing to do with it. I really did some searching and thought back on what I could have done differently to prevent the injury in the first place. My back was strong. In fact, I had the strongest back on the team. No one on the team can squat as much as I can, and no one can do hyperextensions, which are really reverse sit-ups, like I can. Then, suddenly, it was obvious. My back was too strong for my stomach. I didn't have the strength in my abdominals to support my back. My legs were strong. My hamstrings were strong. Everything was strong except for my abdominals.

When you're in a position like I am, if you have any weak points, they're going to be exposed sooner or later. Weak ankles, weak knees, weak shoulders, anything weak is going to go because your body is going to be flexed, stretched, bent, and tested in all varieties of positions. I knew that and that's what angered me because I had neglected my sit-ups and stretching. I always prided myself on how hard I worked and now I had to look at myself and say, *I should have worked harder.*

A lot of good it did then but I promised myself that I'd never let that happen again. *I'm not leaving anything to chance. I'm going to stretch my ass off, take karate for flexibility, and work my abdominals to death. I'm going to work, work, work, work. If the back eventually goes, I'll be miserable, but at least I'll know that I left nothing unturned.* And I couldn't say that last year.

It had cost me the Redskin game. But I did what I could to help the team and that meant getting Erik Howard ready to play my position. Erik was activated from injured reserve and was going to start ahead of Jerome. I knew center Jeff Bostic and the Redskins' line by heart. I tutored Erik on what keys to look for, how to read run or pass. He was nervous going into the game; who wouldn't be in that position, a rookie making his first start ever in the most important game of the regular season. He had problems with stamina because he had played only sporadically during the season, but he did a fine job, especially since we do more slanting against the Redskins. He's strong, he's got a great motor, and he's going to be a great player. Not too soon, of course, if I can help it.

While I was preparing Howard, Leonard was busy drilling Brad, who, according to John Madden, was involved in one of the two key matchups of the week—Brad against their fast-talking defensive end Dexter Manley, Joe Jacoby against Lawrence Taylor. Sack or be sacked: that's how Madden saw the game. He who gets to the quarterback shall reap the spoils. Leonard did his part by impersonating Manley in practice and by psyching Brad all week, telling him he was going to kick Dexter's ass.

Manley did his part just by opening his mouth, which he does so well. Before Joe Gibbs could sprint over to him and gag him, Manley told reporters that he had "a vendetta" to settle against Brad and the Giants, and that our offensive line coach, Fred Hoaglin, would know what he meant. Who really ever knows what Dexter is talking about? All Brad knew was that the pressure was on him. When it was over, he said the week had been hell for him, though he did manage to tell Madden the day before the game that he was going to name his pet dog "Dexter." I'll say this for Brad. Sunday, December 7, 1986, was his finest hour. And no one was happier for him than I was.

Right there, on the game's first play, Dexter put on a bull rush and Brad put him on his ass, which is exactly what you have to do with a momentum player like Dexter. Shut him off early and you've got him. Well, Brad owned him. Dexter didn't even smell Phil the rest of the game and Brad, with that ugly boil on the bridge of his nose caused by the rubbing of his helmet, became an instant celebrity—recognition that was long overdue.

There was a long story behind what happened that afternoon and since. It goes back ten years, which was how long Brad had to put up with hearing how he supposedly wasn't big enough or talented enough or whatever. People just never believed in Brad. I've gone through a lot myself, but it was nothing compared to what Brad went through. They always downplayed him, always moved him around to a different position, always looked to get somebody in to replace him. They even drafted William Roberts on the first round in 1984 and he still couldn't take Brad's job away, even though they gave him his chance.

It's a known fact that Ray Perkins wanted to run Brad out of there. Bill Austin, the line coach under Perkins, blamed Brad for everything, like he was some sort of dog. How those tables have turned. I remember how Brad suffered under Austin and still, he was such a nice guy that he invited Austin to his wedding. And Austin almost got in a fight with Brad's best man when he said that Brad was a lousy player, right at Brad's reception. Yet Brad stuck it out through all of that.

I just don't know if I could have survived like he did. One thing I demand is respect. I couldn't play if I didn't get it. Brad never got it, yet from the day I came to the Giants, I always thought he was a good football player. The bad rap didn't break Brad but it wore on his confidence. Brad's the kind of person who tends to doubt himself anyway. In fact, he always psyched himself up for games by getting deathly afraid of his guy beating him. Sometimes that worked in reverse because he was afraid to make a mistake, which the coaching staff would surely let him hear about.

Brad's confidence began to rise when Austin was replaced

Colleen, Jimmy, and me at the Pro Bowl in Hawaii.

Who said Mark Bavaro never smiles? *(Blair Holley)*

Joe Morris pulls away from Ken Woodard of the Broncos. *(Ira N. Golden)*

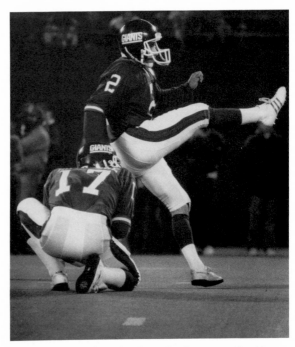

Raul kicks a field goal to beat the Broncos. *(Ira N. Golden)*

Brad Benson answers questions about his nose.
*(Jerry Pinkus)*

Lawrence sacking Steve Pelleur of the Cowboys.
*(Blair Holley)*

Phil drops back early in his MVP
performance. *(Bill Cummings)*

John Elway on the run in the second half of Super
Bowl XXI. *(Bill Cummings)*

Mark Bavaro crosses himself after his TD catch in Pasadena. *(Bill Cummings)*

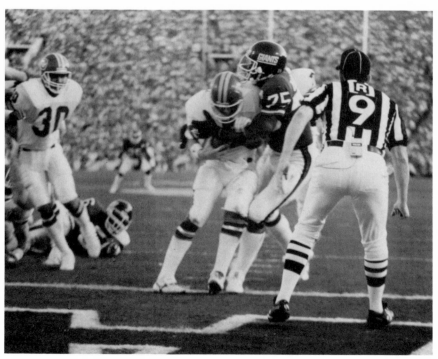

Pops has Elway in his grasp for the safety. *(Bill Cummings)*

At the Pro Bowl (*left to right*): Harry, Mark, Sean, Joe, me, Leonard, Lawrence, and Brad. I'm sure Sean tried to get the phone number of the Hawaiian woman in the middle. *(Chris Schwenk)*

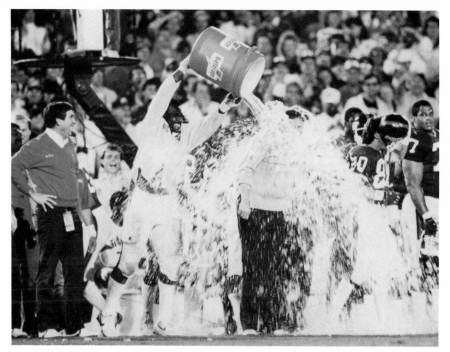

Harry gives Bill his bath as the seconds tick off on our Super Bowl victory. *(Bill Cummings)*

High-fiving fans on the way to the Rose Bowl locker room. *(Bill Cummings)*

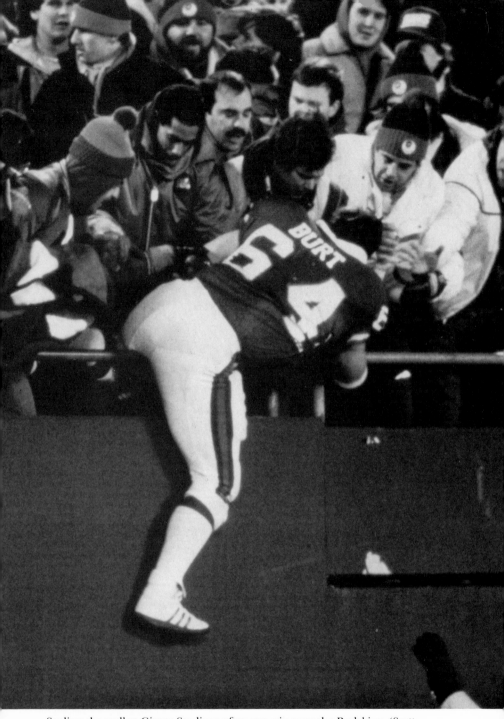

Scaling the wall at Giants Stadium after our win over the Redskins. *(Scott Cunningham/NFL Photos)*

by Tom Bresnahan, a coach who finally treated him as a good player. It continued when Hoaglin took over for Bresnahan in 1985. All of a sudden, Brad didn't look that bad to a lot of people. And you know what? He really was the same player. If he wasn't successful in his early years it was only because he had no self-confidence.

Well, that all changed for good at RFK Stadium. Brad played like a champion. Everyone did. And if certain people didn't feel it until then, they knew it after the game: we were the best team in football, and the Redskins were probably next after us. For more than a quarter of scoreless football, we slugged it out like a couple of prizefighters feeling each other out. But our defensive game plan was working. We needed to flush Jay Schroeder out of the pocket, then dare him to throw deep. Clark didn't matter. We'd be there covering him. And with Lawrence undressing Joe Jacoby, Schroeder was under constant pressure. Even when Lawrence wasn't making one of his three sacks, he was an intimidating force on Schroeder, who couldn't seem to keep his mind off our pass rush, for good reason. When the day was finished, Schroeder had given up six interceptions and was sacked four times as our defense attacked in waves.

Our offense got on course with our first possession of the second quarter. Mark Bavaro made the first big play of the game, by tipping and controlling Phil's pass, then rumbling for a 27-yard gain to the Redskins' 37. Joe got ten yards and a first down in two carries. A 19-yard completion to Bobby Johnson out of a moving pocket on third and 14 got us to the Washington 13. Joe got four more before Mark freed himself on a quick post and caught Phil's first touchdown pass of the day.

It could have been 14−0 had Mark not inexplicably dropped a pass at the Washington 18 after the Redskins' secondary left him wide open. That break led to the Redskins' first touchdown. Washington moved seventy-five yards for the tying TD but fifty-four of those came on a flukey Schroeder-to-Clark completion. Headen hit Schroeder just as the ball left his hand and it fluttered downfield. Clark came back to the ball to make the catch and spun away from Perry Williams all the way to our 26. Kelvin Bryant, who later was reduced to being the Redskins' only weapon, finished off the drive with a four-yard run. It was 7–7 and less than 2:00 remained in the half. Time for Phil to explode another myth, that he couldn't direct a 2:00 offense. This one was perfect.

Phil worked a no-huddle offense from our 19 to a third and seven at our 40. The offensive line gave him great protection and Phil made a great throw to Bobby up the right sideline for a 34-yard gain. Thirty-nine seconds remained. The Redskins went to a safety blitz but Maurice picked it up, Stacy Robinson made the sight adjustment and Phil zipped a quick out to him for nineteen yards to Washington's seven. Twenty-nine seconds. Brad forced Manley upfield, Phil stepped up in the pocket and found Bobby alone in the back of the end zone. The touchdown gave us all sorts of momentum going into the locker room. Nothing like a successful 2:00 drill for that.

The third quarter, as usual, was ours. Lee Rouson slipped into the backfield for one play and made a 21-yard catch. Bavaro picked up twenty-two and Phil hit a couple of key third-down passes. We held onto the ball for thirteen plays and went up, 17–7, on a field goal by Raul. Our defense took the field knowing the next series was critical. Schroeder had been bringing the Redskins from behind all year long and a touchdown here, in front of the RFK Stadium crowd, could send the momentum on a U-turn.

We didn't allow that to happen. On the very first play from scrimmage, Schroeder looked for Clark but Harry made an alert, veteran play. He didn't bite at Art Monk, who was running an underneath route, but stayed back in his zone and made the interception when Schroeder never bothered to check him off. Harry's 20-yard return set us up again at the 14-yard line of the Redskins. Two plays later, from the 16, Phil Mc-Conkey gave Darrell Green an inside move, then headed back out for the corner to make an over-the-shoulder, juggling catch of Phil's pass. Bavaro picked McConkey up in the air to celebrate a 17-point lead. As for me, I bent forward to peer up the sidelines and when I saw McConkey in Bavaro's arms, I lifted mine over my head. I wasn't going to get carried away again, like I had in San Francisco.

Still, there was 3:11 left in the third quarter, plenty of time for the Redskins to get back in the game. Like I said, Schroeder had been a comeback quarterback and by using Bryant out of the backfield he picked his way up to our 12-yard line, where it was second and three. Once again, Old Reliable, George Martin, made the big play at the critical time. This time, he got inside on his pass rush and with Schroeder looking for a wide-open Monk and the first down, George stuck his hand up there to bat away the pass, right into Leonard's hands for another interception.

The Redskins were through for good on their next series, when Andy Headen made it six interceptions off Schroeder, the same quarterback who had been intercepted just eleven times in the thirteen previous games. A fourth-quarter touchdown by Bryant made little difference as we practically locked up the division with a 24–14 win. At 12–2, we were tied for the best record in football with the Bears, but we held the advantage over Chicago in any tie-breakers that decided home-field advantage in the playoffs. We needed only one more win, or one Redskins loss, to officially clinch the NFC East. Washington obliged us the following Saturday by losing to the Broncos in Denver.

Personally, the pressure was off. I had two weeks left to rest my back if need be, and I recovered fast enough to play in our last game of the regular season against Green Bay. The fun was starting now, for both me and Brad. It was amazing what that one game against Manley did for Brad's confidence. He was like a new person after that. It was funny. During the game, Brian Johnston was trying to boost Brad's confidence, so he kept telling him how well he was playing against Dexter. At first, Brad downplayed it and told Brian he was just playing okay, but later, Brad let something slip that he probably wished he could retract as soon as the words left his mouth. "Yeah," he told Brian. "It's the best against the best out there." I made sure, of course, he would be reminded of that statement as the season wore on.

In fact, on our first day back, I schemed with the other offensive linemen, and they all wore No. 60 jerseys and Band-Aids on their noses into the line meeting. Brad loved it. It was probably the best week of his life. The papers finally came through for the baby boy he and his wife Lisa were adopting, he had that great game against Manley, and he received all that attention from Madden during the broadcast. He was named the NFL's Offensive Player of the Week, the first time a lineman ever got it. To cap it off, he was named to the Pro Bowl along with me, Lawrence, Harry, Leonard, Joe, Bavaro, and Landeta.

When we got the word, Brad and I looked at each other as if to say, Can you believe this? As two free agents, we probably enjoyed it most of all. I know I was flying on a cloud that day, thinking back to the tough times. Because of the injury, I hadn't been sure whether I was going to make it, so it was sort of a surprise for me. I called Colleen from the locker room and told her, "We did it. We made the Pro Bowl."

Respect, as I said, is so important to me and to be chosen among the best at my position by the league's players is something I was very proud of. Before that, the only all-star team I'd made in the pros was the All-Madden team selected by John

Madden himself. Oh yeah, my teammates call him my "Uncle John." I like him because he likes underdogs and that's what his All-Madden team is all about, battlers like me.

John even likes nose tackles because it's an underdog position. He explains it this way:

"No one wants to be a nose tackle. You can't go out for a pass, can't throw, can't run. You just stand over the center. It's like when you were a kid and nobody wanted to play right field. It was always the kid who couldn't play but who had the rich father and brought the ball. You always put him in right field. That's a nose tackle."

The day I made the Pro Bowl, I felt like a rich kid. One of my goals was complete. One more remained.

As for Brad, well, I think one story says it all. Ever since I'd known him, he always whined about how his body was falling apart and how he'd have to retire and how he had a degenerative hip and how he couldn't perform squats because of it. After he made the Pro Bowl, we didn't hear one word about his degenerative hip and he started doing squats again. Before, when I kidded around with him, he really freaked out. Now things weren't bothering him.

When the time came for our third game against the Redskins in the NFC championship, Brad had a totally different approach to Manley. He stayed low-key, of course, but by looking at him, you knew that he knew that he was going to whip Dexter again. It's amazing what confidence can do. Although I bust Brad's balls a lot—I was even more merciless after the Washington game—I was genuinely happy for him. He deserved it more than Simms. He deserved it more than me. He deserved it more than Taylor. I know a lot of people talked about how long George and Harry waited, and it's true, they deserved it more than most. But what about Brad? That guy deserved it more than *anyone* else. And that's the damn truth.

Our final two games of the regular season weren't without any meaning, and that's the way we played them. No letdowns. As soon as we beat the Redskins to win the division, we began to concentrate on the home-field advantage. No one wanted to go back to Soldier Field, and we all longed to get a shot at the Bears in our backyard. And all we had to do was beat the also-ran Cardinals and Packers in our final two games, both at home. By doing so, we could also set a club record for wins in a season with fourteen. The scores, 27–7 over St. Louis and 55–24 over Green Bay, tell most of the story.

I could have played against the Cardinals and I was so miffed that I didn't that I didn't say a word to anyone all week. Had we not taken control of the game so early, I might have gotten in but Bill, against my pleas, decided to hold me out to be safe. World gained 179 yards on the afternoon, outgaining the entire St. Louis running game by ninety-five, and we got ready for the Packers.

That one was no ordinary season finale. I was happy to return to action and give my back a clean bill of health. But let's put it this way. It wasn't one of the cleanest games ever. I don't know the reason for that but I do know that the Giants don't play dirty football. I don't know what the Green Bay players were told to do but it seemed that, more than in any other game, their players were trying to hurt our players.

It really was weird. I realize they were fighting for their jobs but cheap shots weren't going to help them, and that's what they were doing all day with late hits and cutblocks. Then to top it off, they got miffed when we worked a fake field goal and they started exercising their middle fingers in our direction. It was quite odd because we played the Packers before and we never experienced anything like that. But that game was a dirt fight, and it must have been directed that way by the coaches.

As for the game, we got off to a 24–0 lead early in the

second quarter, thanks in part to a blocked punt by Tom Flynn, one of two players on our team who started the season with Green Bay, Phil McConkey being the other. Our defense fell asleep for a while and the Packers pulled to within 24–17, but from then on, we turned on the jets and blew it wide open. World had 115 yards to break his own record for yards in a season—1516—and Phil finished strong with 245 yards on 18-of-25 passing. Five of those completions went to Bavaro, who finished the season with 1001 yards, highest ever by a Giant tight end.

We were ready for the playoffs and even more primed for the week off we earned by winning the division. That opening-night loss in Dallas seemed very far away.

# 14

## EAST RUTHERFORD

## Over the Wall

**H**ome for Christmas and we didn't even have to think about football. Two years earlier, we were away in Fresno, getting ready to play the 49ers. One year earlier, we were preparing for the 49ers in the wild-card game at home. This season, with five days off from Bill Parcells, we opened presents, ate Christmas dinner, and got ready to watch the Rams play the Redskins in the NFC wild-card game.

We still weren't sure who our next opponent would be. If the Rams won, they'd play us. If the Redskins won, we'd see the 49ers for the second time in the season. I didn't have a preference, but most of the guys would rather have played the Rams, who are basically a running team, and not the 49ers, who are more diverse with an experienced playoff quarterback in Joe Montana. Naturally, in a season where nothing came easy for us, the Redskins beat the Rams and left us with the 49ers, who also had that first week off after winning the NFC West.

For some reason, everybody was picking the 49ers. John Madden. Allie Sherman. Every expert on every program. Who was the 14 – 2 team, anyway? Why, we were, of course, but their thinking was that the 49ers were the hottest team coming into the playoffs. Huh? So we got mad, which was easy because of the electricity in the air that week. The week off really helped recharge us mentally. We felt the pressure, but it was good pressure and we adopted an attitude we never had a right to take before—that we, the New York Giants, deserved to win Super Bowl XXI and that the 49ers and whoever else followed them into the Meadowlands would be viewed as thieves, trying to take what was ours.

I didn't sleep that week, or the week after, for that matter. I kept thinking we *had* to win. It was like when I worked for my dad on the Pepsi truck and he'd give me a dollar. It might not sound like much, but that dollar meant a lot to me and whatever I spent it on meant a lot because I'd worked so hard for it. It was the same thing here. We worked for something and we couldn't throw it away, or the season would have meant nothing.

The day before the game, I watched the Redskins beat the Bears, and while disappointed that our chance for revenge was gone, all I could think about was the 49ers. And just watching that game got me ready to play.

Colleen helped, too. Once the most noncompetitive person in the world, my wife was getting into it by this time. I must have rubbed off after all those years. Anyway, she shocked me at the breakfast table the morning of the game by blurting, "Now go kick some ass today."

I figured that everybody on our team would feel the same way. But when I got to the stadium, a certain individual was still missing. He had been out late screwing around the night before and he didn't show until after warm-ups. Imagine that, in a big game like this. Like I've already said, though, our team is made up of a lot of character individuals and we quickly turned this into an internal matter. He was tried and convicted by his peers, the players. Just about everyone was jumping down his throat, saying, "Hey, man, that's f——ed up." The coaches didn't say one word to him. They didn't have to because the players were saying enough.

The other thing that bothered me that week was a story out of San Francisco in which a local newspaper diagrammed the play the 49ers use to cut defensive linemen down from behind, a practice that was made illegal for the 1987 season. The 49ers were actually bragging about it. They called it the Great Neutralizer. Bill Walsh said it's what they teach and they had been teaching it since 1981 when I first came into the league. It's their trademark to cut you down from behind where you're not looking. They talked about how defensive players don't like it and how it takes away their aggressiveness.

To be honest, it only helped fire me up. "If these guys want to play like this, *we* can play like this," I told a few guys, spreading the word. And on a few of our interception returns that day, we went after them and they knew it. There were more than a few of their people on the ground. When Jerry Rice, their Pro Bowl wide receiver, did some crack-back blocking on Robbie Jones, one of our backup linebackers, Kenny Hill stepped in and retaliated by spearing Rice. Kenny was later fined for it by the league, but in truth, he was acting in defense of a teammate. He hadn't started anything.

Though I didn't like them bragging, I wasn't that concerned because the Niners had always played that way and I expected it. I was more worried about the effectiveness of their running game. I'd seen them gain over a hundred yards in the first half while on the sidelines in Game 13. We had some problems on our left side that day.

Belichick and Parcells worked hard on Carl Banks all week until he got sick of watching the film. At our Saturday film session, Belichick kept telling Banks, "You're better than this. You're better than this." Carl's a hard worker and a dedicated athlete, and he really prepared himself for this one. Meanwhile, I suggested a small adjustment to George Martin.

Until that game George had been playing off the ball and whenever he was knocked back, it created a pile. I would try to scrape behind him to pursue the play outside but would only get caught up in traffic. I suggested that George overplay the outside and leave the inside to me. Secondly, I told George to move up on the line of scrimmage and to fire out on the 49er tackle, Keith Fahnhorst, as soon as the ball was snapped so that Fahnhorst couldn't get his momentum working on George.

"Don't worry about getting hooked," I said. "If he cuts you off to the inside, don't worry. I'll make up for it. Just get in there."

That's what he did and it worked great. I was able to slide, *whoosh*, with a clear lane to the outside and that helped shut down their running game. That and the fact that Banks totally dominated Russ Francis, who had given him problems in the previous game. Their final total on the ground was twenty-nine yards on twenty carries. We made sure they weren't going to get anything extra. Once we hit them, that's where they stopped. If anything, they were falling backwards. We could just feel that kind of performance building in the pre-game warm-ups, where I do my stretching right next to Lawrence. It's become a tradition for us to line up in the same spot in the back row. Then, coming out of the tunnel for the pre-game introductions, Lawrence and I butted heads. He was wearing his helmet. I wasn't.

I was ready. But it didn't exactly start out in a mad-dog way.

Our offense fizzled after three plays and Montana went to work. A quick play action pass worked for nine yards to Roger Craig, who only had the worst game of his life against us in the playoffs the year before when our footsteps echoed in his head. Then Craig hurdled his line for four yards and the first down. When the 49ers get their running game going, that really makes Montana dangerous because he can then hit short passes until his arm falls off. When you give Montana too many options, he's too good a player not to take advantage of something.

Here was that something. A two-step drop and a quick slant at midfield to Jerry Rice, who got inside our cornerback, Elvis Patterson, and was at least *looking* at six points, if he wasn't already counting them. I trailed the play, mainly as a spectator when, without being touched, Rice attempted to switch hands and dropped the ball at the 25-yard line as if one of those ghosts from our past had a pang of regret and stripped the ball away. I remember thinking, *There'll be more plays like this today. We can't turn guys loose like this.* But as far as changing the game, no way, even though the 49ers might have thought that as Kenny Hill recovered in our end zone. Maybe the final score would have been 49–10. Had Rice continued in for the touchdown, it just would have made us play harder. For this was our day, and our intensity level would have broken any thermometer. We were operating on a level above anything we'd ever played at before.

As it was, we marched eighty yards on the legs of Joe Morris. Bill had dubbed the offensive line, actually the entire running game, "Club 13" because we had totalled only thirteen yards on the ground in San Francisco. Joe surpassed that with his first carry of the series, a 15-yard gain on the flow play. Carries of six, six and eleven followed immediately. Bavaro got the touchdown by outmuscling cornerback Tim McKyer—no contest at all—for the 22-yard score.

Montana brought the Niners back to 7–3, after we stopped them at our nine-yard line to force a field goal. And that was as close as they got the rest of the day. The avalanche began to overtake them in the second quarter when they forgot to pick up Banks on a blitz—that happens a lot because teams are so concerned with Lawrence—and Carl nailed Montana head on in the midsection, the ball flapping into the air like a wounded bird. Herb Welch, the twelfth-round pick from UCLA who filled in for Terry Kinard at free safety, made the interception and that set up a 45-yard touchdown run by World on the very next play, a perfectly executed flow 38 play by the Club 13 contingent, which would end the day as Club 216.

Following a punt, we hit the 49ers with another ARAPA-HOE play. As Raul lined up for a 45-yard field goal, Rutledge, our normal holder, shifted into a shotgun formation and pulled the trigger with a pass to Bavaro for twenty-three yards. The 49ers were so confused that they picked up Raul Allegre, who lined up as a wide receiver, and forgot all about Bavaro, who was wide open. That set up a second Simms touchdown pass on third down as Phil was flattened by Riki Ellison, a blitzing linebacker.

A lot of quarterbacks would have ducked away but Phil hung in there and bulleted that pass to Bobby. When Phil got up, he didn't even know it was a touchdown. He needed smelling salts. He kept asking me, "Was it tipped? Was it a touchdown?"

The answers were "no" and "yes" and if anyone had said then that Phil had no guts, he would have had to answer to *me*. We were taking the game by the throat and led, 21 – 3.

In a matter of moments, it would really be over. Montana was at his 18-yard line and looking to get something as the end of the half drew near. We rushed three guys with our linebackers deep in that stinking prevent defense that I hate. I mean, it's terrible. When we rush just three men, two of them are getting double-teamed and the other guy is triple-teamed. With maximum protection, a quarterback can't help but complete the pass.

But what happened shocked me, and, I'm sure, Montana as well. Fred Quillan, their center, engaged me, and Randy Cross, their right guard, started to come down on me. But to my surprise, there was no one on my right side since that guard, Guy McIntyre, was double-teaming Leonard. I grabbed Quillan's pads and made a move around him to get myself through their gap. I couldn't believe I was free. There was Joe Montana right in my face and I just ran right through him, creasing him in two as he barely managed to let go of the ball.

My momentum came underneath Joe's shoulder pads and I felt him leave his feet. He went flying and I just jumped over him. By the sound of the crowd, I knew it was quite an impact. The ball never reached its target. Instead, Lawrence jumped inside Jerry Rice and had a clear 45-yard path to the end zone for our fourth touchdown of the day. I turned around, saw the interception and just sprinted over to mob L.T. I didn't see Montana laying there until the play was over. I went over to see if he was okay and when I saw that he was unconscious with what turned out to be a concussion, it really bothered me. I respect the guy a lot. He had come back from back surgery and I know how tough that can be. And he's always shown a lot of class. In the two years he beat us and went on to the world championship, he never talked any trash afterwards. A lot of guys throw a little in your face. He is never like that. He is always a gentleman. Despite being a two-time Super Bowl MVP, he has never been cocky.

It may be a contact sport but it's played by people and you hate to see a guy laying there on a cold day like that. It was an eerie feeling. McIntyre, who didn't even see the play, threatened me. "We're gonna get you for that," he said.

"Why don't you go f—— yourself," I said. "It was a clean shot and if you want to start something, go right ahead."

I knew it was no cheap shot and I'm glad they made that clear on TV. I always try to avoid hitting a quarterback low. I don't want to hurt anybody's knees. I try to hit him as high as possible and if he's running away from me, I dive at him so he knows I'm coming. There's no reason to deliberately hit anyone low. You're there to make a play and sack him. You don't need to cripple the guy or end his career.

When Montana left the game, we knew we had taken control. "We just dropped the H-bomb on them," Lawrence said. They would have had to play in an awesome way to beat us and they were without their best player. Even our amazing comeback at Candlestick wouldn't have been enough for them. Instead, we were the awesome ones in the third quarter, adding three more touchdowns to create the final score, 49–3. Unbelievable, especially against a team like the 49ers. "We were shattered by a great team," said an embarrassed Bill Walsh.

At that point I figured what goes around comes around, because the most embarrassing losses I ever experienced came back-to-back in 1984, 33–12, against the Rams in Anaheim, and 31–10 at home against the 49ers the following Monday night, when they jumped off to a 21–0 lead in the first quarter. Had we come a long way. We were clicking on all cylinders now. Phil, who threw four of his nine completions for touchdowns, was frighteningly efficient, and Joe, with 159 yards against the 49ers, was running with a vengeance out of our winterized game plan. And our defense, well, I don't think anybody, not even the Bears of 1985, had played defense any better. Yet, though our victory over the 49ers was so complete and so dominant, no one felt comfortable or secure. Our job was hardly over and that locker room was more businesslike than jubilant.

And I couldn't stop thinking about Joe Montana. I felt bad. Here he was, left behind in the hospital and I felt as if I had gotten something at someone else's expense. Besides, I had to warn him about the food over there. If it was somebody I didn't like, I wouldn't care, but I like Joe. I grabbed something to eat, got clearance, and headed straight for the hospital in New York. That's how I celebrated our playoff win.

I guess Joe was surprised to see me. We talked for about half an hour about our two common interests, football and backs.

Joe was added to the list of the four quarterbacks we KO'd

during the season. I know a ridiculous story surfaced during Super Bowl week that we had a bounty on quarterbacks, but it was just one of those things. We're going to have more hits on the quarterback than a lot of other teams because we're coming from all directions. If the quarterback doesn't step up and move around, he'll get hit. It just depends on how and where that happens. The bounty stuff was bullshit.

Joe knew it was a clean hit, too. "Go for the ring," he said, even though he later picked the Broncos to beat us in the Super Bowl. *Yeah, the ring,* I thought, now closer to it than ever before. But first the Redskins. Always the Redskins.

It was a strange week preparing for the Redskins because really, what is there to prepare for? We know them, they know us, it's like playing your brother in one-on-one basketball. We concentrated a lot on their two playoff games against the Rams and Bears. I concentrated on being low-key. I avoided the press corps, which was growing larger and larger like some runaway amoeba and asking every question imaginable, from Jay Schroeder's rifle arm to Ed Koch's ticker tape parade. I didn't even want my name in the paper that week. I didn't want anything to break my concentration on the game because I was trying to build up to a pitch that I had never attained before. I kept thinking back six years when our defense first started taking shape and our team wasn't very good at all. I kept thinking how far we had come—indeed, to the team's first championship game since 1963 with an opportunity to win the Giants' first championship since 1956. Thirty years.

The only departure I made from my tunnel-vision approach was to give the occasional needle to Brad. I mean, how could I resist, and besides, it served to break up the tension in the locker room. Billy Ard had already started on him the previous Saturday night, after the Redskins beat the Bears. Brad didn't feel well. "You've got the Dexter flu coming on again, huh?" Billy asked him. Brad, who always used to flip, just flipped him the bird this time. There really was a big difference in how he approached Manley now. He knew he would kick his ass. I knew I could have some fun with it. So when the swarm of reporters got loose for their half-hour interview sessions at lunchtime, I got on the locker PA to announce Brad's arrival from the lunchroom.

"Now entering the locker room, Brad Benson," I said in a John Facenda-like tone. "The man who named his dog Dexter. The best against the best."

Brad took his chaw of tobacco and sat down. "Another week of hell," he said. For the Redskins, maybe.

That Sunday, January 11, had "Giants" written all over it. The Hawk had flown over from Chicago to join our team and was sending gusts up to thirty-five miles an hour bouncing around Giants Stadium like never before in a game. Inside, where we sat on the brink of destiny, the locker room walls reflected our mood, stone-cold and mean. I had accomplished my goal of fever pitch and I noticed that everyone else felt likewise. I walked around the locker room, making sure to say something to everybody, nervous but ready to explode. I'm always able to turn on the switch and start a flow of adrenalin. I don't need uppers to get ready for a game. I've got an internal drugstore and for this one, I was soaring.

I knew I would be a focal point for the Redskins' attack. They had whammed the hell out of Rams' nose tackle Shawn Miller in their first playoff game, and I was ready for it. A wham, one of the classic plays of nose guard football, is exactly how it sounds. The center hits me then turns back on the end, in this case Leonard, causing me to take a step along with him. That freezes me up and if it works the right way for them, I'm standing there flat-footed while their lead blocker, with a full head of steam from lining up in the backfield, is snorting and taking dead aim at me, hoping to knock my ass to Hackensack, creating a hole that's too big for the linebacker to fill. My key is to read it and squeeze the hole by standing up the wham guy, and forcing the runner in an arc to the outside, where the pursuit makes the tackle.

Before I got to all that fun, the Redskins made a key mistake. They called tails, or rather the spokesman for their six co-captains called tails. Harry, our lone representative for the coin toss, had been given instructions by Bill: "Forget the ball. If we win the toss, take the wind." Harry knew, because while the linebackers were trying to play catch in the warm-ups, the ball kept floating away from them. "This is like trying to catch a knuckleball," he said. So when heads came up, Harry used his: "We'll take this side of the field." The Redskins got the ball, our cutthroat defense, and the wind all at once.

Then they rolled out their surprise for me. Raleigh McKenzie, their six-foot-two, 262-pound tank of a backup guard, lined up in the backfield, with the assignment of whamming the shit out of me. "McKenzie's in the backfield," somebody shouted on our side of the line. My first reaction was shock, because they'd never done that before. That was more like a short yardage offense. My second reaction was to rub my hands together and say, "Great." I knew they were coming with the power game. That would make it easy to read. I buckled my chin strap tight and said, "Here we go."

Here they went. On the first play from scrimmage, McKenzie came charging through and kind of jolted me. Still, I stood him up and Banks tackled George Rogers after a two-yard gain. I guess maybe I got the better of our collision, because on the second play from scrimmage, McKenzie came in a little softer. Lawrence made the play. By the third time they tried it, McKenzie was like a marshmallow. Eventually, they junked it. And in the second half, in fact, they tried only one running play.

After the Redskins got only four yards in their first three

plays, the wind became a factor for the first time. Steve Cox, their punter, got off a kick that hit a stone wall of wind after twenty-three pitiful yards. Our ball at their 47. All we really needed was a 14-yard run by World as he turned the right corner and a five-yard carry on the next play. Raul took the field with the hurricane at his back and launched a 47-yard field goal through the goal posts with just 3:22 gone in the game.

The Redskin offense was out there for just three more plays before Cox came out to face the wind again. He did better this time. Twenty-seven yards. Our ball at their 38. It looked as though we would have to settle for another field goal when on third down, Phil's pass to Stacy Robinson was incomplete. But fate interceded. Our center, Bart Oates, was called for holding and the Redskins decided to move us back ten yards to the 36, which would have made it a 53-yard try for Raul. Instead, Phil faded back and found Lionel Manuel, our long-lost wide receiver, running a post for a 25-yard gain to their 11-yard line. On third and 10, Phil found Lionel again, this time for the touchdown. Phil did a good job of stepping up in the pocket away from the pressure and Lionel moved with him, left alone when the Redskins messed up on a switch. The Redskins could already sense their doom with the game just 9:28 old. It was 10 – 0 and nothing seemed to be going for them. Even our friend Gary Clark couldn't beat us. With steps on Elvis Patterson, a big gainer went off his fingers at our 30-yard line.

Maybe the Redskins thought things would change when they got the wind in the second quarter. They didn't. With the second period less than 2:00 old, Sean Landeta waddled out to try his luck with the teeth of an all-too-familiar wind. Cox had done no better than a 27-yard effort and with Landeta punting from midfield, the Redskins figured to take over at about their 25. Landeta took the snap and got off the most amazing punt I've ever seen. The ball exploded off his leg and soared incredibly high, never losing its tight spiral, but rather cutting through the air for fifty-five yards. It finally came to rest at their four-yard line. I'd never seen anything like it.

"Makes up for Chicago," someone said.

"I wouldn't go that far," I said. But it was incredible.

Unfortunately, we couldn't keep the Redskins in the hole Landeta had dug for them, for on the first play, Art Monk got behind Elvis Patterson up the right sideline and Schroeder, glad to have the wind, dropped it into his arms for a 48-yard play. They reached our 36 with a first and 10 and Rogers gained a quick four off right tackle. Second and six. I lined up in the gap between the center and guard and they went with their sweep to our right. Being off the center, I was able to shoot in and get penetration. I met Rogers two yards behind the line of scrimmage and planted him there for a loss. Schroeder missed with a bomb and Jess Atkinson, one of our old kickers, came out to try a 51-yard field goal with the wind at his back. Except he never got the chance. The snap bounced past Schroeder, who was holding, and Banks recovered at their 49-yard line.

With one 30-yard pass to Bavaro, we were at their 17. A couple of plays later, Phil ran a naked bootleg to their one, and Joe finished the drive from there. Giants 17, Redskins 0. Washington had one more threat before the half was over, but we stopped Rogers on a fourth and one call from our 28-yard line. No one scored in the entire second half, although it took long enough because the Redskins ran only one running play while exhausting Schroeder's arm with thirty-four passes. That wasn't Redskins football. But the shutout was Giants football. Two playoff games against two of the best offenses in the league and we had allowed only a field goal. For seven quarters in a row, we threw a shutout. And as the end of the game drew near, along with the Giants' first title in thirty years and a trip to Pasadena to play Denver, a storm of paper rained from the upper decks, giving the place a surreal look.

There's nothing like the feeling when you know that you're headed for the Super Bowl (except, of course, when you know that you've *won* the Super Bowl), and for our team and our fans this was something special. I even grabbed my first Gatorade bucket in two years and emptied it over Harry, who had already doused Bill. The coach had smuggled a water pistol under his jacket but was outmatched. It was wild. And then, I decided to do what I did next.

With the Giants, season tickets get handed down from generation to generation. For six years, the same people have been sitting behind our bench, yelling encouragement. I can't say I knew their faces, but I certainly knew their voices. And being a Buffalo Bills fan for so long, I knew their frustration, as well. I don't know what possessed me, but when I looked back into the stands and saw Colleen, I figured, *What the hell.* I tossed my helmet to one of the equipment men and headed for the wall, a ten-foot-high barrier with a thick railing on top. But after all, I am an amazing athlete, contrary to the scouting reports. Somehow, I jumped up, grabbed the railing with one hand and pulled myself up and over into the stands.

I was just so happy for us and for the people who had waited thirty years. I started high-fiving hands in a sea of fans that was spilling down in droves from above. My initial plan was to make my way up to the top, but that became impossible. As for getting hurt or squashed, I had no fear. At that point, I could have been clubbed with a bat and I wouldn't have felt a thing. It was marvelous. But finally, I said, "Hey, I'll see you," and hopped back down to the field. I got them all riled up and left. But as I made my way to the locker room, I did a goofy dance, making up the steps as I went, spinning, hopping, and pumping my arm.

And suddenly, I was back in Buffalo, hopping from rooftop to rooftop with my friends after ringing somebody's doorbell and running. There's nothing as exhilarating as the thrill of being chased, or the thrill of finally winning the chase.

Bring on the Broncos.

# 15

## COSTA MESA

## Almost Heaven

California, here I was, seven days away from the Super Bowl, as close as I've been to this game of games since Elbert Dubenion.

Yes, that's right. Elbert Dubenion.

What a receiver. What a Buffalo Bill. What a letdown.

It was New Year's Day, 1967, as cold an afternoon as Buffalo could muster and my Bills were playing the Kansas City Chiefs for the American Football League championship and the right to play the Green Bay Packers in the very first Super Bowl. I was seven years old and my dad and I were huddled among a crowd of 42,000 in the end zone seats at old War Memorial Stadium. I was as psyched as I was cold. We, the Bills that is, had a powerhouse offense that season, led by quarterback Jack Kemp and a backfield of Bobby Burnett and Wray Carlton.

I was a pretty happy kid when Kemp unleashed his arm and connected with Dubenion for a 68-yard touchdown pass that tied the score, 7 – 7, in the first quarter. We were on our way. My Bills were going to the Super Bowl! My Bills were going to the Super Bowl!

Well, not quite. Len Dawson took over the game and in the

fourth quarter little Mike Garrett got loose for a couple of TD runs that turned the game into a rout, 31 – 7, Kansas City. And *Giant* fans thought they'd suffered long.

I remember at one point turning to my dad and saying, "Dad, I can go down there and play. I can do that." And I was serious. That's how early I started carrying this dream around with me, a dream I would finally realize in one short week. It was a dream that faded at times, a dream I wasn't sure was realistic. But it never went away.

It was funny. All week, my mind kept flashing back instead of looking ahead. I thought about the 1982 season, when the dream started coming into focus. The Redskins won the Super Bowl that season and we should have beaten them twice. Instead, we lost in overtime on a squib kick at home, then lost at RFK Stadium when Mark Moseley kicked a late field goal. When Washington won the Super Bowl that year, I said, "Hell, if they can win it, *we* can win it."

Then came 1983, our 3 – 12 – 1 disaster, but it was only a temporary setback. I knew we had a lot of work to do. I just hoped that I could stay healthy until the year we'd be good enough to make it. I was thinking about those feelings during Super Bowl week as my memory conjured up stories I'd long forgotten, mostly to do with the tough times when things could have gone one way or the other. There were so many of those, maybe a hundred, and it seemed as if I remembered them all.

Mostly, I thought about the great opportunity I had now and that I didn't want to blow it, because you never know when another chance will come along. Look at my favorite player, O.J. Simpson. As great as he was, he never did get to play in a Super Bowl.

At the same time, I couldn't imagine us losing. I thought how I wouldn't be able to live with myself if we lost, that I wouldn't be able to listen to everybody saying that we should have won. It's weird but it's almost better *not* to get to the

Super Bowl than to get there and lose. As happy as people in New York were when we won, they would have been just as angry had we lost. That would have been a tragedy. *All or nothing*, I kept thinking, *all or nothing*.

It made for a lot of pressure and even though there wasn't much said about it, we were all walking around like little time bombs, ready to play the game on Tuesday or Wednesday. People were always wondering why we never seemed to celebrate after our victories. That's because there wasn't anything in our minds but winning the ring. Anything short of that this year wasn't going to be good enough. There was a sign hanging from the control tower at Newark Airport: Giants #1. It was the last thing we saw of New Jersey as our plane lifted off for California. We wanted it to be there when we came home.

I was also scared. We were 8½-point favorites and that got us nervous. I had no doubt in my mind that we were the better team. We were ready to play. We knew we should win. But the football can take funny bounces and the momentum can change quickly. For instance, a team can start playing over their heads. I know that happened to us this year, that we played over our heads, maybe to the point where we really got to be that good.

With all these thoughts playing catch in my head, it would have been too easy to be overwhelmed by the magnitude of the Super Bowl. My approach was to have as much fun as I could for a few days, then put everything aside at the end of the week to concentrate on the game. I didn't want to get too psyched too early, even though I was already itchy to play because of the week off we'd already had after the championship game. So I had fun. In one short week, I almost had Brad arrested and Johnny Parker picked up in a gay gym. I caught a record seagull on a fishing expedition and I even told an off-color joke on the Joan Rivers Show.

Our plane ride to destiny was a little unlike any we'd taken all year, even though it got off to a slow start when a snowstorm turned a regular fifteen-minute bus ride from Giants Stadium to Newark Airport into a forty-five-minute haul. Most of us took it in stride, except for the hyperactive McConkey. He wanted to jump ship and walk to the airport, until Bavaro settled him down.

Once we got airborne, I felt hungry so I sat next to William Roberts, our six-foot-five, 280-pound backup tackle. If you want extra food on a plane, just sit with Willie. He butters up all the stewardesses so they slip him bonus portions. On this flight, they were giving out shrimp cocktail appetizers. Willie must have gotten twenty or thirty extra plates. I love shrimp so I didn't even bother to eat the meal, though Willie did eat his entree. In the meantime, we were sharing the shrimp. One for me. Two for him. Two for me. Four for him. Willie's mouth is a lot bigger than mine. So is his stomach.

Finally, Willie got full, so he stashed a bunch of full dishes underneath his seat for later—Willie eats every hour on the hour. In the meantime, I was picking at his shrimp when he wasn't looking. In the sixty minutes it took for him to regain his appetite, I cleaned out his reserves. When he reached underneath again, he came up empty. Then he saw me chewing on the last one. He started screaming in a high-pitched voice, "My shrimp! My shrimp!"

The whole plane ride was a little unlike any we'd taken all year. You didn't see any nervousness. It was almost a party atmosphere. We had a big card game going. Lawrence, Gary Reasons, Eric Dorsey, Damian Johnson, Erik Howard, Elvis Patterson and Andy Headen were all playing at one time or another. I sat in there for about forty minutes and won four hundred dollars. The big losers were Dorsey the tightwad and Howard the amateur. We were teaching Howard how to play as we went along. He didn't know that a flush beat a straight. He was in trouble. We took no pity on his second-round salary.

We landed late in the afternoon at Long Beach Airport. Or was it Newark? Giants fans seemed to be everywhere. Although we got straight off our plane and onto a bus, we could see them climbing the chain link fences, acting like animals. That was a tip-off they weren't Californians. Some of them followed us on the ride over to the hotel, the South Coast Plaza in Costa Mesa. One car rode alongside our bus with people hanging out the sunroof. Another lunatic followed us by bike. Our bus made a wide turn to get on the San Diego Freeway and that forced the biker into the opposite lane, where he was riding head-on into traffic. But he didn't care. He kept pedaling and pumping his arm into the air as cars swerved to avoid him. He didn't even seem to notice them. Sometimes, you'd like to put some of these fans into a uniform.

The hotel lobby was jammed, too, but we avoided the crowd by entering through the back door to the kitchen. Bill said that if we wanted go down to talk to reporters it was up to us. The first guy downstairs was Landeta, who never can resist a little ink. He told them he had to use the phone to call his girl-friend, which one in his harem of two hundred I don't know. He didn't say why he couldn't use the phone in his room. Every paper in the country had a Sean Landeta story the next day.

By dinnertime, the place was a mob scene and it took us about thirty minutes to make our way through the lobby to our cars. There was no curfew until Thursday night but we weren't near anyplace that resembled Bourbon Street. The hotel restaurant required jackets—this was California?—and across the mall from our hotel was a newly constructed Center for the Performing Arts. Talk about contrasts. We were sharing the hotel with the New York City Opera Company.

It didn't surprise me that everything was first class, including an arrangement that provided one Super Bowl car per room. Brad, Billy Ard, Brian Johnston, Karl Nelson, Erik Howard and I took three of them to a Mexican restaurant. Dinner was good. Nelson scrutinized the bill, of course, and after everything was in order, we headed back to the hotel.

Howard was driving in one car with me. Billy was driving my car with Brian. Brad was driving Karl. Howard—he's crazy anyway—started playing chicken with our car so Brad just had to show what a great driver he was. You know Brad, alias Mr. Car. He was swerving from one lane to the next like he was A.J. Foyt.

Suddenly, Billy Ard and I spotted a police car waiting in ambush up the street and I motioned to Billy. No one alerted Brad. He swerved from the far left to the far right lane, right in front of the cop. All of a sudden, we saw the lights start flashing as he pulled Brad over. I mean Brad of all people— Mr. Car, Mr. Hunter, Mr. Dog. Of course, we all felt sorry for him. We rushed to his aid and laughed our asses off while he squirmed his way out of it. He avoided a ticket because the cop saw the Super Bowl logo on the car. Still, it instantly became part of Brad Benson lore.

Monday night brought our first meeting with that herd of cattle otherwise known as the national media. You hear all sorts of horror stories about what a circus this part of Super Bowl week can be but let me tell you, that's all overblown. A player is only obligated to do interviews for an hour each day and there are no interviews from the Thursday session until after the game. Sure, there are a lot of press people around but it's all in the way you approach it. I've never had problems with reporters. A few of them are even nice guys. My attitude coming into the week was to have fun with them and enjoy the attention. Of course, it never ended out there unless you made it end. Everybody and his brother wanted to do a TV spot, especially the New York stations. But that was up to you. You could always say no if it got to be too much.

The first night, five of us were led into this big ballroom at our hotel, where it was wall-to-wall with microphones, cameras, and notebooks. It looked just like our locker room. Really, I was used to it. They led us to these elevated platforms, where we sat at tables. It was kind of dangerous. I heard that one of the Broncos leaned back against his chair and fell off the platform. That would have been difficult for me. I had reporters in front of me, on the side of me, and in back of me. And I was really enjoying it, especially since Steve Serby from the *New York Post* was running back and forth between Brad and me, trying to re-create Sunday's Mr. Car incident. When the papers came out the next day, Brad slammed them in front of me on the breakfast table. "Look what you're doing to me," he moaned.

Hey, I was only trying to help Brad get some ink because he'd need it. Earlier in the week, Parcells was asked to name the player most likely to emerge as the media star of the week. "I'd have to pick McConkey," Bill said. "We've designated him the number one self-promoter on the team. He's passed Burt, who's still in the top five, and of course there's Landeta, who has always been in the top five."

Hmmm. How about Bill as No. 1? You should have seen him at his press conferences, basking in the attention, going through his standard repertoire, which we call S.O.S., code for Same Old Shit.

In fact, most of the questions I was asked had to do with my strange relationship with Bill, the Gatorade thing, and my dance in the stands. Somebody wanted to know what my first thought was when I heard the name Bill Parcells. I told him "Hemorrhoid." He couldn't believe it. Most of the national reporters couldn't understand how we get away with dumping on Bill like we do, but that's part of what makes our team click.

The dumbest question of the week came from a guy who wanted to know about sex the night before the game. I told them that on this team, there were a lot of guys who preferred to have sex with themselves. Bavaro had a better answer for the same guy. Deadpanning all the way, Mark told him, "I wouldn't know. I'm a virgin."

Bavaro was something that week. Most guys become media stars at the Super Bowl because of what they say. Mark became a celebrity because of what he didn't say. It got so bad that there were guys from New York area papers assigned not to interview Bavaro, but to cover his non-interviews with the press.

For Mark, the circus began on Tuesday, when we had to dress in uniform for something the NFL officially designated as Photo Day. Of course, reporters had access to us at the same time, which shocked the hell out of Mark. We were all lined up in a row on a football field at some junior college when they opened the gates for the media. They looked like an army of little ants as they descended upon us from the grandstands. Mark must have freaked. He stuck around for two minutes, then headed straight to the team bus, followed by a trail of press guys. He got on the bus and told the driver to lock the door. That's where he stayed for the next hour. "It was Picture Day," he explained. "I got my picture taken and left."

Later in the week, a writer asked Mark about his early-season foot injury.

"Broken toe," Mark said.

"Which toe?"

"Big toe."

"Which foot?"

"Right foot."

"Where'd you break it?"

"Philadelphia."

Photo Day was also Lawrence's big date with the media. He was cool, sitting up there on his own platform, leaning back and wearing shades. He made a lot of reporters' days when he said, "You know you're ready for the game when you feel like slapping your momma."

The guy I really noticed was Landeta, Mr. Hound himself.

He had made a beeline for a bunch of junior college cheer-leaders who were brought in for the occasion, and talked himself right into the middle of their kick line. Let's just say he had his hands full. When it was over he told me, "I got seven out of eight numbers." He said he was going to make the hay while the sun was shining. In California, the sun was shining a lot.

I don't know what Landeta did when that media session was over, but I took advantage of our day off by going deep-sea fishing with some of the offensive linemen and Tim Burke, a sea captain from New Jersey who takes Bill Parcells out on shark-hunting expeditions. We had Tuesday off because of Bill. The usual routine for Super Bowl teams is to arrive on Monday night and work out Tuesday through Friday. Bill, as he always does, did a lot of research and came to the conclusion that we'd be better off sticking to our regular season routine. We came out Sunday to get acclimated, had a good workout on Monday, then, except for that media obligation, we had Tuesday to ourselves. Captain Burke told us we were going after bonito, which is like a tuna—the fish, not Parcells. Bill was more like a piranha this week. The first thing I wanted to catch, however, was some sack time.

When I finished my nap we were well out on the Pacific. I climbed up on deck and said, "Bet I know who caught the biggest fish. It's gotta be Brad." After all, if he was Mr. Dog and Mr. Car, he had to be Mr. Fish, too.

I walked over to Brad and said, "Here, gimme that thing." I grabbed his rod and cast it off the side to see what I could come up with. Sure enough, I got a bite and by the struggle it was putting up, I knew it was a real whopper. Slowly but surely, I reeled in my prize bonito. Then it came into view. Bonito, hell. I'd hooked myself a seagull. Definitely not a keeper. Bart Oates let the lever go and the thing flew off until the line ran out, then, *boom*, it dropped straight down into the water. Finally, we got it close enough to the boat to get a good look at it. I'm telling you, those things are mean. I said, "Here, Brad" and handed him back the rod. Finally, the thing got itself unwound and flew off.

We weren't finished with Brad that week. Even though I was feeling sorry for him because of the car incident, Johnny Parker had a score to settle. Brad had stung Johnny good the week before by arranging for a friend of his to pose as a sportswriter in a phone interview. Bill Parcells might call McConkey, me, and Landeta self-promoters, but the worst has to be Parker—and Brad wanted to get it all on tape. Johnny's wife Jane answered the phone and since Johnny wasn't home, Brad's friend got Jane to go on and on about how totally dedicated Johnny was to his job.

When Johnny got there, Brad's friend talked to him for over forty-five minutes. He asked him, "Johnny, what do you think about your program compared to the rest of the NFL teams?" And Johnny said, "Well, I'll say it this way. In 1983, the Giants had forty-six documented injuries. In 1986 we've had three. What does that say about my program? I think my program speaks for itself."

Later, Brad's friend asked him if he would entertain the thought of going to the Tampa Bay Bucs. Johnny sighed and said, "Well, I'm under contract to the Giants right now, but if they made a reasonable offer, well, I'm just a country boy from Mississippi, and it would be awful un-country of me not to listen. Fact is, it would be a sin to my wife and myself not to listen to what they had to say."

Johnny just kept getting himself in deeper and deeper with each question. A couple of days later, Johnny found out that Brad had nailed him, so he really wanted to strike back. Johnny, McConkey, and I had planned out a sting for Simms. We had him contacted by a photographer claiming to be from *Muscle and Fitness* magazine. He asked Phil if he would pose for some beefcake shots. Well, Phil denies it. He says he saw right through the scheme, but in truth, he got all fired up. I know because he went as far as to brag about it to our agent, David Fishof.

Still, we didn't follow up on the Simms sting because Johnny pulled out, figuring that it was not the time to jerk around the Super Bowl quarterback. But any time is the right time to get Brad, and Johnny was hell-bent for revenge.

So, we used the same setup for Brad, and of course he fell for it. The photographer we got told him he would pay him $15,000 for the pictures and that he also wanted some beach shots once Brad got to Hawaii for the Pro Bowl. Now Brad's not the best-built guy around, but the photographer told him not to worry, that they can touch things up just like they do with the *Playboy* centerfolds. At the last minute, we decided we couldn't go through with it. Not even to Brad.

I did the Joan Rivers show Tuesday night, when we got back from our six-hour fishing excursion.

I had a whole bit prepared for whatever Joan would ask me. The producers had told me to get together a joke to tell on the air and the only one I could think of was one that had been going around ever since Landeta whiffed the punt in Chicago.

I told Joan that I had experienced a nightmare about that game. In it I was walking in New York City and came across two bums who were arguing back and forth about who was the bigger Giant fan. One bum said he was. The other bum insisted it was him, so he pulled down his pants and showed off his rear end, which was decorated with two tattoos.

"See the tattoo on this right cheek?" he says. "That's Phil Simms. See the tattoo on this left cheek? That's Y.A. Tittle. What do you have to say now?"

"I don't give a damn about who's on the right cheek, who's on the left cheek," said the other bum. "But the guy in the middle, that's Sean Landeta."

A couple of us got together to watch the show later that night and Brad was shocked by some of the things I said about Bill, particularly my line about picking on the chubby kid. He told me I'd better watch what I say. "Bullshit," I told Brad. "If they want to fine me, let them fine me." Brad just doesn't understand me sometimes.

When Wednesday came, we were glad for the Tuesday off. Bill was super-tight all week. You could tell. He paced. He pouted. He complained about stupid things. He was a general pain in the ass. When he's nervous like that, he can drive us hard. The previous week's practices back home were no picnic, but in California, Bill didn't let up. Even on Monday when we were in shorts, he worked us full speed like dogs so that we'd get used to the heat again, shocking the jet lag right out of our systems. Practice ended with more wind sprints. I didn't like it. I thought he'd flipped. But this was the Super Bowl so nobody really complained.

Besides, I really did know why he did it. Monday was also the day he had an audience. John Madden, Pat Summerall, and Sandy Grossman of CBS were watching practice, so Parcells tried to coach his ass off. He was ripping into everybody, particularly the offensive linemen. He saw me giggling on the sidelines and screamed at me to get my ass on the field.

"It's showtime, boys," I said, pointing to Madden and Summerall. I knew we were in for it.

When we got to practice Wednesday, I thought I'd try to loosen up the coach a little, so you wouldn't need a tractor to pull a pin out of his ass. "Well, we can take it easy today, guys," I said, loud enough for Bill to hear. "We're not gonna get much coaching today because I don't see Madden, I don't see Summerall, and I don't see Sandy Grossman. We can take it easy."

"That ain't got nothing to do with it," Parcells growled. As it turned out, it didn't get much easier. But that was also the mood we were in. The concentration on everyone's part was intense. No one wanted to screw up in practice. Even the injured reserve guys who were playing on the scout teams were giving it everything, so that we could have what we call "a good look." That means that what we're going up against in practice is as close as possible to what we'll be seeing in the game.

There was a lot more hitting than usual and with the sun beating down on us, it almost made for that training-camp atmosphere where tempers can fray easily. I almost got into a couple of fights, one with the mild-mannered Karl Nelson on Wednesday after he pushed me at the end of a play, another the next day with Leonard because of something he said that came out the wrong way.

But bad moods weren't the only things that were brewing during the week. From the time he stepped onto the field on Monday, Phil threw the ball as well as he ever had. It had been a while since Phil had played in warm weather, and though he's as good a bad-weather quarterback as you'll find, he really took to the sunshine. He said he was feeling the ball better and the receivers knew it. Our practices must have looked like NASA space projects from the outside. Phil was firing spiral after spiral, right on target.

Knowing Phil, I knew what he was thinking. For every boo, for every criticism, for every time some idiot said he couldn't win the big one, Phil was preparing an answer. I was thinking back to that time in 1982 when we were both trying to salvage our careers and Phil told me, "If I ever get the chance, I'm gonna light 'em up." This was his chance. Early in the week, a sportswriter asked him about his skeptics. "Those people can kiss my ass," Phil said. And on Sunday he would moon them all.

Naturally, the golden boy all week wasn't Phil, but John Elway. That whole week long, in fact for two weeks, all we heard and read was Elway, Elway, Elway. Phil was the "other quarterback." Elway was supposed to be the guy who could win the game single-handedly. He had the golden arm, the pizzazz. But I knew Phil had more than that. I knew all about his competitiveness.

Frankly, I was happy as hell that everyone was talking about Elway, because I knew all this "John Elway is so great" talk was pissing off Phil. I knew what was going through his mind: I'm gonna show these sons of bitches who the quarterback is.

Besides, the defense had its own plans for Elway. We knew well from the November 23 game that Elway passed better on the run than in the pocket. Although our plan in the championship game was to flush Schroeder out, we wanted to contain Elway in the pocket. He had shown tendencies for throwing the ball deep whenever he scrambled. That's what made him so tough. He had great vision while on the run and his arm was so strong that he could get it downfield as soon as the coverage broke down or started to force. Some quarterbacks can't throw it forty or fifty yards. Elway can bomb it so your defensive backs must stay with their assignments.

The way I looked at it, our job was to stop their running game cold because that would only open things up more for Elway. When the Broncos ran the ball well during the season, they were able to crease things up the middle and force the safeties to come up in their zones. That gave Elway more of a chance to go over the top. We wanted to take care of their running game up front so that our secondary didn't have to force. That was the game plan. Stone the run. Keep Elway contained.

As for my own state of mind, well, I was in a peculiar situation. Just take note of the following description: This is a guy who gets *everything* out of what he has, is a real scrapper, not overly big, maybe 255-260. Very quick feet, very good technique . . . Sounds like me, right? Actually, I'm talking about the guy I went up against in the Super Bowl, Billy Bryan, the

Denver center. In a sense, he was an offensive Jim Burt. He even wears the same number as I do, 64. He'd made the Madden team, too.

The last time we faced each other in the regular season, it got pretty intense. Watching the films, I couldn't help thinking that Bryan did some of the things I would have done if I were playing offense. He went all out, and did whatever he had to do to get the guy in front of him. If that meant leg-whipping him, he'd leg-whip him. If it meant tackling him, he'd tackle him.

I didn't have to be worried about being overpowered. That's not Bryan. But I knew that he really stayed after his opponent and that when the fourth quarter came, he'd still be fighting me.

By Thursday night, I started really concentrating on the game and by Friday, I was getting on my game face. I wanted to put the funny stuff behind me. But somehow, I couldn't avoid a few more laughs.

On Friday, we were moving to a hotel in Beverly Hills because fans were mobbing the lobby and it was getting too crazy and distracting at our place in Costa Mesa. There were supposed to be two buses leaving after practice, one for the guys who were lifting that day and had to stay longer, and an earlier one for the guys who were going straight to the hotel. Somehow, we ended up with only one bus.

I was pretty ticked off about it because I have a thing about doing my squats on Friday and I sure as hell wasn't going to forget about them before the Super Bowl. I stayed as long as I could and was the last one on the bus. Parcells, of course, said something like, "You always gotta push it, don't you?" That's what I mean about him being tight and bitching about stupid things. I just gave him a look and headed to the back of the bus. Anyway, I told Johnny Parker that we had to find a gym once we got to the hotel so that I could do those squats.

Johnny asked about a gym at the front desk and they recommended one that was just a short walk from the hotel. As we went over there, I had a hard-ass attitude. Like I said, I was getting my game face on by then.

Johnny, however, just can't keep his mouth shut around people. He's got to gab and be friendly, talk shop. But in the meantime, I noticed something strange about the guys working out in this place. A lot of them had short-shorts stuck up their asses and these tight little muscle-shirts without the sleeves. One guy even had on eyeliner. I knew right away what we had walked into, but Johnny was still yakking away.

It was obvious that the guys didn't know who I was, because one of them tried to keep up with me doing squats. I blew him away at 315 pounds and stopped myself at 405, not wanting to push it. That freaked out a lot of them, but then again they weren't really looking at me. They had their eyes on Johnny, who was squatting along with me.

One guy was doing the spotting for Johnny and when Johnny was done with the set, the guy put his arm around him and said, "Gee, that was a nice set." By this time I had to drop my hard-ass approach. I took Johnny aside and said, "Johnny, you know California. I was talking to that guy over there and he told me this is a totally gay gym. See that guy over there? He's trying to pick you up."

Well, Johnny turned nine thousand colors. He's from Mississippi, after all, and where *he* comes from they don't cotton to that stuff. Another guy watched Johnny lift for a while and said, "You have to use the proper techniques, otherwise you're going to have problems with your genitals."

I played it for all it was worth. I draped towels over the equipment as if I didn't want to touch anything. Johnny didn't even want to change the weight for me. "Johnny," I asked him, "what weight should I use here?"

"Jim," he said, "for once I don't care how much weight you use. Let's just get out of here."

Going back to the hotel, Johnny made me swear I wouldn't tell anybody. "If you do, I'll deny it and put it on you," he said.

Naturally, I spread it around the rooms pretty quickly. It couldn't have happened to a sweeter guy.

# 16

## PASADENA

## Heaven

**"B**us leaves in five minutes."

Too early, even for the Super Bowl, I thought. It seemed everyone had left by the time the security guard came knocking on my door. I had the room to myself ever since Billy Ard left early as usual, taking a cab over to the Rose Bowl at 9 A.M. Just before he left, we forced Father Moore, the team's Catholic chaplain, to rush through the quickest Mass he had said since seminary school. Why the rush? I couldn't understand it. And people couldn't understand why I couldn't understand.

"I'll be down. I'll be down," I told the guard. "You've got five minutes," the guard repeated, urgency in his voice. Four minutes later, I went downstairs.

I hate leaving early. It only means that I sit around the stadium and get more nervous. Sometimes, I'll even miss the late bus and take a cab over. For Super Bowl XXI, I was the last player on the bus, and one of only four players who hadn't already left: Lawrence, Robbie Jones, Byron Hunt and myself. It was a quiet, meditative trip to the Rose Bowl, with what seemed like another full day to go before kickoff.

I didn't know our locker room was going to be so cramped, and that only made me feel the anxiety more. We were sitting

261

inside, all bunched up—just like the feelings that we each held inside ourselves, on edge because of the buildup, the two weeks off, and most of all, the anticipation. Football is such a routine-oriented sport that you can tell by your internal clock when it's time to take the field. But because of the elaborate pre-game, we were delayed by about ten more minutes than we were used to. I was sitting next to Bavaro and losing my mind.

Mark, a picture of serenity, tried to settle me down. In a nearly hypnotic voice he said, "Try to be as calm as you can, Jim, try to relax." So I said to myself, *Okay, take it easy.* That worked for about five more minutes until I couldn't take it anymore. I jumped up and let loose a primal scream that broke the tension. "Let's get the f—— out and play!" Bill Parcells, who was in the middle of the room, just looked at me and smiled, happy to see a little emotion leak out. Once I got out of control, people started to pace. Naturally, McConkey was one, then another and another. Before long, we had twenty-five guys pacing the floor like expectant fathers. Even Bavaro started to pace. We were like a bunch of caged animals. We nearly broke the door down when they let us loose.

McConkey played the rabbit as he led us out of the gates for the introductions. He sprinted to the far end of the field, waving his towel helicopter-style, and knocked over one of the pylons at the goal line. The Giant half of the stadium—our fans seemed to turn the Rose Bowl into a blue Meadowlands West— went nuts.

When I stepped out of the tunnel it was as if I was walking into my television screen. The Super Bowl was just as I always pictured it. The Rose Bowl is huge and when it's packed, it's as impressive as a stadium can get. The end zones were brightly painted in blue and orange. The playing field was a lush green, and fast—so much for the bullshit speculation that Joe Morris couldn't run on anything but Astroturf. The sky was a perfect blue and I even noticed the mountains in the background.

As I looked around the sidelines, I saw a bunch of guys with a lot to prove, a lot to play for. Phil Simms, the most underrated quarterback in the league, not even appreciated by his own fans. Joe Morris, a pack of dynamite they said was too small. Brad Benson, the free agent who defied yearly attempts to run him off the team. George Martin and Harry Carson, two talented players who seemed stuck when it looked like the Giants would forever be losers. Lawrence Taylor, who was proving Bill Parcells' faith in him. And Bill Parcells himself, who after one bad season in 1983, almost never got the chance to bring this team to the Super Bowl.

We were all ready. Maybe too ready. We had so much nervousness to work off that we forgot to concentrate on our assignments. I don't know how the Broncos were feeling before the game but they must have come into the first half in a better state of mind. As it turned out, they had a good chance to take control of the game before we ever settled down.

It was Elway, of course, who sparked Denver, though this day would prove that you can't depend on only one guy. It couldn't be "If Elway does this" or "If Elway does that." Elway did as much as he could for one half but found himself a great quarterback up against a great team.

We also saw what Elway could do if we didn't stick to our game plan. On the game's first play, Lawrence got a little deep with his pass rush and Elway scrambled underneath him for ten yards. If we kept breaking contain like that, it would be a long day. Two plays later, on third and long, we were unable to get any heat on Elway and he hit Mark Jackson for a first down.

The man of the drive for us was our left outside linebacker, Carl Banks. He'd already made two big hits before the Broncos lined up at our 31-yard line on third and two. "Killer," so named because he used to dig graves as a summer job in college, shot past tight end Orson Mobley with an inside move. I saw him bury Sammy Winder for no gain. The Broncos settled for a 48-yard field goal by Rich Karlis for the game's first points. We didn't feel all that bad coming off the field.

Then Phil Simms finally got his hands on the ball. *Click, click, click.* Four plays, three pass completions. Two first downs. I could tell from the sidelines that Phil was in command, that nothing was going to stand in his way, even our first penalty of the game, a holding call against Bavaro that wiped out Joe Morris' 11-yard run to the Denver 28. No problem. On third and 10, Phil sensed a cushion on Stacy Robinson's side and hit Stacy for an 18-yard gain. Two plays later, it was Phil to Bavaro for 17 and on the next play, with two tight ends in the game, Phil got the touchdown with a six-yard flip to Zeke Mowatt.

Normally after our offense strikes back like that, our defense takes out the sledgehammer. It happened that way most of the year, but again Elway made things happen with our defense still just running around aimlessly. We were playing hard but we weren't doing a good job of thinking; it only took three plays before Elway had the Broncos at our six-yard line. Harry was called for a late hit on Winder on the tail end of a screen pass and they nailed Lawrence with an unsportsmanlike conduct for picking up the flag and flinging it down.

Still, the Broncos couldn't run against us. They tried it on first down, and Steve Sewell met Carl Banks up close and personal about three yards behind the line of scrimmage. Elway got five back to Vance Johnson. Now it was third and goal at the four. The Broncos brought four wide receivers into the game, indicating pass, as Elway took his position in the shotgun.

My pass rush lane was to the left of Bryan. Usually when I go left, two other men, including a linebacker, shoot the right gap. But by the time I made my move between the guard and center, there was a big hole and no one was filling it. All the other pass rushers were upfield, too. But Elway wasn't throwing the ball. He was running a quarterback draw and no one laid a finger on him until he dived into the end zone.

I'd been had. I was trying to get off the ball quickly to get some penetration and I should have known better. In a similar situation late in the season against Washington, Elway ran the same play. It even stood in my memory because he made a great run on it. I should have anticipated the draw. I should have stayed home.

The Broncos had done what they needed to do, strike early and stay in the game. And on their next possession, with the score still 10 – 7, they continued the pattern. Again, we were to blame because we got away from Bill Belichick's game plan.

Elway was playing very well but he hadn't done anything we hadn't seen on film. All the short stuff he was hitting was no problem, because we'd been conceding that throughout the season, only to stop teams once they crossed into our half of the field. But the deep stuff: we knew if he broke the pocket, he loved for his guys to get deep, yet we were allowing the Denver receivers to slip behind us. Elway was burning us.

This time, he completed a 54-yard bomb to Vance Johnson. Then he picked a little more and the Broncos were looking at first and goal from our one. A touchdown here and it would have been 17 – 7. Even a field goal would have put us down by six. And then it began.

For some strange reason, the Broncos thought they could pound it in against our goal line defense, instead of using Elway's talents down there. I was shocked. I'm in no position to tell Coach Dan Reeves what plays he should have called, but after Elway lost a couple of yards trying to sprint out and find an open receiver, I would have come right back with him. Instead, they tried a trap play on second down, thinking our linebackers would blitz. Our line just hit the deck and Harry came up to fill the hole. No gain.

The third down call was really bizarre—a delayed toss to Winder. Banks got penetration and caught him from the back side for a loss of three. Another bad call. When you're on the goal line like that, any runs have to be quick hitters, because we're penetrating.

Stopping them like that was a big lift for us but what really killed them was when Karlis came in and missed a 24-yard field goal. Even that early in the game, still trailing, I said to myself, *We got it. We're gonna take it.*

Now we were starting to turn the game around. The next time Denver got the ball, we got two points when George sacked Elway in the end zone. It was another veteran play by Pops. As the defense was coming to the line, George yelled some nonsense over to Erik Howard, who was in for me on the play. It was what we refer to as a dummy call, done to fool their left tackle, Ken Lanier, into thinking that George and Erik were going to work a pass rush trick. When Lanier favored his inside, anticipating Howard on a loop, George blew straight past his right shoulder and rode him so quickly that Elway didn't have a chance of escaping. Another big play by George. When the season was over, I'm sure Elway was seeing George in his sleep.

Elway did bring the Broncos downfield one last time in the first half, thanks to an incredible throw where he sprinted out to his left and threw back across his body to the right sideline, nailing us with a 31-yard completion to Steve Watson just as I was getting ready to hit him. While we could marvel at the strength of Elway's arm, we could kick ourselves in the pants for not preventing the completion. It was another play Elway had used during the season and our DBs had seen it on film.

I got the Broncos five yards closer by jumping offside. With eighteen seconds left, Karlis came on the field again to try a 34-yard field goal, a chippie considering he had made ten straight field goals coming into the Super Bowl. But he pushed it wide right with his bare foot again and by the looks on the Broncos' faces, they knew they might have wasted one too many opportunities. It's demoralizing to drive upfield, look at easy points, and come up empty. All the Broncos could show for three trips inside our 20—the red zone—was seven points.

I had two thoughts as we headed into the locker room. We were damn lucky to be down 10–9 and there was no way in hell we were going to lose the game now. They'd just played their best half. We'd just played our worst.

I know after the game there were so many people asking what adjustments we made at halftime. Actually, there were no adjustments to be made outside of discussing our mental glitches in allowing Elway to break contain and his receivers to slip behind us. We were all pissed off because we were losing, but that helped settle us down.

I sat with some of the offensive guys at halftime and they were very calm. They felt that the Broncos had done nothing to stop them; that when they stalled, they had stopped themselves. Phil's three incompletions in the half had come on one drop, one slight overthrow off Bavaro's fingertips, and a play where McConkey was upended and could have gotten an interference call. Otherwise Phil was perfect. "We're gonna kick ass," Phil told Bart Oates. He didn't know how much ass he really would kick—that for the rest of the game, he wouldn't throw one incompletion; that when it was over, he would have played the best game any quarterback ever has in a Super Bowl. The man people said would never win the Big One carved himself into history with a 22-for-25, 268-yard game to remember in the biggest one of all.

When we took the field for the second half, the sun was behind the mountains and the cooler air somehow told us that things might change. They did, in a hurry. We played the best single quarter of football I can ever remember. We did it both ways, offensively and defensively, and when the third quarter ended we left the Broncos with no chance. We were simply dominant and it wouldn't have mattered what team we were playing. We had succeeded in raising the caliber of our play to that extra level, where a team can do anything it wants.

Anything. Soon after the second half kickoff, our offense looked at a fourth-down situation, two feet away from a first at our 46. It was time again for ARAPAHOE. Bill sent Sean Landeta onto the field and that brought out the Broncos' punt return team. But Bill had also smuggled backup quarterback Jeff Rutledge into the formation as the upback. Jeff slipped under the center and we had the Broncos beaten for the first down. Without their short yardage team in there, there was little chance they could stop Jeff's two-yard sneak behind Oates.

That first down got things rolling. Simms came back in and started to utilize his backs in pass patterns. Pressured, he dumped to Joe for twelve, then with Lee Rouson in the game for a play, he found him for twenty-three. That made three first downs in three straight plays and it was only moments later when Phil threw the go-ahead touchdown pass to Bavaro, who crossed himself and flipped the ball behind his back to the referee.

We had the lead again and now our defense was back, facing the same challenge as in the first half when we last took the lead. We couldn't let Elway get things rolling again. Now was the time when we had to apply the stranglehold. I felt it was the most critical defensive series of the Super Bowl.

We had them back at their 14 following the kickoff. Elway tried a short look-in pass on first down but George got up in the air to bat it away. Our fans started chanting, "Elway, El-way." *Keep it up,* I thought. We pushed the pocket straight back into Elway's face and he dumped off for five. Again under quick pressure, he tried to hit Gerald Willhite but the pass fell short.

Now the pattern was set. Joe got it going on the ground and

we moved in for a 21-yard field goal for a 19–10 lead. Again, we stopped the Broncos in three downs. Then Bill Parcells went for the jugular. He call for a flea flicker that the offense had been preparing all week, and the Simms-to-Morris-to-Simms-to-McConkey connection worked for forty-four yards to the Broncos' one. In a little bit of irony, McConkey tumbled over Mark Haynes, who but for his contract problems could have still been a Giant.

When Joe followed Chris Godfrey's block to score on the next play, we all felt we had won the game. We had overwhelmed them, 163 yards to 2 in the third quarter, and after another touchdown in the fourth quarter, that statistic was up to 210–2. By that time, we led 33–10, but Bill was trying to stop any premature celebrating on the sidelines.

But that was the best thing about it. We had time to enjoy it. With about 3:00 left, I went into the game one last time. Bill came down and started preaching. "Jimmy, it's not over yet, it's not over yet." And I yelled back, "Bullshit. We kicked their ass. It's over. The game is over. Forget about it. We just won the Super Bowl."

I guess Bill wouldn't believe it until Harry dumped his bucket of Gatorade on him—not once, but twice. Phil got doused, too. Right after he was announced as the game's Most Valuable Player, Brad and Bart grabbed a bucket and got him. Phil didn't say much but you could tell by his face that he finally was sticking it to his critics.

I came across Bill Belichick about the same time. Bill never shows much emotion but he was just jumping all over the place. I remember him saying to me, "Two free agents here, a free agent coach and a free agent player. Let me tell you something," he said. "You have come a long way. From free agent to Pro Bowl to Super Bowl." And I said, "Congratulations, Bill. Congratulations to *you*. A free agent coach." Belichick didn't play any college football. He started in this business breaking down films and some day I'm sure he's going to make a great head coach.

And so it went, each man in his personal fog, sometimes sharing it with someone else for a few minutes, then getting lost in a private world again.

With 2:00 left, Lamar came up to me and said, "Great job, boy. We're puttin' the young guys in." Finally happy to hear anything Lamar had to say, I said, "That's great." I took off my shoulder pads. I took off my helmet. I laid them down on the ground, tore off my elbow and hand guards and hurled them into the stands.

That's when I thought, *I gotta find Jimmy*. And that's what I cherish the most out of the Super Bowl, sharing it with him. He might not have understood it fully, but someday he will. He was talking to the guys, slapping hands with Joe Morris and Chris Godfrey and at one point, with Jimmy up on my shoulders, we were actually two yards out on the field while the game was still going on. Even Bill had loosened up by then. When we walked past him on the sidelines, Bill said, "Hey, Jimmy."

It seemed to last an eternity and when the game ended, I remember meeting up with Mark Cooper, the Broncos' offensive guard who played with me at Miami. "Shake hands with my friend," I said to Jimmy. But he wouldn't. "Daddy," he said, "he plays for Denver. I don't want to shake his hand."

"It's all right, I said. "He was a teammate of mine in college." So they shook hands.

We walked behind Bill as he was being carried off on Brad and Chris Godfrey's shoulders and we tried to push him off. It just seemed like a good idea at the time.

Eventually, I had to give Jimmy back to Colleen. I couldn't take him into the locker room, which was strangely subdued. And that's how it stayed the rest of the night—sort of a Twilight Zone. We'd been pointing to this for so long, and now that we got there, we couldn't believe we had done it.

The strangest part of it all? You're going to think I'm sick. As I was walking into the locker room after the game, I was thinking, *We've got to do this again. We've got to repeat*—and I said to myself, *There must be something wrong with me.* I slapped myself on the side of the head to tell myself, *Stop that shit.* I'm always trying to push and do a little more, never satisfied. But I was satisfied, about as satisfied as I've ever been in my life.

But later at our team party I said it again to Colleen.

"Oh, no," she said disgustedly.

"You're right. I *am* an asshole," I said. "I can't believe I'm thinking that."

And then I saw Bill Parcells and I went over to him and gave him a hug. "Jim," he said. "Come here, sit down."

"I know what you're going to say, Bill," I told him. "We've got to do it again next year."

"Jim," he said, "we could make history. Only two other teams have done it back-to-back."

"I've already thought about it, Bill," I replied. "I know I'm sick just like you're sick. We're both sick bastards, because I was thinking about that in the locker room and I thought of you. I knew you were thinking the same thing."

That's how the night ended. And that's why I wouldn't bet against the Giants this year.

# 17

## WALDWICK

## That Feeling

It's been a couple of months since Pasadena and I still get chills thinking about it.

I was making an appearance at a local banquet the other night when they played "The Star-Spangled Banner." It was the strangest thing. Before long, I got glassy-eyed and covered with goose bumps and as I listened to the music, I actually thought I was back at Giants Stadium, waiting for the start of our NFC championship game against the Redskins. I was in some sort of trance, my head tilted straight up as if I was staring into the upper deck.

When the anthem was over, someone jarred me back to my senses, that's how strange I must have looked.

"You all right?"

Actually, I couldn't be better. We're getting our Super Bowl rings at mini-camp next week and I'm sure that moment will hit me harder than anything. That's when it will all become real. But as sweet as last year's championship was, I'm starting to think that No. 2 will be even sweeter. There I go talking about No. 2 again, but it's true. I know what the feeling is like now, and I want that feeling again. Only the Packers and Steelers have won Super Bowls back-to-back. I really think we'll join them.

The signs are already there. It's true that the endorsements and appearances have been there for the taking but I don't think they've overwhelmed us. Personally, my agent David Fishof has done a good job of scheduling those things in perspective. I haven't let anything interfere with my workouts.

I have a real good feeling that my back will be fine. Shortly after the Super Bowl, I got some good news from Dr. Warren—that I wouldn't need further surgery. I just have to rest for a few days as soon as I feel it start to spasm. We'll see how Bill reacts to that. In the meantime, I'm doing a lot of abdominal work in the weight room as well as Tae Kwon Do for my flexibility. I think it's working, because usually my back is stiff in the morning and so far, it hasn't been stiff at all.

In fact, Johnny Parker's weight room has been buzzing in the off-season. Bill, who should be signing a fat new contract soon, has been been walking around with a big grin. He's really got control of the players now. I've kidded him, "Boy, oh boy, you're really in command." I've started calling him "Commando."

The Pro Bowl was a nice break with the family in Hawaii. I also got to know some of the people I've been playing against. In fact, the Redskins' Russ Grimm and I nearly pulled off the heat-balm-in-the-jock trick on Jay Schroeder. We also rigged the pants of Rams' center Dennis Smith so that when he leaned over the ball, they'd split right up his rump.

Meanwhile, the Redskins' coaches couldn't get over Sean Landeta's punting, while Sean couldn't get enough of the Hawaiian women. The hot weather suited everyone.

At one of our practices during the week, Lawrence and I were watching Sean kick only about fifty, fifty-five yards.

"C'mon, Sean, what's the story?" I teased. "I'm just loosening up," he replied. All of a sudden, he started rocketing them out seventy-five yards on the fly, nine miles in the air. We couldn't help but notice Joe Gibbs on the sidelines, standing with his hands folded, looking Sean up and down, from those skinny legs to that big belly. Sean kicked five or six perfect spirals.

After practice I called Gibbs over. "Hey Coach, what do you think of Landeta? Were you sizing him up like I thought you were?"

Gibbs was still scratching his head. "How the hell does he kick? What the hell is he doing? What the hell does he take? The guy is unbelievable."

After the Pro Bowl—I think we lost to the AFC, but who really cared?—I stayed an extra week in Hawaii for the Super Teams competition. The best part of that was Brad challenging Joe Frazier's record in the swimming event—the record for sinking like a cinder block, that is. Poor Brad. Poor us. He told us he was a championship swimmer.

One guy who won't be poor is Bill Parcells. Just before the Pro Bowl, word leaked out that the Atlanta Falcons were interested in Bill to the tune of $1.4 million a year. When asked for my reaction, I told reporters I was all for it. "The guy deserves it," I said.

Of course, Bill stayed a Giant and when I got home I just had to bust him about turning down all that money. "You are an example to us all," I teased.

After Hawaii, it was home for our team meeting with President Reagan at the White House. The Pro Bowl guys like myself had all missed our celebration at Giants Stadium—as it turned out there was no ticker tape parade down Broadway—and I almost missed our flight to Washington. I had scheduled a lunch date with Paul Rotella and didn't want to stand him up. "You crazy?" he said. "This is the *President.*" So he raced me over to Newark Airport at the last minute. Wouldn't you know it? When we got to the airport exit off the New Jersey Turnpike, Lawrence was in the car ahead of us.

It's going to be an important season for me. Erik Howard's

an up-and-coming player and there is going be tough competition between the two of us. He's a hell of a player. My contract is up again and I'm looking for security. I don't know how many more years I'm going to play but the thought has crossed my mind. Maybe one more Super Bowl and that will be it. This may sound strange, but as much as I love the game, I don't think I'll have any trouble leaving it behind me. I'll just go on with the rest of my life, enjoying whatever I'm doing. And it's important for me to leave the NFL while I can still walk.

Meanwhile, back at the Don Burt household in Orchard Park, things haven't really changed. A second generation of kids has kept the place a zoo. Dad, who's mellowed out anyway, can't be bothered by the racket from the eight grandchildren. He has a hearing aid now, but he'd rather not wear it so that he doesn't have to put up with the noise.

I'm still sure, though, that if someone yelled, "Grandpa!" loud enough from the basement, he'd be there, standing at the top of the stairs.